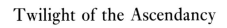

Twilight of the Ascendancy

By the same author

All a Nonsense
Paradise Escaped
Nothing in the City
The Remarkable Irish
Palaces of the Raj
Clive of India
The Cavaliers
Burke's Country Houses of Ireland
The British Aristocracy
(with Hugh Montgomery-Massingberd)
The Viceroys of India
Ancestral Houses
A Guide to Irish Country Houses
The Catholic Families

Mark Bence-Jones

TWILIGHT OF THE ASCENDANCY

Constable·London

First published in Great Britain 1987
by Constable and Company Limited
3 The Lanchesters, 162 Fulham Palace Road
London W6 9ER
Copyright © Mark Bence-Jones 1987
Reprinted 1987, 1989
Paperback edition 1993
Reprinted 1995, 1998
ISBN 0 09 472350 8
The right of Mark Bence-Jones to be
identified as the author of this work
has been asserted by him in accordance
with the Copyright, Designs and Patents Act 1988
Printed in Great Britain by
St Edmundsbury Press Ltd
Bury St Edmunds, Suffolk

A CIP catalogue record for this book
is available from the British Library

Contents

Illustrations

Preface

The lords and other landowners of Ireland, known, together with their relations, as the Ascendancy long after they had ceased to be in the ascendant, entered a twilight period just over a century ago when they lost most of their political power at the same time as their economic foundations were eroded by agricultural depression and agrarian disturbances. This is their story during the hundred years of their decline; a decline which, while it can to some extent be blamed on their own extravagance, mismanagement and political obstinacy, was largely the result of economic and social upheavals beyond their control. It is easy enough to say that if only they had farmed their lands more efficiently they would still be able to maintain their ancestral homes; but during the past century just as many well-farmed family estates have been sold up as neglected ones. It is again easy to say that if only they had not on the whole been so loyal to the Crown and so determined to maintain the Union with Britain they would have been able to play a more significant part in the life of the new independent Ireland; but while there were always some Nationalists among the Ascendancy, their families are now just as much outside the mainstream of present-day Irish life as those with a Unionist tradition.

In short, the Ascendancy was a 'doomed aristocracy', as the novelist George A. Birmingham called it. Its fate seems all the sadder in that its sons and daughters were far from decadent – 'no petty people', in the words of Yeats. The sons fought and died bravely in two World Wars; the daughters showed no less courage, whether in the face of nocturnal raiders during the 'Troubles' or in trying to keep up large and dilapidated country houses with little help and less money. And while they suffered misfortunes, they never ceased to enjoy life; along with the tragedy went a light-hearted gaiety, with an abundance of absurd, bizarre and hilarious incidents.

Elizabeth Bowen has written of how her family home in County Cork had the look of 'a house in which something important occurred once, and seems, from all evidence, to be occurring still'. It was a characteristic of the Ascendancy world that quite minor incidents assumed an importance; so that survivors from that world have – or had – a rich store of memories. Such memories have inspired this book and constitute one of my chief sources of material; many of those to whom I am indebted for them are no longer alive, notably my father, the late Colonel Philip Bence-Jones, and Elizabeth Bowen herself. To Elizabeth Bowen I am also indebted for the help and encouragement which she gave me when I first started writing and for her book *Bowen's Court*, perhaps the best history of an Ascendancy family ever written.

As well as talking to me about the past, people have given me access to papers and permission to quote from them; they have provided me with illustrations and helped me in other ways; they have also made my work more enjoyable by their hospitality. On one or more of these counts I must express my gratitude to each of the following: The Marquess of Dufferin and Ava; the Marquess of Waterford; the Earl of Dunraven; the Earl and Countess of Rosse and the Birr Scientific Heritage Foundation; the Countess of Wicklow; Count de la Poer and Mr Nigel de la Poer; Lord and Lady Dunleath; Lord William Taylour; Lady Katharine Dawnay; Lady Jennifer Bernard; Lady Betty Clarke; Lady Anthea Forde; Lady June Hobson; Sir Christopher Coote, Bt., and Lady Coote; Sir Hercules Langrishe, Bt., and the Hon. Lady Langrishe; Sir John Leslie, Bt., K.M., K.C.S.G.; Sir Cecil Stafford-King-Harman, Bt.; the Hon. Mrs Marcus Crofton; the Hon. Desmond Guinness; the Hon. Mrs Mariga Guinness; the Hon. Mrs Charles Moore; the late Captain the Hon. Valentine Wyndham-Quin; Mr Patrick Annesley; Miss Clodagh Anson; Mr and Mrs Richard Ball; Mr and Mrs Derick Barton; Mr Donal Begley, Chief Herald of Ireland; Mrs Edmund Boyle; Mr George Boyle; Mrs Gilbert Butler; Mr Hubert Butler; Mr James Byrne; Miss Grace Carroll; Colonel Kendal Chavasse, D.S.O.; Mr George Chowdharay-Best; Miss Catharine Clements; Mr Marcus Clements; Mr Adrian Cosby; Dr Maurice Craig; Miss Lydia de Burgh; Major and Mrs Hugh Delmege; Mrs Robert de Winton; Brigadier Denis FitzGerald, D.S.O., O.B.E.; Brigadier Bryan Fowler, D.S.O., M.C., and Mrs Fowler; the late Lt-Colonel Hubert Gallwey; Mr William Garner; Mr Daniel Gillman; Mrs Owen Guinness and Mr Charles Guinness; Major Walter Joyce; Mrs Robert Keane; Mr and Mrs Robert Kennedy; Mrs Richard Lee; Miss Elinor Longfield; Miss Margaret Longfield; Mr Charles Lysaght; Mr Malcolm Lysaght; Mr Henry McDowell; Mr Gerald McSweeney; Brigadier Edmond Mahony; Mr Gordon St George Mark; Mrs Collis Montgomery and Mr Arthur Montgomery; Captain Peter Montgomery, V.L., J.P.; Mr Hugh Montgomery-Massingberd; Mr Edward More O'Ferrall, K.M.; Mr Andrew O'Connor; Mr Peter Pearson; Mrs George Phipps; the late

Mrs Henry Phipps; Mr Harry Ponsonby; Mr Henry Ponsonby; Mr Claud
Proby; Mr Richard Shackleton; Mrs Susan Sharpe; Mr John Skidmore; Mr
Peter Smithwick, K.M.; Mr Colin Smythe; Mr David Synnott; the late Major
Pierce Synnott, K.M., C.B.; the late Group-Captain Rudolph Taaffe, K.M.,
O.B.E.; Miss Toler-Aylward; Mr Richard Tottenham; Mr Richard Wood.

A special word of thanks must go to Mr Donall Ó Luanaigh and Mr Brian
McKenna of the National Library of Ireland; to Dr Anthony Malcomson, Mr
Paul Brennan and Mr Andy Harrison of the Public Record Office of Northern
Ireland; to the Knight of Glin for giving me the benefit of his knowledge, his
library and his collection of photographs and for letting me have the verses from
his cousin Hilda Blennerhassett's scrapbook; to Mr Homan Potterton for
permission to quote from the William Orpen letters in the National Gallery of
Ireland and to reproduce pictures in the Gallery; to Miss Marye Pole-Carew and
her sister Mrs Peter Du Cane for their childhood memories of Kilkenny Castle and
some magnificent illustrations; to Mrs David Thomas for generously allowing me
to make use of the typescript of her mother, the late Mrs Solly-Flood, and also for
illustrations; to Dr William Vaughan for his guidance over the Irish land question;
and to the Committee and Secretary of the Kildare Street and University Club for
giving me access to records.

Since much of this book consists of narrative and of glimpses of the life of
individuals at various periods, I have taken the liberty of referring to people by
Christian names or nicknames where this seems natural in the context; even at the
risk of appearing unduly familiar. Also for stylistic reasons, I have dispensed with
the title of Honourable; and I refer to senior Service officers simply as Admiral,
General or Colonel as the case may be, even where Vice-Admiral, Major-General
or Lieutenant-Colonel would be more accurate.

'The happiest country I ever knew'

— I —

Such was the reputation of Irish hunting towards the end of the 1870s that the most exalted as well as the most dashing and glamorous huntswoman in Europe, the Empress Elizabeth of Austria, came to Ireland to hunt. For a month at the beginning of 1879 and for another month a year later she rented Summerhill, a splendid Palladian country house which stood in its glory of crisp grey stone, Corinthian columns and domed pavilions on a hilltop overlooking the broad grasslands of Meath. Its owner, the thirty-year-old Lord Langford, stayed on as a member of the Empress's house party during her visits, accompanying her on her days with the Ward Union, the Meath and the Kildares, when there would sometimes be more than a hundred people out riding. Himself a celebrated rider to hounds, he nevertheless found it hard to keep up with her as she galloped across

Summerhill

the fields, a slender, elegant figure on her black horse Domino, the finest of the twenty-one hunters which she brought to the Summerhill stables, taking the banks and ditches more recklessly than the most daredevil Irish. With her beauty and her courage, everybody lost their hearts to her, except perhaps Lord Langford's neighbour Robert Fowler of Rahinston, who when told that the Empress wished to buy a horse belonging to his young daughter said: 'I'm not going to have any damned Empress buying my daughter's horse.'[1]

At a supper party at Summerhill the hunting gentry from round about serenaded her as 'The Queen of the Chase' with verses composed by one of them for the occasion. The country people put up triumphal arches for her; they lined the roads and the railway waving flags as she passed by; they went miles in the hope of catching a glimpse of her. The tiny lace handkerchiefs which she took out with her when hunting, used once and then threw away, were picked up and treasured as souvenirs.

The Empress, who had travelled the world in a vain quest for happiness, spoke of her days in Ireland as having been among the happiest in her life, a tribute which Lord Langford and his sporting contemporaries would not have found particularly surprising. One of them, Barnie FitzPatrick, afterwards Lord Castletown,* writing some forty years later towards the end of a life in which he had, like the Empress, seen a great deal of the world, remembered the Ireland of those days as 'the happiest country I ever knew: and the people, my own countrymen, most thorough gentlemen when left in peace'.[2] Happy seems hardly the word for nineteenth-century Ireland; yet in the 1870s Ireland would certainly have seemed happy to a high-spirited young nobleman whose family was reasonably prosperous and on good terms with the country people around. It seemed happy indeed to the Marquess of Waterford's three younger brothers, the sailor Lord Charles Beresford and the two soldiers Lord William and Lord Marcus, when they came on leave to their family home, Curraghmore in County Waterford, a Georgian house built on to an old castle in the middle of a vast demesne of hills and woods that was part of the primeval forest. More than a hundred horses were stabled in the great forecourt which 'resounded with the cheery bustle of a jovial company coming and going';[3] in winter there was hunting six days a week and the house was always full of guests. The Beresford brothers were as famous for their horsemanship as for their pranks, which included riding down Piccadilly on a pig and taking a horse upstairs to their mother's bedroom. In 1874, when Lord Charles, Lord William and Lord Marcus were together at Curraghmore, they rode against each other in a steeplechase long remembered as the 'Three Brothers' Race'; the whole countryside turned out to watch and cheer.

* A title which had nothing to do with the well-known country house of this name in County Kildare, nor with the other country house named Castletown in County Kilkenny.

The Beresford brothers with their mother outside Curraghmore in about 1874. The Marquess of Waterford and Lord Charles Beresford are on the left of the group, Lord Marcus and Lord William on the right.

The carefree hunting life existed in most parts of Ireland at this time, if not in so grand a manner as at Curraghmore. Even in Kerry, a county not usually associated with hunting, various gentlemen kept hounds; Sir John Godfrey of Kilcoleman Abbey had a pack and so had Arthur Blennerhassett of Ballyseedy and Francis Chute of Chute Hall, whose huntsman, wearing an old red coat and ill-fitting breeches, would ride up and down the streets of Tralee blowing a twisted horn to advertise that there was to be a hunt. Francis Chute's cousin, Lord Ventry, kept a small pack of harriers at his home on the shores of Dingle Harbour, where he also kept hawks and a pet seal. He also had a yacht managed by an excellent boatman, the quiet and impassive Tim Devane. Once, on the way back from Valentia Island, darkness fell; Lady Ventry, who was in the boat, started making anxious enquiries about the Crow Rock, until Tim Devane, at the tiller, broke his silence and said firmly: 'You leave the Crow Rock to me, my Lady.'[4]

Retainers like Tim Devane, who while never lacking in respect for their masters

A page from the scrapbook of Barnie FitzPatrick's wife Clare, recording a shooting party at Moore Abbey. Photographs of the host and hostess, Lord and Lady Drogheda, are pasted above the view of the house; while on the right is a list of the guns, who include Lords Bandon, Monck, Drogheda, and Cloncurry and Hugh Barton, as well as Barnie himself, who by then had become Lord Castletown.

(*opposite*) Castle Bernard.

would speak plainly to them if necessary, were a feature of Irish country-house life. At Granston Manor, Lord Castletown's home in what was then known as Queen's County, there was Boyce the gamekeeper who was a raconteur and a humorist; after a hard day's shooting he would get the whole house party dancing to the reels and jigs which he played on his fiddle. When Queen Victoria's son, the Duke of Connaught, was shooting at Granston, his equerry tried to get a rise out of Boyce by asking him if he had not said that His Royal Highness 'had shot damned badly', to which Boyce replied: 'Not near as bad as yourself.'[5]

In those days of large estates and no shortage of keepers, the shooting in Ireland was as good as the hunting. Among the shooting house parties at which Barnie FitzPatrick was a guest were those of the Earl and Countess of Carysfort at Glenart Castle in County Wicklow, famous for its woodcock and its high pheasants, of Sir Arthur and Lady Olive Guinness at Ashford Castle in County Galway, no less famed for its woodcock, and of the Marquess and Marchioness of Drogheda at Moore Abbey in County Kildare. He also stayed for the shooting at Straffan House in the same county, where Hugh Barton and his wife 'gave one the best of sport and the best of claret', and at Castle Bernard in County Cork, which he described as 'one of the cheeriest houses in Ireland'.[6]

Castle Bernard, a rambling, ivy-covered, castellated mansion overlooking the Bandon river near the town of that name and containing an unusually fine collection of Old Masters, was the home of the young Earl of Bandon and his wife, known as Doty, who was the daughter of Lord Carbery, another West Cork peer. They were married in 1876; after their wedding somebody made a list of the

presents and it ran to sixty-four pages: a gold-and-turquoise-topped smelling-bottle from the Vicereine, the Duchess of Marlborough, vases from a former Viceroy, the Duke of Abercorn, a silver casket from the Earl and Countess of Bantry, a 'photobook' from Harriet Viscountess Midleton, a Bible in an oak case from Lord Clonbrock, biscuit china groups from Lady Colthurst, a cameo from Sir Oriel Foster, an 'exquisite illuminated book' from the children of the local school. The bridegroom gave the bride a gold and diamond locket with a coronet in pearls; he also gave her, by way of a joke, 'two tiny spitting kittens'. [7] Lord Bandon's fondness for practical jokes led him to do things like substituting a live cockerel for the necessary article of china in the bedside cupboard of one of his guests at Castle Bernard. 'There was a good deal of practical joking and bear fighting going on and we danced each night till all hours' Lady Alice Howard wrote of a Castle Bernard house party early in 1880. They also 'played a game called rounders on the grass in the morning' and 'most of the party amused themselves coming down the fire escape'. [8]

This last diversion Lady Alice refrained from trying; at thirty-four she may have considered herself past such juvenile frolics. She was the youngest of the three unmarried sisters of the Earl of Wicklow; they lived with their mother in a moderate-sized country house in the part of County Wicklow nearest Dublin. Here they gave tea and tennis parties for the neighbouring gentry, which were on the whole a success apart from the vagaries of the Irish weather – the view of the mountains would be hidden by a sea fog and people would have to play tennis in the rain. By the end of the 1870s, the Ladies Howard would have been regarded as being on the shelf; yet such was their popularity that they continued to go the rounds of country house parties. Lady Alice spent the Christmas of 1879 in County Cork with the Earl and Countess of Listowel; then, after returning home, she went to the Bartons at Straffan for the Naas Ball and for a ball given by the young Earl of Mayo at his newly-built house, Palmerstown; then, before going south again to Castle Bernard, she stayed at Moore Abbey with the Droghedas.

The great houses of County Kildare, such as Moore Abbey, Palmerstown and Straffan, were always full of guests for Punchestown, the race meeting held by the Kildare Hunt every spring which by the 1870s had become one of the chief events in the Irish social calendar. Particularly lavish were the Punchestown parties at Bishopscourt, the home of the Earl of Clonmell, known as Earlie not because he was an Earl but because his courtesy title before he succeeded his father had been Lord Earlsfort. Earlie was inclined to do his guests and also himself rather too well; there are many stories told of his exploits when in his cups, such as when Queen Victoria smiled graciously on him at a garden party and he rushed over to her, shook her warmly by the hand and assured her that he knew her face but could not for the moment remember her name.

The dining room at Shelton Abbey, County Wicklow, seat of the Earls of Wicklow, in 1875.

Another hard-drinking Irish peer of this time was Viscount Massereene and Ferrard, who at his shoots at Antrim Castle and at Oriel Temple in County Louth would give drinks to the beaters, filling a glass for each of them, then tossing it off himself to make sure he had poured out what the man wanted before refilling it and handing it to him. There is a story of how he was once nearly pushed off the platform of a small station near Belfast by a couple of drunken farmers; they were reprimanded by a porter who said: 'Don't you see it's Viscount Massereene and Ferrard?' To which one of the farmers replied: 'And both of them drunk.'⁹

Very different from Earlie and Massereene was their contemporary, the Earl of Rosse, whose castle backed on to the elegant little town of Birr in the very middle of Ireland and faced over an idyllic demesne in which stood a Gothic observatory containing the largest reflecting telescope in the world. This had been built by his father, whose scientific genius he had inherited; he devoted his life to various branches of astronomy, particularly the measurement of lunar heat. His days were spent in his workshop at the back of the castle, inventing such devices as a camera-mounting for star photography; he spent the long winter nights making observations through his father's great telescope, assisted from 1880 onwards by

Birr Castle.

Dr Otto Boëddicker of Göttingen University whom he put in charge of his observatory. He was a Fellow of the Royal Society and belonged to the most learned of London clubs, the Athenaeum, where the members included at least one other Irish landlord, William Bence-Jones of Lisselane in County Cork.

Like Lord Rosse, Bence-Jones was scholarly rather than sporting; his leisure was spent neither in the hunting field, nor with a gun, but in his library writing articles for serious journals such as the *Nineteenth Century* and the *Contemporary Review*. His chief interest was agricultural science: improving his estate, which his father had thoroughly neglected, was his life's work. Now, after thirty years of draining bogs, planting trees, erecting farm buildings and introducing German methods of dairying with the help of a German dairymaid imported for the purpose – a humbler counterpart of Lord Rosse's German astronomer – his estate was one of the best run in Ireland, with an attractive demesne and a new house which he had built in the style of a French château where, in 1878, he and his wife gave a tenants' dinner to celebrate their son Willy's coming-of-age and the marriage of their daughter Carry.

Lord Rosse in the Great Telescope at Birr. The bearded figure on the right is Doctor Otto Boëddicker.

Lord Rosse shows the Bishop and a lady through the Great Telescope.

Some forty or fifty tenants sat down in the dining room, the family silver was all out and the dinner 'very much as if prepared for gentlemen'. In his speech, Bence-Jones told his tenants 'how he had wished to help them and what good will he felt towards them'; the conviction that his life's work had improved their lot and indeed benefited the whole countryside was an even greater source of satisfaction to him than the knowledge that it had improved his own family fortunes, for he was deeply religious with a strong sense of duty towards the less fortunate of mankind. At the dinner, he and his wife felt prosperous and happy. It pleased them especially to see that although the tenants had been given porter and a glass of whiskey each, only one of them was 'a little too merry' – and he happened to be a teetotaller.[10]

This was a modest celebration compared with that held in 1873 when Captain Chambré Ponsonby brought his bride to Kilcooley Abbey on the borders of Tipperary and Kilkenny. The happy couple were greeted with illuminations and a triumphal arch in the neighbouring town and a bonfire at the entrance to the demesne; their carriage was pulled by cheering tenants and there was music and dancing all night. Whiskey and beer were provided for all comers by the bridegroom's uncle William Ponsonby-Barker, the then owner of Kilcooley, who though a stern Evangelical did not object to the country people enjoying themselves. Nor did his religious beliefs prevent him, in his old age, from taking a maidservant to bed with him as a 'human hot water bottle'; indeed he is supposed to have justified himself on the Scriptural precedent of King David. He would choose a maid for this purpose after family prayers; on one occasion the maiden of his choice offended his olfactory sensibilities, so he sprinkled her liberally from what he took, in the dark, to be a bottle of eau-de-Cologne, but which in fact contained ink.[11]

The Evangelical with a well-ordered estate was a not uncommon type of Irish landlord in the 1870s. At Athavallie in the plains of Mayo, a long, low, creeper-clad house surrounded by a demesne of woods and rhododendrons kept up as though it were one vast pleasure-ground, Sir Robert Lynch-Blosse presided over family prayers, as his grandson recalls, 'with the solemnity and grimness of a hanging judge'.[12] He ran his household and estate 'with the discipline of a Prussian Guards regiment';[13] meals had to be on the dot, the doors between the drawing room and dining room being flung open and dinner announced on the last stroke of the gong, not a moment before or after. With the exception of his wife, Lady Harriet, who was a sister of the Marquess of Sligo and therefore his superior in rank, everybody was terrified of this gaunt, unsmiling, white-haired autocrat; yet, like William Ponsonby-Barker, he was an excellent landlord and in his own way fond of the people and anxious to help them. Every morning after breakfast Lady Harriet would emerge from the hall door and go slowly down the long line of people waiting to see her, listening to sorrows or complaints, dealing out advice as well as money, food and medicine.

On the other side of Ireland in County Carlow, the people would go in crowds to talk to their landlord, Arthur MacMorrough Kavanagh, who though born without arms and legs had taught himself to ride, shoot and sail his yacht, had travelled in remote parts of Asia and become an MP. When the weather was fine he would receive them sitting beneath an oak tree in the courtyard of his turreted ancestral mansion, Borris House, dressed in a black cloak and with his pet bear chained nearby. If great landlords like MacMorrough Kavanagh were able to maintain a close relationship with their tenants, so even more were the smaller ones, such as George Burke of Danesfield, whose estate was an oasis of good land in the wastes of Connemara. He would sit in his study, which went by the imposing name of Magistrate's Room, a bearded, patriarchal figure with his small daughter curled up in a chair beside him, and the people would come to consult him, or to bring their disputes to be settled by him, arguing them out in Irish, which he could speak and understand. They would also come to pay their rents and he would put what he received from each of them into one of the wedge-shaped drawers of the rent table, a piece of furniture then to be found in most Irish country houses. 'My father, who knew all of them and all their affairs, knew who was speaking the truth when he or she declared their inability to pay' his daughter afterwards recalled. 'Rents were often forgiven or reduced. Frequently they were paid in kind and we adjourned to the yard to see a load of turf from the bog tipped out of its cart and measured.'[14] There was not much money at Danesfield, but the family lived quietly: entertainments were few and far between, the drawing room was shabby, faded and very little used. George Burke asked for nothing more in life than to spend the day out in the fields sitting under a large cotton umbrella watching his men at work, with a sandwich for his lunch.

The austerity of Danesfield was just as typical of the smaller gentry of this time as the atmosphere of easy-going plenty such as a young Englishman, who served in Ireland with the Constabulary from 1873 to 1878, found at Riddlestown Park in the west of County Limerick, which belonged to a branch of the Blennerhassetts less well-endowed than their kinsman at Ballyseedy in County Kerry:

The large entrance-hall was filled with tables, littered with newspapers, novels, hunting-crops, walking-sticks, hats and coats, in endless confusion; chairs with broken legs and rickety cabinets loaded with priceless china, never cared for, and never dusted. The household consisted of only two or three good-natured, but absolutely inefficient servants, though devoted to the 'ould' family. At Riddlestown there was always the most cordial of welcomes and the truest hospitality – the best of everything that was going, a good bottle of claret after

Riddlestown Park

dinner, which was at once whipped off the table the moment the ladies disappeared and replaced by a bowl of steaming whiskey punch. The one thing always lacking was 'money', but that did not seem to affect life.[15]

As well as supporting the servants, the workers on the place and other dependants, most Irish country houses gave occasional sustenance to a following of people who were not beggars in that they did not actually ask for help, but turned up from time to time knowing that they would be given something if they did not come too often. Mrs Brooke of Summerton in County Dublin, a sister of Viscount Monck, had a large clientèle of this kind. The more privileged members were allowed to tap at her sitting-room window to give notice of their arrival. She would open the window and engage in conversation which varied in length with the visitor's standing; she would then dispense a few coppers and send the visitor round to the back door for cold meat sandwiches and – if it was a lucky day – a bowl of soup. The lesser members of the clientèle would sit patiently on the steps of the hall door until Mrs Brooke came out for her morning walk, it being not done for them to ring the bell. When she emerged, they received the same treatment as those enjoying the privilege of tapping on her window. Some of the visitors sang for their supper: either literally, or by playing a musical instrument such as the pipes, or else by regaling Mrs Brooke with the news of distant friends and relations whose houses were on their beat. Pipers were among the hangers-on of many Irish country houses, like Corley the Piper who would visit the Gregory family at Coole Park in County Galway.

Corley the piper outside Coole at a somewhat later period. Also in the picture is Augusta, Lady Gregory, with W.B. Yeats on her right.

— 2 —

The Earl of Bandon, Sir Robert Lynch-Blosse, plain Mr Blennerhassett of Riddlestown – they and others like them, together with their relations, constituted what was known as the Ascendancy; it continued to be known as such long after it had ceased to be in the ascendant. The term originated with the Protestant Ascendancy of the eighteenth century, when Catholics were debarred from all share in government and suffered many other disabilities, leaving the Protestant aristocracy with a monopoly of power and privilege in Ireland. With the repeal of the anti-Catholic Penal Laws – a gradual process which started in 1778 and ended with full Emancipation in 1829 – Protestant Ascendancy became a thing of the past, and Catholic landowners took their place alongside their Protestant neighbours in Parliament, on the Bench of magistrates and on the Grand Jury which managed the affairs of the county. The nineteenth-century Ascendancy included Catholics as well as Protestants: in County Kerry in 1879, the Queen's representative – known in Ireland as Her Majesty's Lieutenant, the equivalent English title of Lord Lieutenant being held only by the Viceroy – was the Catholic Earl of Kenmare; while out of the sixteen Deputy-Lieutenants of that county, four were Catholics, including the grandson and the nephew of Daniel O'Connell.

That the Catholics were greatly outnumbered by the Protestants is a matter of history. As a result of the wars and rebellions of the sixteenth and seventeenth centuries the old Catholic landowners, who were either of Celtic-Irish or Anglo-Norman stock, suffered wholesale dispossession; their lands passing to Protestant settlers from Britain. Of the Catholic families still holding land in the eighteenth century, many 'conformed' to Protestantism as a result of the Penal Laws, which had rather the same effect as present-day capital taxation on the property of Catholics, so that those who kept their faith tended to become impoverished. Among the Irish landowners of the 1870s, Catholics like George Burke of Danesfield were on the whole poorer than Protestants of similar standing. There were, however, exceptions. Lord Kenmare could afford in 1872 to build himself a vast new red-brick Tudor-revival mansion overlooking the lakes of Killarney. Count de la Poer, a kinsman of the Marquess of Waterford holding a Papal title, had also recently rebuilt his ancestral seat, Gurteen le Poer, in a style that was baronial as well as Tudor. While the de la Poers or Powers of Gurteen had, like the Kenmares, managed to keep their inheritance reasonably intact during Penal times, the cousinhood of Powers who lived grandly in various country houses on the shores of Waterford Harbour and elsewhere are an example of a Catholic family that became rich through business and acquired landed estates after the worst of the Penal Laws were repealed.

The Protestant majority of the Ascendancy was not, as many would imagine, descended exclusively from English land-grabbers who came over with Cromwell and Presbyterian Lowland Scots who settled in Ulster under James I. Though the families of English and Scots settler stock together constituted the largest group in the Ascendancy, they nevertheless did not amount to more than 60 per cent of the total; and of their number, only about 10 per cent were of Cromwellian origin. The rest of the settler families were established in Ireland at different periods from the sixteenth century onwards; for example, the Earls of Bandon and Rosse, the Bartons and the Blennerhassetts were all descended from settlers of the time of Elizabeth I.

Rather less than 40 per cent of the Ascendancy families were of old Celtic-Irish or Anglo-Norman stock; but this minority included some of the most important. The Duke of Leinster, Ireland's premier peer, and the Marquess of Ormonde were the heads, respectively, of two historic Anglo-Norman families, the FitzGeralds or Geraldines and their traditional rivals the Butlers. The Marquess of Waterford had inherited the estates of his ancestors in the female line, the de la

Poers or Powers, Norman barons who in the later Middle Ages became 'more Irish than the Irish', as did the de Burghs, whose descendants included the Marquess of Clanricarde and the Earl of Mayo, as well as Mr Burke of Danesfield. Lord Inchiquin was descended from the O'Brien High Kings, Arthur MacMorrough Kavanagh from the MacMorroughs, Kings of Leinster, Lord Castletown from ancient Kings of Ossory who took the name of MacGillapatrick. The Earl of Dunraven was an O'Quin. Even in Ulster, where almost all the Ascendancy families were of Scottish or English settler stock, there was the Earl of Antrim and Lord O'Neill, both descended in the female line from illustrious Celtic forebears whose lands they still held. And Ulster's premier peer, the Duke of Abercorn, though his roots were undoubtedly in the Scottish Lowlands, differed from other descendants of Lowland Scots settlers in that his seventeenth-century ancestors were Catholic and Jacobite.

The ethnic diversity of the Ascendancy – which also included, among the settler families, some descendants of Huguenots and other continentals – together with its apparently conflicting allegiances and its predominantly if by no means uniformly English manner of speech, has given rise to much argument as to its true nationality. The more extreme Irish nationalists have always been liable to brand the Ascendancy as English or 'West British'; while English writers tend to use the rather misleading expression 'Anglo-Irish', though they would never think of calling a Scottish laird who was loyal to the Queen and spoke English without a Scots accent 'Anglo-Scots'. But the vast majority of Ascendancy people in the 1870s would have considered themselves as Irish. They did not feel any less Irish for insisting, as most of them did, that Ireland should remain in the United Kingdom, of which she had been an integral part since 1800. Their Unionism came from the head rather than from the heart: in present-day terms, it was like supporting the Common Market. Their allegiance was not so much to Britain as to the Crown.

As an indication of how the Ascendancy indentified itself with Ireland, when an Irish equivalent of the I Zingari cricket club was founded – under the presidency of William Ponsonby-Barker's cousin Frederick Ponsonby, afterwards Earl of Bessborough, who was, incidentally, of Cromwellian stock – it was given the Irish name of Na Shuler. The fact that this Irish rendering of 'The Wanderers' is not quite correct may be taken as typical of the Ascendancy's somewhat haphazard approach to the language. Barnie FitzPatrick picked it up during his holidays from Eton, from a little Galway fisher-girl with whom he was in love; for others, learning Irish was, in the words of one of them, 'a phase much like the stamp-collecting of a schoolboy'.[16] Yet even if the Ascendancy had only a little Irish, it was probably more than what the educated Catholic middle-class of Ireland had at that time.

The Ascendancy could not stand any sort of superiority on the part of the English towards Ireland and the Irish. A conceited English officer, out shooting in County Monaghan with the wild young Lord Rossmore – known to everybody as Derry – found himself abandoned by his host in a water-filled bog hole, to be fished out later by a farmer; for years afterwards the country people would speak of 'the bog where Masther Darry drowned the Englishman'.[17] The wife of John La Touche, a prominent County Kildare landowner, spoke for many others in the Ascendancy when she told a friend: 'I could not live in England. You will think it horrid of me, but I hate English ways, manners and customs, tight respectable virtues, clattering voices and nasty contemptuous ways of speaking of my country.'[18] Maria La Touche was of Celtic-Irish stock on her mother's side, but on her father's side her roots were in Cornwall, Wales and Jamaica and her husband was of Huguenot descent. She was a Protestant and a staunch upholder of the Union, as loyal as any of Queen Victoria's subjects; she was on the best of terms with a host of English relations and friends. But her country was Ireland and she thought of herself without any doubt as Irish.

— *3* —

In the 1870s, it was still possible to think of the Ascendancy as the ruling class. The leading landowners of each county met every so often on the Grand Jury and settled all matters of local government; they usually managed to get through a fair amount of business as well as enjoying an excellent luncheon. Derry Rossmore's brother once held a cock-fight in the kitchen of Monaghan Court House while he was acting as Secretary of the Grand Jury, but this was very much frowned upon. As Justices of the Peace, the Ascendancy acted as unpaid magistrates, though much of the power formerly exercised by the landowners in this respect had been taken over by the police force and by full-time Resident Magistrates – Irish RMs. Gone were the days when the maintenance of law and order in the country districts was entirely in the hands of people like Gerald Blennerhassett of Riddlestown and his future father-in-law the Knight of Glin, who in 1819 brought to justice the murderer of the Colleen Bawn. And if the landowners had lost much of their power as the guardians of law and order, they or at any rate the Protestant majority of them had gained a new sphere of influence since Gladstone had disestablished the Anglican Church of Ireland in 1869. Disestablishment had been fiercely opposed in Ascendancy circles, notably by High Churchmen like William Bence-Jones who feared that the disestablished Church would be taken over by the Evangelicals; but it meant that from having been a department of State, the Church was henceforth controlled by an Ascendancy-dominated Synod responsible in particular for ecclesiastical appointments.

In the Parliamentary field, the Ascendancy continued to hold its own despite the electoral reform of 1850. In 1868, seventy-three out of Ireland's hundred or so MPs came from landed families; the number was still impressive even after it had been reduced to fifty-two in 1874, for as well as the constituencies actually represented by members of the Ascendancy, there were others where the candidates, though not of the Ascendancy themselves, owed their election to Ascendancy influence. Victorious in the 1874 election was the twenty-eight-year-old Lord Charles Beresford, who at the request of his brother Lord Waterford took time off from the navy to stand as a Conservative for County Waterford, a constituency represented by two members. The other candidates included the Whig sitting member Sir John Esmonde, a Catholic landowner from the neighbouring county of Wexford who held minor office under Gladstone. There was also a Home Rule candidate named Longbottom, which caused a Catholic priest, himself a Home Ruler, to remark to his congregation: 'As for this Mr Long-what's-'is-name, I wouldn't be dirtying me mouth by mentioning the latter end of him.'

At one of Lord Charles's meetings, an elderly heckler complained that whereas he had been 'up to the knees in blood and whiskey' on the last occasion when a Beresford stood for the County – which was in 1826 – this time 'devil a drop of either' had he seen. Apart from this alleged two-fold deficiency, it was a campaign very much in the Irish tradition. Lord Charles challenged the car-boys of Waterford city to a race on the quay and won by the simple expedient of stuffing some straw into his horse's harness and setting it alight; he was afterwards to maintain that the horse, though stimulated, had been quite uninjured. Then there was his encounter with a man pasting up posters which said: 'Vote for Longbottom, the Friend of the People.' Having given the wretched man a lick across the face with his own paste-brush, Lord Charles helped himself to the brush, the paste and the posters and made off with them back to Curraghmore where he arrived late at night to find his younger brother Bill in bed and asleep. Without waking him, he pasted the posters all over Bill's room, even on his towels and on his trousers. In the morning Lord Bill appeared looking pale and solemn. 'Charlie, there's some bold men among the enemy,' he said. 'Why, one of them got into my room last night.'[19]

Charlie Beresford's victory was due not only to Lord Waterford's popularity as a landlord and to Longbottom's name, but also to the fact that he had the support of some of the Home Rulers because, though a Protestant himself, he shared the

Catholic Church's views on education. Afterwards, attempts were made to persuade him to join the Home Rule party; surprising though it may seem in the light of subsequent history, they might have been successful, for of those who sat in Parliament as Home Rulers during the late 1870s, no less than half were of the Ascendancy. Among them were the Earl of Kingston's cousin, Colonel Edward King-Harman of Rockingham in County Roscommon, one of Ireland largest landowners, and, of course, Charles Stewart Parnell, the eventual Home Rule leader. Both Parnell and King-Harman were Protestants of English settler stock.

On the whole, however, the Home Rule movement had little support from the Ascendancy, even though it stood for only a very moderate degree of political independence. The Ascendancy was inclined to take a romantic view of the rebels of the past, such as the the Duke of Leinster's great-uncle Lord Edward FitzGerald, but it had little sympathy for present-day Nationalist aspirations. It was usual in Ascendancy circles to hear people spoken of disparagingly as Union peers, because their forebears had obtained peerages as a reward for voting for the Act of Union of 1800; yet in the same circles almost everybody was determined that the Union should, at all costs, be maintained.

And so the Home Rule movement, which could easily have been dominated by the Ascendancy had there been more people like King-Harman and Parnell, became instead a middle-class challenge to the Ascendancy's political power. By 1874 the movement was gaining ground: the General Election of that year brought Home Rulers to Westminster in strength; they took the place not only of Conservatives but also of Whigs like the Catholic County Meath landowner Edward MacEvoy of Tobertynan, who during his years as an MP had espoused many popular Irish causes but would not support Home Rule.

Even before 1874 the Ascendancy had been challenged by Home Rulers in some constituencies. In 1872 there was a by-election in County Galway in which a Home Ruler opposed the Conservative candidate Captian William le Poer Trench, who was a younger son of the Earl of Clancarty, a Galway magnate. One of Trench's supporters was the elderly James Martin of Ross, whose estate was close to the town of Oughterard where the poll took place. Martin had always been on the best of terms with his tenants, who in previous elections voted whichever way he wanted; he felt confident that they would do the same this time. But as he was driving into Oughterard on the morning of the poll, he was stopped by a man who advised him to turn back. Ignoring this advice, he drove on into the town, where there was a seething crowd. Soldiers kept the way open for the wealthy Sir Arthur Guinness of Ashford Castle, who led a small party of his tenants to vote for Trench, the oldest of them on his arm; but when Martin tried to muster his own tenants, they were nowhere to be seen.

All that morning he 'ranged through the crowd incredulously, asking for this or that tenant, unable to believe that they had deserted him. It was a futile search.' With a few exceptions, the Ross tenants, like most of the constituency, voted for the Home Ruler, who was elected by an overwhelming majority. He was later to be unseated on petition, but this did not alter the fact that the tenants voted for him.

When Martin came home to Ross on the afternoon of that election day, as his daughter Violet recalls, 'even the youngest child of the house could see how great had been the blow. It was not the political defeat, severe as that was, it was the personal wound, and it was incurable.'[20] The election was in February; in March he caught a cold while on tour of inspection as Auditor of the Poor Law Unions. Pleurisy set in and he lay ill at the Galway Club; he kept saying plaintively: 'If I could hear the cawing of the Ross crows I should get well.' He was brought home one day towards the end of April, and later on that same day he died; his tenants mourned his death by keening or wailing at his funeral. James Martin was not the only County Galway landowner to die after being let down by his tenants in that fateful election; there was another, a Catholic, who on his deathbed desired that not one of his tenants should touch his coffin.

$$- 4 -$$

While the Ascendancy of the late 1870s hunted and generally enjoyed life, not only was its political power being challenged, but the long period of agricultural depression which was to cause its economic collapse was already beginning. With a few notable exceptions, such as the Earl of Dunraven, who owned coal mines in South Wales, the brewing Guinnesses and the Bartons of Straffan whose income came largely from their French wine business, the fortunes of the Ascendancy were based on Irish land. The Duke of Leinster owned 73,000 acres and there were other territorial magnates such as the Earl of Kenmare who owned over 100,000. However, most Irish peers did not own quite so much; the Earl of Wicklow with his 28,746 acres was nearer the average while Lord Langford's splendid mansion of Summerhill was supported by an even more modest 9745 acres. The County Kerry baronet Sir John Godfrey, Robert Cole Bowen of Bowen's Court in County Cork, and the FitzGerald who held the romantic title of Knight of Glin were typical landlords of consequence not in the magnate class; they owned 6092, 6740 and 5693 acres respectively. Among the lesser gentry, something like 1000 or 2000 acres was usual; thus George Burke of Danesfield owned 2759 acres, Gerald Blennerhassett of Riddlestown 1142, and his County Limerick neighbour James

Cooper of Cooper Hill 1075. At the bottom of the tree, there were some hopelessly run-down families such as the Briscoes of Tinvane in County Tipperary whose patrimony had dwindled to less than 500 acres.

A government valuation made earlier in the century gives a figure for the income received by each landlord from rents; thus the Duke of Leinster is supposed to have received £55,877, the Earl of Wicklow £15,719, Lord Langford £9281, Robert Cole Bowen £3795, James Cooper a mere £941. These figures, however, are only theoretical; on some estates the rents were lower than the valuation, on others they were higher. They tended to be higher in the 1870s, when Irish agriculture was still enjoying the long if not unbroken period of prosperity that had begun soon after the terrible potato famine of the late 1840s; for example, the Earl of Mayo's rents in 1877 came to £9605, some £2000 more than the valuation.[21] During this period, landlords whose estates were in good order had a comfortable income from their rents, and many of them supplemented their rental income by farming profitably on their own account. In County Galway, most of the gentry farmed some of their own land; the Ballinasloe October Fair was a great social event. The Galway Club took a house in Ballinasloe for the fair week, staffed it with servants and stocked it with claret, and here each night, after a day spent in buying and selling livestock, the assembled gentry would dine at a long table.

But while plenty of Irish landlords in the 1870s were genuinely well off, the air of prosperity was often deceptive. Among the Ascendancy, it was regarded as vulgar to talk of money; it was no more done to bemoan one's poverty than to boast of one's wealth. In those days of low wages and cheap and plentiful food, appearances could be kept up on a very small income; and although the estates of the lesser gentry may have theoretically brought them in more than £1000 a year, their real income was in most cases very small indeed; a writer of 1868 put it at something between £200 and £500 a year.[22] James Cooper of Cooper Hill certainly did not have the £941 a year he is recorded as having; his sons went barefoot up to the age of twelve and his daughters had to take turns to go to balls because there were not enough ball dresses to go round.[23] This discrepancy between theoretical and actual income was to some extent caused by rents being lower than the valuation; but it was more frequently due to the mortgages and other charges with which so many Irish estates were burdened. The large and medium-sized estates were just as encumbered as the smaller ones. Colonel King-Harman and his cousin by marriage, Anna Countess of Kingston, each received no more than about £8000 a year from their respective estates which, but for encumbrances, would have brought them in £40,000 a year and nearly £18,000 a year. When the young George Moore succeeded his father in 1870, his 12,000 acre Moore Hall estate in County Mayo brought in nearly £4000 a year, out of which, after paying mortgage interest, he had only £500 a year left.

These mortgages were the result of extravagance, bad management and in some cases philanthropy. It was usually earlier generations that had been extravagant – the Regency bucks, the Charles Lever characters; their worthy mid-Victorian descendants had to suffer the consequences. The money might have gone on high living, on building or gambling or racehorses or on an expensive election campaign; or it might have been squandered in a more original way; thus the Earl of Donoughmore's estate in County Tipperary was reduced because a forebear had run a theatre to oblige an actress friend. But though it was generally a case of the sins of the father, there were plenty of Victorians who overspent. The talented and highly respectable future Viceroy of India, the Earl of Dufferin, as he was then, was obliged in the 1870s to sell 18,000 out of the 26,000 acres which he owned in County Down because he was so heavily in debt; he had brought this on himself simply by maintaining a standard of living that would have been by no means excessive for an English peer of his importance, but which his Irish patrimony could not support.

Another great Irish landowner who was in financial difficulties in the 1870s was Henry Herbert of Muckruss, an estate bordering on the Killarney Lakes and almost as beautiful and extensive as that of the neighbouring magnate Lord Kenmare. Nobody seems to have known where the family fortunes went – Henry's father had, it is true, built a large Elizabethan-revival mansion where he had entertained Queen Victoria in tremendous style – but even after that there was still plenty of money. Some attributed the collapse to reckless spending, others to a sharp reduction in rents, others again to Henry Herbert's business ventures, which included prospecting for copper and making birch trees into cotton reels.

In about 1840, when the new Muckruss House was built, building was still a favourite pastime of the Ascendancy; but by the 1870s it was no longer fashionable to outbuild one's neighbour. The mansions of Lord Kenmare and Count de la Poer, Sir Arthur Guinness's baronial additions to Ashford Castle, Colonel Robert Cosby's grandiose Italianate remodelling of Stradbally Hall in Queen's County, Lord Mayo's fine new Queen Anne-revival house in County Kildare – paid for by public subscription as a tribute to his father, the Viceroy of India who was assassinated in 1872 – were exceptional; the Irish landlord of those days generally made do with the house he had inherited.

Henry Herbert of Cahirnane, whose estate was much smaller than that of his kinsman and namesake at the nearby Muckruss, would certainly have made do with his pleasant old house had it not been for his neurotic and domineering wife, who came from England, was inordinately proud of her illustrious lineage and despised all things Irish. When she first came to Cahirnane as a bride in 1865, she was dismayed to find that the only sanitation consisted of a row of outdoor privies approached by a path through wet laurels. An old man would accompany her on her walks along this path, holding a carriage umbrella over her head, and when she had reached her objective he would insist on waiting for her lest she should get wet on the return journey. 'I made your father see how much I disliked it, and everything else about the place,' she told her daughter many years later. 'The first present he gave me after our marriage was a wc from Cork, which he had fitted up in time for Christmas.'[24]

Even then she was not satisfied, and in the following decade her husband built her a new house, a monster of grey cement with an interior of pitch-pine. It cost far more than he could afford, for his rents were declining; he had to skimp the furnishings, so that some of the high plate-glass windows lacked curtains. From then on he was burdened with a debt which grew more harassing every year, for though nothing was spent on luxuries or amusements and he and his family dressed in coarse Kerry frieze woven of wool from his own sheep, he was determined to keep up appearances; the servants, gardeners, gamekeepers, horses and carriages at Cahirnane continued to be as numerous as ever. He lived in constant dread that the bank would ask him to reduce his overdraft; 'he would sit alone in the large, bleak dining room with an oil lamp giving too poor a light to read by, and brood over his financial worries, a glass of whiskey and cold water by his side.'[25]

The Land War

On 2 April 1878 when the Earl of Leitrim was driving near the northern Donegal coast, where he owned a large estate, he was shot dead together with his driver and a young clerk who was accompanying him. The assassins escaped in a boat and were never brought to trial, though it was generally believed that the whole countryside knew who they were. Leitrim fancied himself as an improving landlord, but he was greatly disliked in the locality being a miserly and inconsiderate tyrant: for example, he would shoot his tenants' goats, or have them shot, on the pretext that they were bad for the land. His murder seems to have been occasioned by a dispute over the building of a school; the popular legend that it was an act of vengeance on the part of a farmer's son whose sister had been violated by the seventy-year-old bachelor Earl is without foundation. With his lifelong talent for quarrelling – he had even once engaged in open warfare with the reigning Viceroy – Leitrim had managed to fall foul of the police, whose reports on his conduct as a landlord are consequently far from favourable; yet they contain no mention of his having had designs on the local girls, though they are full of his other misdeeds.[1]

'I am very very sorry we shot Lord Leitrim,' Maria La Touche wrote on hearing of the crime, showing by her use of 'we' instead of 'they' the extent to which she regarded its perpetrators as her countrymen. 'Sorry, but not at all surprised. It was certain to happen sooner or later. And I am sorrier still for the two poor boys who were with him.'[2] Other members of the Ascendancy were no more surprised than she was. 'The wretched old man has been practically working for his own destruction for many years,' wrote William Hart, whose brother was a County Donegal landlord on a smaller scale than Leitrim yet nevertheless of consequence.

'He has been a curse to his country during his life, and his death has been equally a curse to it, if his cruel murderers escape the extremity of punishment. Personally however, I feel more horror at the assassination of his unfortunate clerk and car driver, who were so causelessly murdered, than at his.'[3] Hart was not alone among the Ascendancy in regarding Leitrim as one of the worst of those responsible for giving Irish landlords a bad name.

There were, of course, plenty of good Irish landlords, particularly among the magnates; the Duke of Leinster and the Marquess of Waterford were both extremely popular with their tenants, while it used to be said that if a man was a tenant of the Earl of Kenmare it was as good as a dowry for his daughter. But despite the many good ones among them, Irish landlords by the 1870s had come to be regarded as hard-hearted evictors and rack-renters, an image that has persisted down to the present day, though it has been considerably modified by recent historical writing.[4] Certain notorious individuals such as Lord Leitrim undoubtedly contributed to this image, but what helped more than anything else to give rise to it was the fact that so many Irish landlords were chronically impecunious, if not necessarily through their own fault. They all too often had to get what they could out of their estates to keep their creditors at bay; there was no money left to be ploughed back in the form of improvements, such as were carried out as a matter of course by landlords in Britain and elsewhere. They were in no position to help their tenants when times were bad, however much they might have wished to do so.

This was tragically apparent at the time of the Famine, which resulted in no fewer than 50,000 evictions between 1847 and 1850, though not all of them can be blamed on Ascendancy landlords, many of those evicted having been tenants of larger tenant farmers or of people like shopkeepers or country lawyers who were landowners in a small way. The landlords responsible for evictions mostly had no choice in the matter; it was a 'miserable necessity'[5] to save themselves from ruin. Many landlords were in fact ruined by the Famine, for their tenants were not only unable to pay them any rent but had to be provided with free food in order to be kept alive. For the more prosperous landlords – like Maria La Touche's husband who fed the starving people with meat from the deer in his park – this might not have been so difficult, but for the poorer ones it was usually more than they could afford; James Martin's straitened finances could barely support the soup-kitchen which he and his wife established outside the gates of Ross House. The contemporary journalist and politician A.M. Sullivan, a Home Ruler who was no friend of landlordism, pays tribute to those landlords 'who at every sacrifice sustained and retained their tenantry' over the Famine years;[6] and to those who, like Barnie FitzPatrick's uncle, died of 'famine fever' caught while working to relieve the people's distress. There were others among the Ascendancy equally heroic: Vere Foster, the brother of a County Louth baronet, endured the horrors of an Atlantic crossing in an emigrant ship while campaigning to better the conditions of the Famine emigrants.

Irish landlords never really recovered their reputation after the Famine, though their record during the three decades that followed is not nearly as bad as the traditional picture would suggest. Rack-renting – that is, obtaining the highest possible rent for a farm even if it meant turning out the tenant and putting in someone else – was allowed by law, yet the overall increase in rents during this period was no more than about 20 per cent as compared with an increase in agricultural profits of as much as 78 per cent, which shows that not many landlords were guilty of this form of oppression. Evictions, despite certain much-publicized cases, were at a low level; the Irish agricultural tenant of the time was statistically less likely to be evicted than the industrial worker of contemporary Britain was to become destitute through injury[7] or the self-employed British town-dweller was to be sold up by his creditors. After the passing of Gladstone's Land Act of 1870, tenants evicted for reasons other than the non-payment of rent could claim compensation for any improvements that they might have carried out.

As for the droit de seigneur of which Lord Leitrim was accused, a present-day historian of Irish landlordism has found only one instance of it in the second half of the nineteenth century, the landlord in question being an obscure figure of the 1860s. Ascendancy morals were improved by Evangelicalism, William Ponsonby-Barker and his 'human hot water bottles' notwithstanding, while those undeterred by the sanctions of religion now felt constrained to go to Paris, London or at any rate Dublin for their amorous escapades. 'Taking one's pleasure on the country' or even 'sowing one's wild oats in one's own county town' had come to be associated in the Ascendancy mind with people who had rather gone to seed, like Henry Briscoe of Tinvane, of whom it was said that he dared not throw a stone at any child in the town of Carrick-on-Suir for fear it might be his own.[8]

There may have been hard-hearted landlords like Leitrim, but there were also plenty of soft-hearted ones like the Home Rule MP Colonel King-Harman who, although his estates were heavily encumbered, was always ready to let his tenants off their rent if he thought they were in difficulties. On one estate in County Mayo tenants unable to pay would ask their landlord's wife for 'a loan of the rent' – a polite fiction which did not establish any precedent. In this case the lady dispensed the so-called loans with her husband's connivance, but Robert Cole Bowen, who was 'as sharp as a fox and as hard as iron', never knew that his wife would sometimes 'wait on rent days, inside the glass door to the passage, to slip the required sum, from her own pocket, into some hand that came empty and damp with fear'.[9] Their seventeen-year-old daughter, Sarah, who used to be sent by her father on an outside car to collect the rents from distant farms, would not press for what was due if she felt that the tenant had difficulty in paying, though it meant that all the way back to Bowen's Court, she would be in dread of her father's wrath.

The landlord's compassion – or that of his womenfolk – was naturally less easily aroused in the case of the absentee. Charlie Beresford, who was very much against absenteeism though an absentee landlord himself – having inherited an estate in County Cavan which, on account of his naval career, he was only able to visit sporadically – tells in his memoirs of how he would have been guilty of rack-renting had he not gone to talk to one of his tenants. His agent had assured him that he could raise his rents all round, but after hearing that this particular tenant had raised the value of his holding by his own labours and those of his sons, he was determined to do nothing of the sort.

The absentee who never visited his estate and whose only concern was to get as much income as he could from it was even more responsible for giving Irish landlords a bad name than the resident tyrant like Lord Leitrim, but by the 1870s this person was no longer typical of the Ascendancy. In earlier times, when travel to and from Ireland – and also within the country – was extremely difficult, many Irish landowners had deserted their estates, particularly in the years immediately after the Union, which reduced Dublin from being a capital, the seat of the Irish Parliament, to being a provincial city, so that those of the Ascendancy who had a taste for politics and high life tended to be drawn to London. Later in the century, as transport improved and the beauties of the Irish scenery came to be more widely appreciated, the absentees, or their children, returned. The wealthier families still had London houses, as had the richer landowners of Britain, but when the London season was over they went home to Ireland which, thanks to railways and steamships, they could now reach almost as easily as their British friends reached Devon or Scotland.

By the 1870s the typical absentee landlord was someone not necessarily of Ascendancy background living in a Dublin suburb on the income from a few hundred acres bought as an investment, like stocks and shares. The eccentric and miserly Marquess of Clanricarde, who never went near his County Galway estate after inheriting it in 1874 but lived in London where he was to be seen shuffling about the streets of St James's, a down-at-heel figure frequently mistaken for a tramp, is generally cited as a notorious example of absenteeism at this time, but among the Irish territorial magnates of his time he was one of the exceptions. Of the 150 or so landowners who in 1878 owned more than 10,000 acres in Ireland, at least 120 resided principally on their Irish estates. In the case of two of them, Lord Carysfort and Arthur Hugh Smith-Barry of Fota Island in County Cork, the traditional picture of absenteeism is reversed, for while they both owned large estates in England in addition to their Irish properties, their interests were chiefly in Ireland.

Desert Court

Naturally there were those among the Ascendancy landlords of the 1870s who for some reason or other lived away from their estates, but so were there among the landowners of Britain and elsewhere. The young George Moore preferred the bohemian world of Paris to County Mayo. Robert Percy ffrench of Monivea Castle in County Galway also preferred to live on the continent; he moved in cosmopolitan society and was married to a Russian heiress. The Earl of Desart, an impecunious young man with marital problems, was living away from Desart Court, his beautiful Palladian house in County Kilkenny, when Maria La Touche, who was his half-aunt, came here in 1879. 'All the familiar walks were obliterated, the stones of the terrace and balustrades were lifted out of their place by seedling trees' she reported in a letter. 'The greenhouse was a tangle of passion flowers within and ivy and honeysuckle from without. Flowering shrubs trailed and twisted and caught at one another across what used to be trim avenues. The old lawns were waving meadows . . . There was something very sad about it from the human side. But yet I never saw the place look so beautiful, or so stately and calm.'[10]

There were some good landlords among the absentees, such as Viscount Midleton, who owned the town of Midleton in East Cork and over 6000 acres in the vicinity, but whose principal family seat was in Surrey. His popularity with his Irish tenantry was shared by his agent, James Penrose-FitzGerald, the brother of another prominent East Cork landlord. Land agents like Penrose-FitzGerald were considerable personages in the Ascendancy world; many were themselves landlords, such as the Hamiltons of Hamwood in County Meath, who for generations were the agents and confidants of their illustrious neighbours the Dukes of Leinster. It was usual for agents like Penrose-FitzGerald to be Justices of the Peace; Major John Humphreys, agent to the Earl of Wicklow in an earlier period and father of the hymn-writer Mrs Alexander, became a Deputy-Lieutenant.

— *2* —

The agrarian agitation known as the Land War, which started in Connaught in 1879 and spread to other parts of the country during the following year, took the Ascendancy by surprise. Despite Lord Leitrim's murder and some other less-publicized crimes, the Irish countryside was on the whole peaceful in the late 1870s. It is true that agricultural prosperity was giving place to a depression, caused by bad harvests and falling prices; by the beginning of 1879 some landlords already felt obliged to reduce their rents, among them the husband of Maria La Touche, who consequently had to get rid of his agent and steward and make other economies. Maria's pony-carriage and ponies had to be sold. 'We have altogether come down in the world' she wrote, but added: 'This is not one of the things that make me sulky. Quite the reverse.'[11]

There had, however, been an even worse agricultural depression in the early 1860s and that did not cause a land war. But when hard times came again in 1879, bringing in their wake the inevitable tensions between landlords and tenants over demands for reductions in rent, the tenants were backed by political forces such as had not existed during the previous depression – those same forces of Nationalism that were sweeping the Home Rulers to victory. Under the dynamic leadership of Parnell – himself the brother of a landlord – and of Michael Davitt, the Irish National Land League was formed to organize the tenants in their demands and to conduct a general agitation against landlordism.

The Land League's policy was to prevail upon tenants to pay no rent at all unless the landlords agreed to the reduction which they demanded. If a landlord retaliated by evicting tenants who refused to pay, the League endeavoured to make it impossible for anybody else to take their holdings by the method which came to be known as boycotting after being used in November 1880 on Captain Charles

Boycott, an English farmer and land agent in County Mayo. The activities of the League inevitably led to violence, and there was a sharp increase in agrarian crime, for which the landlords blamed what they regarded as the weakness of Gladstone, who returned to power with the general election of the spring of 1880. Henceforth, the Grand Old Man was to be the Ascendancy's principal bête noire; chamber pots decorated on the inside with his portrait were to find their way into many an Irish country house.

The disorder was never as great, nor as widespread, as it appeared to be, at any rate in as far as it affected the Ascendancy. Public opinion on both sides of the Irish Sea was shocked by various incidents, notably the murder in County Galway in September 1880 of Viscount Mountmorres, but this obscure and impoverished peer was the only Ascendancy landlord who actually lost his life during the Land War. Others were shot at, but somehow escaped injury; others again were threatened with assassination, such as Viscount Lismore, who had to have police protection and eventually left Ireland for good. George Moore and his neighbour and agent Thomas Ruttledge of Cornfield had a narrow escape during the late summer of 1880 when they attempted to drive across a wooden bridge which had been maliciously sawn through; together with the horse and trap they fell into the river, but suffered nothing worse than a wetting.

For Moore, as for all other encumbered landlords, a more serious aspect of the Land War was the threat of financial ruin through the reduction or withholding of rents. The menace of the Land League hangs heavily over the assembled company at Dungory Castle in his early novel *A Drama in Muslin*. 'Every mind was occupied by one thought – how the pleasure of the dinner party had been spoiled by that horrible Land League discussion.' Since the Land War was more in the nature of a series of skirmishes than a campaign on a preconceived plan, nobody knew who the next victim would be; a landlord might flatter himself that he was on the best of terms with his tenants, only to find that the League had put them up to asking for a rent reduction such as he or she could not afford to give.

Catholic landlords suffered as much as Protestant ones; indeed, the League's first target was actually a Catholic priest. There was no question of landlords being singled out for attack because they were descended from Cromwellian or other English settlers, as is sometimes suggested. The Duke of Devonshire, whose estates in Ireland had come to him by descent from the ultra-Protestant Elizabethan English settler Richard Boyle, Earl of Cork, had very little trouble during the Land War for the simple reason that his vast English income enabled him to be very generous to his Irish tenants. On the other hand, many of the victims of the Land War were of Celtic-Irish or Norman descent. Lord Lismore (who, incidentally, had no connection with the Duke of Devonshire's County Waterford seat Lismore Castle, but lived in the neighbouring county of

Tipperary) was an O'Callaghan. Sir Robert Lynch-Blosse, whose sufferings at the hands of the Land League caused him to retire with his family to Folkestone – leaving his County Mayo estate in charge of his agent, with a body of armed constabulary encamped on the lawn in front of the house – was of Norman ancestry, descended from one of the medieval civic families of Galway, known as the 'Tribes'.

Among the landlords of impeccable Celtic-Irish descent who suffered during the Land War was the armless and legless Arthur MacMorrough Kavanagh, though when the Land League tried to stop his rents, some of his tenants paid him at dead of night, or sent him the money by letter from a post office twenty miles away. But what for him was far worse than the loss of revenue was the outcome of the 1880 general election. He had sat in Parliament as one of the two Members for County Carlow since 1869; he was convinced of his popularity with his County Carlow tenantry and the other people living on and around his estates. Although he had known before the election that many of his erstwhile friends would, under the influence of the Land League, be voting for his Home Rule opponents, enough of his people had assured him of their support for him to count on at any rate a narrow majority. On the polling day he himself went to vote in the neighbouring county of Kilkenny; as he returned to Borris that night he could see bonfires on the hills and felt certain that his people were celebrating his victory. But in the village at his gates he found that the crowds, with their torchlight processions, were celebrating his defeat. 'It is not so much the defeat or the loss of the seat that I mind, although they bring with them their own stings,' he wrote in answer to a letter of sympathy. 'But to feel that almost every one of my own men who met me with kind expressions and cheerful promises were traitors, is the hard part of the burden and the poison of the sting.'[12]

In County Kildare, where Punchestown Races competed with the election as a source of excitement, the 'Home Ruiners', as Maria La Touche called them, were likewise victorious. For this, Maria blamed the local gentry: 'Few of them consider anything worth living for that has not to do with horses.'[13] At Portarlington in the next county, however, the Home Rule candidate was soundly defeated by Barnie FitzPatrick, who was carried in triumph through the streets, a beggar woman supporting his head and kissing him repeatedly 'with vigour'. His electoral victory was followed by threats on his life as the Land War grew fiercer; he refused police protection and engaged two 'stalwart Northerners' as a private bodyguard, telling them that if he were fired on, they were not to mind about him but concentrate on shooting his assailant. He also put it about that if he saw anybody crouching behind a hedge he would shoot first and apologize afterwards. These precautions were efficacious, though he and his wife Clare had to be shadowed by the two Northerners for nearly a year, which rather got on their nerves.[14]

In December 1880 the Land League struck at William Bence-Jones of Lisselane in West Cork, whose career as an improving landlord had, for all his good intentions, brought him a measure of unpopularity. Having improved his tenants' land, he expected them to pay a higher rent; to him this seemed fair enough and he argued that even though they had to pay more on account of his improvements, they were much better off than they had been previously, but some of his tenants did not see it in this way. And as a well-known writer on landowning and agriculture, he had made himself unpopular by his rather offensive comments on what he considered to be the character defects of the Irish tenantry.

His troubles began in the usual way with his tenants demanding a reduction in rent which he would not concede. A grave was dug outside the Lisselane hall door and he received threatening letters, then he was boycotted and most of the workers on his estate were made to leave. This was serious, for he farmed a thousand acres on his own account; there were a hundred cows to be milked and what with cattle, horses and sheep, a thousand animals to be fed. Bence-Jones was himself too old to work on the farm, but his elder son Willy and his unmarried daughter Lily were both at home. Willy and the Scottish farm bailiff fed the animals while Lily took on the milking of the cows helped by the butler and a gardener who were both English and by an Irish housemaid who had remained faithful. 'Poor Willy's back and neck were quite doubled over for one evening and my arms were weak with milking,' Lily wrote just before Christmas to her married sister Carry who was in England. 'And even now we can neither of us sit down in a low chair without groans over our poor legs. However, we are really getting on bravely . . . if that hard-hearted brute Mr Gladstone could only be hung in chains as the officer with the Dragoons from Bandon suggested yesterday we should do very well.'[15]

The Dragoons and also ten policemen with double-barrelled guns had been sent to protect them, for there had been more threats and Lisselane was by now in a state of siege. The family all carried revolvers; the butler let one off by mistake in the house, giving everybody a fright. 'I ask our friends to remember what a Christmas we are having, unable to go to church on Christmas Day without revolvers in our pockets,' Bence-Jones wrote in one of his numerous letters to *The Times*.[16] To make matters worse, they were snowed up, for it was an exceptionally hard winter; a few miles away at Castle Bernard the lake was frozen, so that the Bandons were able to hold a skating party which may have served as a distraction from their own worries, many of Lord Bandon's tenants having refused to pay any rent.

During those weeks, Bence-Jones became a national figure; letters of sympathy and offers of help poured in from all quarters. A stalwart British workman wrote to say that he would work for him 'for no Paye and two bits of dry bread'. Someone else wrote drawing attention to a remarkable new gun: 'It is not expensive and to

Armed Constabulary at Lisselane, the home of William Bence-Jones in West Cork, during the Land War.

Skating Party at Castle Bernard Christmas 1880.

use the inventor's ungodly expression would kill the devil at sixty yards.' A clergyman in Florida offered to sell Bence-Jones an estate there with a mansion which he assured him was commodious 'though in no way comparable to any of the castles the landlords of Ireland are used to'.[17]

By the middle of January a new labour force had been recruited and was at work under the protection of the police. Bence-Jones, accompanied by Willy and Lily, was able to join his wife at their London house. She had been in England since the beginning of December, suffering terrible anxiety on their account, for they had naturally seemed in far greater danger from a distance.

Even from a mere twenty miles away, the special correspondent of the *Daily Telegraph* in the West of Ireland heard exaggerated reports of the plight of Lord Ardilaun, the former Sir Arthur Guinness, who had recently been raised to the peerage. He was said to be beleaguered at Ashford Castle, his life threatened on account of his alleged refusal to allow his tenants to cut turf on their own hills and because he had lent some horses to his neighbour Captain Boycott. The correspondent braved a snowstorm in order to interview him, and on the way

Ashford Castle.

Tea and tennis at Ashford Castle in September 1880. Lord Ardilaun, wearing a bowler hat, is second from the left in the back row. Lady Rosse is in the middle of the back row, Barnie FitzPatrick stands on the extreme right, handing a lady a cup of tea.

talked to the country people who all agreed that he was an exceptionally good and generous landlord, but kept on saying: 'He's not liked, sir, he's not liked.'

At Ashford there was no sign of any siege. No soldiers or police guarded the gates, while inside the beautiful demesne labourers were peacefully at work brushing leaves from the paths. Lord Ardilaun seemed perfectly happy in his brand-new castle of gleaming cut-stone on the wooded shores of Lough Corrib, where his steam yacht lay at anchor. The correspondent asked him if he considered himself to be in any danger. 'Well, no,' he replied laconically.

'Police have been offered me for my protection, but I have a little force of my own consisting of my gamekeepers, who are loyal men and true, and I prefer to trust to them. Besides, my tenants are all on good terms with me, even though they may be frightened by those who are about them. I do not intend to even ask them for their rent until next January. They could pay it very well now, but I certainly shall not press them. Whatever danger landlords are in is owing to the agitation which goes on around us'.

Afterwards, the correspondent had a chance of talking to one of the local leaders of the Land League, who said: 'I consider that Lord Ardilaun would be perfectly safe if he were to walk about amongst his tenants, because he is a good man and much liked here; but his agent is disliked and it is he who is unpopular.'

The wealthy Lord Ardilaun could afford to do without rents for the sake of peace, but Anna Countess of Kingston, who in December 1880 was confronted by a parade of some 1600 of the tenants of her vast Mitchelstown estate on the borders of Cork, Limerick and Tipperary, demanding a rent reduction owing to the fall in the price of butter, was in a much less fortunate position. The extravagance of the two Earls of Kingston immediately preceding her late husband – the first of whom was a larger-than-life Regency character known as Big George – followed by a very expensive family resettlement, had brought the Mitchelstown estate close to ruin; it now carried a crippling mortgage of £236,000. The estate should have brought in nearly £18,000 a year, but after paying the mortgage interest there was only about £8000 a year left for the upkeep of Big George's immense Regency-Gothic castle and its magnificent demesne as well as for the living expenses of Lady

Mitchelstown Castle.

The drawing room at Mitchelstown Castle, in Anna, Countess of Kingston's time.

Kingston and her second husband, who consequently maintained a regime of strict economy. The scarcity of fruit in Lady Kingston's barmbracks – those spiced currant loaves which, sliced and buttered, are a familiar feature of the Irish tea-table – became a byword with her neighbours. Once, when Robert Cole Bowen was having tea with her at Mitchelstown, another gentleman, who happened to get a slice of barmbrack with a currant in it, held it up for him to see, at which he remarked, in his best County Cork French, 'Vous avez raisong.'[18]

Until the end of 1880, Lady Kingston and her husband Willie Webber had been on the best of terms with their tenants. Evictions on the estate were virtually unknown and the rents were very moderate, even in the years of agricultural prosperity. But owing to the mortgage interest, they felt unable to grant the reduction which the tenants demanded; it was only something like 15 or 20 per cent, but would have reduced the net annual income from the estate to a mere £5000. The tenants retaliated by paying hardly any of the half year's rent that had been due since the previous September; in March 1881 when the rent for the next half year fell due, the same thing happened. To emphasize their determination not to pay unless their rents were reduced, the tenants held a great demonstration in the streets of Mitchelstown, processing by torchlight through the square outside the castle gates accompanied by the local band playing Nationalist airs.

Lady Kingston now took up the challenge and served eviction notices on a number of tenants. In the case of some of them, this had the desired effect and they either paid their rent in full or agreed to pay it in instalments. But others organized a resistance and when the first evictions took place at the end of May there was an ugly riot in which policemen were stoned and people injured by charging dragoons. The evictions were deferred, pending the arrival of more constabulary and troops, and in the meantime Lady Kingston dismissed her labourers. By the end of June a small army of about seven hundred soldiers and three hundred police had been built up and was encamped around the castle; but when a new batch of eviction notices was served, the people continued to be defiant. They processed once again, headed by a pipe band and children carrying green boughs and singing the Nationalist marching song, *God Save Ireland;* there were cheers for the Land League and Parnell and groans for Lady Kingston and Mr Webber. Angry stone-throwing crowds gathered at the evictions and had to be dispersed by baton-charges; the entrance to the tenants' dwellings were barricaded with boulders and furze-bushes.

But having at last been formally evicted, their doors broken open and some of their furniture put outside, the tenants, almost to a man, paid the rent and were immediately reinstated. Of the two hundred or so tenants of the Mitchelstown estate who were evicted during the course of that summer, all but about twenty were back in their homes before the day was out having paid what was owing; and of the few who did not pay up on the actual day of their eviction, at least three-quarters paid and duly regained possession at a later date. By September the tenants were more interested in saving the harvest, which promised to be a good one, than in continuing their campaign.

During those summer months of 1881, while Lady Kingston was engaged in her lengthy dispute with her tenants, the Ascendancy continued to enjoy its cricket. There were matches all over Ireland, though the season was marred by the tragic death of the young Cambridge Cricket Blue, Nathaniel Hone, who while on a tour with a Na Shuler team at the beginning of August went into a chemist's shop in Limerick to get a dose of senna and was given carbolic acid by mistake. Hone came of a distinguished Dublin family noted for producing artists and cricketers; there had been no fewer than five Hones in the Gentlemen of Ireland team which toured America in 1879. That team had also included a young County Cork baronet, Sir George Colthurst, whose marriage took place in the same month as Nathaniel Hone's death.

The wedding, in Cork city, was a great event, for the bridegroom was very popular; he was not only a cricketing hero but active in many philanthropic enterprises, particularly in those aimed at providing employment and relieving agrarian distress. He was also a considerable landowner in the county and heir, through his mother, to the celebrated Blarney Castle; while his bride, Miss Edith Morris, was the daughter of another prominent County Cork family. The day was perfect, there was a line of nearly two hundred carriages outside the newly-completed St Fin Barre's Church of Ireland Cathedral. The guests included most of the peers and peeresses of County Cork: the Bandons, the Donerailes, the Carberys, the Fermoys. The best man was Lord Listowel's cousin Thomas Hare, Master of the Duhallow Hunt. After the reception, which was held in a country house on the shores of the Lee estuary, the newly-married couple left in a steam launch put at their disposal by the Admiral commanding at Queenstown; it took them down river to Cork Beg, the seat of the Penrose-FitzGerald family on an island just inside the harbour entrance, where they were to spend the first few days of their honeymoon.

Later that evening, in the opposite corner of the county, some fifty of the tenants of Sir George's Ballyvourny estate together with their womenfolk and children celebrated his marriage with a bonfire and barrels of porter, with singing and dancing to a fiddler. The Ballyvourny lands, which were more than twenty miles away from the principal Colthurst estate, had caused Sir George a certain amount of trouble shortly before his wedding; there had been the usual demand for a reduction in rent, and though he had offered his tenants a reduction of 15 per cent, only a few of them had been willing to accept this. The rest had combined to hold out for more, but he had broken the combination by taking legal proceedings against the ringleaders. The outdoor celebration on his wedding night might have seemed like a happy ending to the affair, but at eleven o'clock, when it was in full swing, the revellers were suddenly surrounded by armed men with blackened faces who opened fire on them, wounding several. Others were beaten up with heavy sticks by their assailants, who then proceeded to drink what remained of the porter.

On hearing of the outrage, Sir George and Lady Colthurst interrupted their honeymoon to visit the people who were injured, taking a doctor with them to attend to their wounds. A newspaper reporter who accompanied them to Ballyvourny saw a woman bless the young baronet and his bride. He also noticed that Sir George was building a fine new house for one of his tenants.

During the first winter of the Land War, the Ascendancy had still been able to hunt. The hunting field had in fact been neutral territory; Parnell, when staying in December 1880 with his friend Richard Power, the Home Rule MP for Waterford city, had actually gone out with Lord Waterford's hounds. But by the end of 1881, hunting had virtually been brought to a standstill through acts of sabotage and violence; in the following spring the Kildare Hunt had to abandon its race meeting at Punchestown. Lord Waterford closed Curraghmore and took his hunting establishment over to England; for those not rich enough to follow his example the remaining winter months stretched gloomily ahead with shooting as the only consolation. And in some parts of the country even the shooting was being spoilt by what were known as 'Land League hunts': placards called on the people to assemble in their thousands and kill all the game on a particular estate.

$$- \; 3 \; -$$

By the summer of 1882, the Land War was more or less over. Although the Land League had succeeded in organizing tenants to an extent hitherto unknown, it was not possible to make them hold out indefinitely against the landlords, who from the autumn of 1881 onwards were inclined to take a tougher line and showed less hesitation in evicting tenants who persisted in withholding their rent. And Gladstone's Land Act of August 1881, which gave a greater security of tenure and provided for the fixing of fair rents by the Government, went a long way towards meeting the tenants' demands, even though it was viewed with some mistrust by Parnell and the other Land League leaders. The landlords also had mixed feelings about it. 'I hope you will find the new Land Act do good, or at any rate do away with a great deal of the evil which has been caused by the unprincipled and reckless agitation of Parnell and Co,' William Hart wrote from England in August 1881 to his brother in County Donegal.[19] But though there were many who, like Hart, welcomed the Act as being likely to restore peace, there were even more who saw it as an attack on private property: in Lord Dufferin's words, 'a further whittling away of the landlord's rights'.[20]

Lord Dufferin was a Liberal and had actually supported Gladstone's Land Act of 1870, but he assured a friend that he would have resigned over the new Act had he not by then been out of politics and on an embassy abroad. He felt grateful that he had sold 18,000 acres of his County Down estate, so little faith had he in the future of Irish landownership. His fears were confirmed in the summer of 1882 when the Government Commissioners imposed a rent reduction of as much as 30 per cent on a neighbouring County Down landlord, which left him with no income at all after mortgage interest and other charges had been paid.[21] There were to be many similar cases of hardship among landlords whose estates were heavily encumbered. Colonel King-Harman's rents were reduced by 20 per cent, which swallowed up the £8000 a year left to him after he had paid his English creditors.

Lord Dufferin feared that his neighbour would have to sell up – in fact he somehow managed to keep going, as did King-Harman – but there were other Ascendancy families ruined as a result of the Land War, particularly among the extravagant devil-may-care gentry of County Galway. Land War victims elsewhere in the country included the Briscoes of Tinvane, who were unable to survive being boycotted. One of Henry Briscoe's daughters fell in love with a labourer who had remained faithful during the trouble; she married him and they went to live in a labourer's cottage a few miles away, where she was to be seen, a shawl over her head, getting water at the well.

For the Ascendancy as a whole, the effects of the Land War were as much political, social and psychological as economic. The Home Rule movement may never have had much Ascendancy support, but what it had it lost almost entirely when it became associated with the Land League. In fact, most of the Ascendancy now felt the same as Sir Robert Lynch-Blosse, who regarded Home Rule as 'the inspiration of the Anti-Christ'.[22] Parnell stood condemned as a traitor to his class; of those other Ascendancy figures who had sat in Parliament as Home Rulers during the previous decade, almost all of them, including King-Harman, had left the party. When King-Harman returned to Parliament in 1883 it was as a Conservative.

Relations between landlords and tenants were never quite the same as they had been before 1880, even though such outward manifestations of cordiality as the presenting of illuminated addresses on the heir's coming-of-age continued and were often a sign of genuine mutual affection. However much the landlords may have tried to convince themselves that the tenants had been intimidated by the Land League, they felt a sense of betrayal. William Hart, whose letters before 1880 show a sympathy for the tenants, wrote bitterly to his brother in 1881: 'It must be sickening to have to go on living among a demoralized tenantry.'[23] Landlords who in happier times would never have thought of evicting tenants unable to pay their rent had shown no hesitation in turning out those who withheld their rent deliberately, or took part in anti-landlord agitations. The months between the autumn of 1881 and the summer of 1882 saw what was probably the worst wave of evictions since the Famine; the memory of these evictions made for bitterness among the tenants and served more than ever to blacken the image of landlordism in the eyes of Nationalist public opinion.

After the Land War, some members of the Ascendancy began to consider the possibility of selling at any rate part of their tenanted land, as Lord Dufferin had already done. Captain Chambré Ponsonby, who had inherited the Kilcooley estate in 1880, so despaired of Ireland's future that he decided to become a rancher in Wyoming, where his wife's brother Horace Plunkett had gone for the sake of his

W the Tenants on your
Lordship's Mayo Estate, and their
friends, have heard with the utmost
pleasure of your Marriage, and in
meeting assembled, unanimously and
with sincere and cordial feelings
have passed the following resolution. ....
........We on this joyful occasion of

Although relations between landlords and tenants were never quite the same after the
Land War, tenants continued to present their landlords with illuminated addresses.
Here is one presented to the Earl of Arran by his tenants on his marriage in 1902.
The picture shows Castle Gore, his family seat in County Mayo.

health. Having paid a preliminary visit to the Wild West, and even made arrangements to take out United States citizenship, he set off back to Ireland to fetch his wife Mary and their four young children, but died unexpectedly on the voyage. So Mary Ponsonby stayed on at Kilcooley, running the estate with the help of her brother Horace, who valiantly tackled the problems of landownership in County Tipperary from his ranch in the Rocky Mountains.

Dramas in muslin

— I —

As the Land War died down, Ascendancy life, never greatly disrupted, returned to normal. Those who moved in Viceregal circles noticed the tighter security following the double murder in May 1882 of the newly-arrived Chief Secretary Lord Frederick Cavendish, a son of the Duke of Devonshire, and the Under-Secretary Thomas Burke, who were stabbed to death by extremists in Dublin's Phoenix Park within sight of the windows of Viceregal Lodge. When Lady Alice Howard stayed at the Lodge in July as a guest of the Viceroy and Vicereine, Earl and Countess Spencer, there was a cricket match and she found it 'so curious to see the whole ground guarded by police and detectives in every direction'.[1] Later that summer, when Lord Spencer was staying with the Earl of Dunraven at Adare Manor for the Limerick Show, a formidable array of constabulary was drawn up outside the house, while inside, in the Victorian-Gothic great hall, the police officer responsible for His Excellency's safety entertained him and the rest of the party by singing a rebel song, 'The Wearing of the Green', at the top of his very fine voice.[2]

Lord Spencer, known as the Red Earl on account of his luxuriant red beard, was popular with the Ascendancy even though he had been sent by Gladstone. He and Lady Spencer went the rounds of the country house parties; they planned to stay with Lord and Lady Drogheda at Moore Abbey in November 1882 but cried off at the last minute on account of what Lady Alice Howard, who was another of the guests, referred to casually as 'some murders in Dublin'[3] – actually an unsuccessful attack on two jurymen by the extremists responsible for the Phoenix Park murders. Those who, like Lady Alice, met the Viceregal couple in the houses of their friends and received visits from them in their own houses as well as staying

Viceregal Lodge.

with them at Viceregal Lodge, where they normally resided – a long, stuccoed Georgian house standing in private grounds within the two thousand acres of Phoenix Park – constituted the real élite. The general run of Ascendancy society only came across them on formal occasions and were entertained not at the Lodge but at Dublin Castle, a combination of palace and government offices extending round two imposing courtyards hidden away behind the houses in the middle of the city.

The Viceroy and Vicereine and their Court – the Chamberlain, the State Steward, the Gentleman Usher, the Comptroller, the Master of the Horse, together with ADCs and Gentlemen-in-Waiting and a host of lesser functionaries – came into residence here for the six or seven weeks of the Castle season, which usually began early in February and ended in March after St Patrick's Day. During those weeks, the gilded State Apartments in the Upper Castle Yard were the scene of a succession of entertainments, starting with the Levee and the first of the two Drawing Rooms for the presentation of ladies and ending with the St Patrick's Ball. There was also the State Ball and the second Drawing Room; there were dinners and smaller dances. In some years there was an Investiture, or a Chapter, of the Order of St Patrick, Ireland's equivalent of the Garter.

The Dublin Castle guest lists were by no means restricted to the Ascendancy, but also included the official, professional, academic and business worlds of Dublin, the services and the clergy as well as visitors from Britain and elsewhere.

The Upper Ward, Dublin Castle. The entrance to the state apartments is on the right.

At the State Ball and the St Patrick's Ball, where there were usually about five or six hundred guests, and at the Drawing Room where twice that number of people might have been present, the Ascendancy was in the minority; thus the list of those who attended a St Patrick's Ball during the Spencer regime includes less than a hundred names from the peerage and other prominent Ascendancy families. 'No respectable people went,' was Lady Alice Howard's comment on a Drawing room of 1882, 'very large but poor as to quality,' her description of one two years later.[4] Regular frequenters of the Castle season from among the Ascendancy mostly lived within easy reach of Dublin, as Lady Alice did; people from further afield tended to come only when they had débutante daughters to 'bring out', it being customary in Ireland for girls – and indeed for married women – to be presented at the Viceregal Court even though they may also have been presented at Court in London.

A few of those who came up from the country possessed Dublin houses, but the vast majority either took furnished houses for the season, or else stayed in hotels. The Shelbourne on St Stephen's Green was the most popular and it was patronized by the Ascendancy on other occasions; Mrs Henry Valentine Macnamara of Ennistymon in County Clare would take a suite here whenever she was having a baby. Many, however, preferred – or could only afford – more modest establishments. Lady Alice Howard and her mother and sisters usually stayed at Maple's Hotel, but during the Castle season of 1883 she twice had the good fortune to be invited to stay at the Castle itself. On the second occasion the Viceregal house party, which was usually about forty strong, included her friends the Bandons, who though they lived far away in County Cork were among the habitués of the Castle.

Among the débutantes of that season was Daisy Burke from Danesfield in County Galway. The small girl who used to sit curled up beside her father in his Magistrate's Room, listening to him speaking to his tenants in Irish, was now seventeen, not especially pretty, yet attractive and very amusing. Her presentation dress, of gleaming white satin with the regulation three yards of train, cost her impecunious family the then considerable sum of five pounds; it was made for her by the famous Dublin dressmaker Mrs Sims, who, thinly disguised as Mrs Symond, appears in George Moore's novel *A Drama in Muslin,* where she is said to have been so grand that nobody below the rank of countess presumed to address her by her Christian name. After Daisy's fittings came the great moment when a mounted orderly clattered up Molesworth Street to Buswell's Hotel where she and her mother were staying, and handed in the large white envelope with the Chamberlain's stamp on it containing her summons to the first Drawing Room.

For most people, going to the Castle for a Drawing Room entailed spending anything up to an hour in the queue of carriages in Dame Street, which would move forward a short distance at a walk and then stop, only four carriages being allowed into the Castle Yard at a time. During these stops, the occupants of the carriages were subjected to a close inspection by the crowd that thronged the pavements, not only by the 'poor little things in battered bonnets and draggled skirts', as George Moore calls them,[5] who waited for hours in the rain so that they might see the ladies in their finery, but also by more robust characters whose comments were loud and frank. 'Mary, come and look at this one, look at the bulgy eyes of her', a 'shawly' once called out to her friend after peering through a carriage window at a daughter of Mrs Brooke of Summerton.[6] The obscure Daisy Burke was, however, spared this ordeal, for the cousin who was to present her was the wife of a high legal dignitary with the much-coveted privilege of the Private Entrée, which meant that they could drive round the back of the Castle and go in by a different gate from that used by ordinary mortals.

Having arrived at the Castle, they had to wait in an anteroom at the top of the red-carpeted stairs, which for Daisy, as for most of the other girls who waited there, was agony. At last an ADC called out their names and Daisy found herself in the Throne Room face-to-face with the red-bearded Lord Spencer, resplendent in Court dress and Orders. She felt that long thick beard tickling her cheek, for it was customary for the Viceroy to kiss each débutante as she was presented to him; Lord Spencer's red beard would turn white with face-powder before the end of the evening. Next, she had to curtsy to Lady Spencer, who with her golden hair, her

The throne room, Dublin Castle.

pink-and-white complexion and her glittering jewels was known as the Fairy Queen. Then the obligatory few steps backwards, which she accomplished without suffering the dread mishap of falling over her train before it was picked up and put over her arm by a footman.

In the crowded Picture Gallery, hung with portraits of former Viceroys, there was a buffet supper. When the presentations were over, Their Excellencies processed along the gallery on their way to the private supper room; they were followed by their house party, two by two, and preceded by the Chief Secretary bearing the Sword of State and by the entire Viceregal staff: the Chamberlain and the State Steward with their wands, Ulster King of Arms in his tabard, the Dean of the Chapel Royal, the Physicians and Surgeons in Ordinary, the Surgeon Dentist, the Surgeon Oculist.[7]

Looking back half a century later, Daisy also remembered her first State Ball, and described the scene in St Patrick's Hall, the finest of the State Apartments

St Patrick's Hall, during a Chapter of the order of St Patrick.

with its Corinthian columns and its painted ceiling depicting George III supported by Liberty and Justice, Henry II receiving the submission of the Irish Chiefs and St Patrick converting the Druids. The great lofty room, as she recalled it that evening, was 'full of light and music and laughter and voices and the soft swish of skirts'. Candles 'lit the white and gold walls, the floating banners of the Knights of St Patrick with their rich sombre colour . . . the brilliant uniforms of the men and the gay dresses and wonderful jewels of the women who moved below'.[8] The scene was enhanced by the fact that such men as were not in uniform were obliged to wear Court dress.

The dancing opened with the State Quadrille, which was restricted to Their Excellencies and a few other grandees; everybody else stood behind a cord, looking on. Lord Spencer, in his blue gold-laced coat and white knee breeches, his Star and Orders on his breast and the Garter round his knee, led the dance. His partner was the Marchioness of Ormonde, 'her delicate, beautifully-cut face under her dark lovely hair. She looked reserved and aristocratic . . . her stiff dressing suited her.' Lord Ormonde, 'good-looking and a commanding presence – a real Butler', was Lady Spencer's partner.[9] When the quadrille was over, the cord was let down and everybody began to dance to the Viennese waltzes which Liddell's Orchestra played to perfection. Dublin Castle managed to combine a pomp and magnificence more regal than Viceregal with a natural Irish gaiety, particularly at the St Patrick's Ball, when instead of the State Quadrille there was a lively Country Dance for which the orchestra played a selection of old Irish jigs.

It was, of course, much easier to obtain invitations to the Balls and Drawing Rooms than to the dinners and to the smaller dances in the Throne Room to which only two or three hundred were bidden. When the mounted orderlies stopped before houses in Merrion Square and Fitzwilliam Square, delivering invitations to these more intimate parties, 'the quiet curtained windows,' in Daisy's words, 'showed no sign of the fluttering hearts inside . . . sometimes, alas, the orderly rode by; and what a tragedy that was, and what woe and tears there were hidden then behind that quiet curtain that never stirred!'[10] Daisy herself received plenty of these much-sought-after invitations for the reason that the State Steward, the young Earl of Fingall, had noticed her at the beginning of the season and fallen in love at first sight. He should have been looking for an heiress, for though he was the head of the historic Danish-Irish family of Plunkett and owned a large ancestral castle in County Meath which dated back in part from the twelfth century, he was

Killeen Castle, Lord Fingall's ancestral home in County Meath.

Daisy Fingall.

not very well off. But he would think of no other girl but Daisy, who at any rate had the advantage of being a Catholic, as he was; they were married in the following May.

Daisy was more fortunate than most of George Moore's débutantes in *Muslin*, who come, as she did, from County Galway; they fail to find suitable husbands after not one but two Castle seasons and one of them suffers a fate worse than death. Moore himself took part in the Castle season of 1884, staying at the Shelbourne and borrowing a Court suit which saved him £45; he told his mother that the State Ball was 'very grand and imposing'[11] and mentioned the now Daisy Fingall's sister as one of the girls he had met. He did not, however, get an invitation to a dinner at the Castle, and in the following January, when he was working on *Muslin*, he wrote in a peremptory way to the Chamberlain, Colonel Gerald Dease, asking to be invited to one during the forthcoming Season, and adding: 'My books, as you are probably aware, are extensively read . . . it would therefore be well to render my picture as complete, as true, as vivid as possible.'[12] The Chamberlain turned down his request, and having been bombarded by Moore with further importunate notes, sent by a messenger who was instructed to wait for an answer, informed him that the lists were closed. Moore's chagrin at this rebuff would explain the rather unattractive picture which he paints in his novel of the Castle entertainments, particularly of the crowded Drawing Room:

> The brain ached with the dusty odour of *poudre de ris*, and the many acidities of evaporating perfume; the sugary sweetness of the blondes, the salt flavours of the brunettes, and this allegro movement of odours was interrupted suddenly by the garlicky andante, deep as the pedal notes of an organ, that the perspiring arms of a fat chaperon slowly exhaled.

He did not confine himself to a fictional revenge, but also published a letter in the Nationalist paper, the *Freeman's Journal*, maintaining that he had a right to go to the dinner because of the public money being spent on the Viceregal Court, and also making fun of poor Lord Fingall:

> I believe that when this somnolent earl is overtaken by that sleep which overtakes us all, and for which, it appears, he is qualifying himself daily as well as nightly, his claim to be remembered will be that he refused to invite me to dinner at the Castle.[13]

The State Steward's tendency to fall asleep during Viceregal functions was notorious; he was even able to sleep standing up, like a horse. Once, soon after their marriage, Daisy noticed him falling asleep at Their Excellencies' dinner table: 'Kick Fingall!' she said with some urgency to an ADC who was nearby, with the unfortunate result that he kicked Lady Spencer under the table by mistake. To some extent his somnolence was owing to his having spent the day hunting in Meath or Kildare, as many others did throughout the Castle season; but it was also due to boredom. He hated society and was only really happy in the saddle; he had taken on the office of State Steward in order that his two unmarried sisters might have the State Steward's house in the Castle Yard as a base from which to find husbands.

Fingall's colleague Gaston Monsell, the Gentleman Usher – the young half-French son of Lord Emly, a County Limerick peer – was also something of an amateur in his position, which carried the particular duty of calling out people's names. He never could remember names or get them right; he is said to have announced a member of the well-known English family of Sclater-Booth at a Levee as 'Mr Scatter Boots'. The Chamberlain, Colonel Dease, who came of an ancient family of Catholic gentry in County Westmeath, was, by contrast, a courtier to the manner born, urbane yet with a heart of stone when it came to considering requests for invitations and for the Private Entrée. This privilege was enjoyed automatically by people like peers and Privy Councillors and by the holders of various offices ranging from the Attorney-General to the Chairman of the Prison Board, but was also granted to others as a much-solicited favour. Lady Constance Leslie was among those whose request for the Private Entrée met with a favourable response, whereas Earlie Clonmell's sister Lady Rachel Saunderson was told that the list was full up.

The Chamberlain and his colleagues had also to deal with requests from ladies to be allowed, for reasons of health, to appear at the Castle in 'high dress' or 'half high dress' instead of the prescribed décolletage. Some of them, such as Lady Harriet Lynch-Blosse, Viscountess Monck and her sister-in-law Mrs Brooke of Summerton, were granted this indulgence on their word alone; others had to produce medical certificates. As well as replying to these requests, the Viceregal courtiers occasionally administered rebukes. 'The Chamberlain presents his compliments to Miss C. Todd Thornton and begs to ask her under what circumstances she appeared at St Patrick's Ball last night, the attendance at which is properly limited to those ladies who attended a Drawing Room during the *current season.*'

They also wrote such ominous memoranda as: 'Beware of a lady, Miss Georgina Corrie, who in Drawing Room Book gives a wrong address.' In March 1886 they noted that a lady who had been presented by the wife of a knight at the recent Drawing Room was 'not a lady of high social standing'.[14]

For all its rules and protocol, the Viceregal Court in Dublin was much more easy-going than the Court of St James's. Occasional cases of over-indulgence were viewed with toleration, such as when Earlie Clonmell went into St Patrick's Hall and sat down heavily on the brocaded lap of a portly dowager, which in his condition he mistook for an armchair. When, however, the holder of an ancient Irish title arrived so drunk at a Castle Ball that he tried to draw his Court sword on someone, there was an inquiry; at which Fingall was asked if he had noticed anything out of the ordinary about the offending Chieftain on that night. 'No,' he replied in his slow voice. 'Nothing out of the ordinary.'[15]

As well as the entertainments at the Castle itself, there were many dances in private houses during the Castle season. The most spectacular were the balls given by Lord Ardilaun's sister-in-law Mrs Edward Guinness at 80 St Stephen's Green, a town house on a palatial scale with sumptuous marble halls and enough bedrooms to accommodate large house parties. The brewer Edward Guinness and his wife sometimes had grander house parties at Number 80 than Their Excellencies had at the Castle; when Lady Alice Howard stayed with them in 1888 for the St Patrick's Ball and Lord Ormonde's Investiture as a Knight of St Patrick, her fellow-guests included not only the Duke of Leinster and his beautiful and talented young Duchess Hermione, but the Duke and Duchess of Abercorn as well.

By the 1880s, the Royal Dublin Society's Horse Show was becoming the occasion for a second if very brief Dublin season in August. For the 1884 Horse Show, Dublin was so crowded that Lady Alice Howard and her mother and sisters could only find rooms in a 'dirty little hotel' in Baggot Street.[16] That year, Lady Alice spent one day at the Show and went to a dance given by the Scots Guards: 'Their farewell, as they go, alas, on Thursday.'[17] In the previous year she did not attend the Show itself, as she had nobody to go with, but she went to a dance given at the time of the Show by the Spencers at Viceregal Lodge. Dances at the Lodge were completely private, with only the duty ADCs in attendance; the other members of the Viceregal staff did not come to them unless specially invited.

To the highbrow Maria La Touche, the Horse Show was of less interest than the lectures held by the Royal Dublin Society at other times of the year, such as 'Professor Barrett's Lecture on Light' which she went up specially to hear.[18] In those days, the RDS occupied the former town house of the Dukes of Leinster in Kildare Street, a few steps away from the red brick Victorian-Gothic club house of the Kildare Street Club. The Kildare Street was not the only predominantly

The Kildare Street Club at the turn of the century.

Ascendancy club in Dublin; there was also the Sackville Street Club, north of the river, which had the young and dashing Lord Charles Beresford among its members, together with an impressive array of peers, mostly from Ulster. But it was the Kildare Street rather than the Sackville Street that was the real centre of masculine Ascendancy life in Dublin, more so than ever from about 1880 onwards, when the north side of the city became increasingly run-down, so that the Sackville Street suffered on account of its situation. Some people belonged to both clubs, including the august Lord Ormonde and Lady Alice Howard's brother Lord Wicklow, the bibulous Massereene and Ferrard and no less raffish Derry Rossmore. By the 1880s, however, the grandees who belonged only to the Kildare Street outnumbered those belonging only to the Sackville Street: they included Lords Drogheda, Bandon, Rosse, Kenmare, Powerscourt and Monck, as well as Colonel King-Harman.

Not only was the Kildare Street Club conveniently situated; it was luxurious and had the reputation of keeping the best table in Dublin. Oysters, when in season, were sent up daily from the Club's own oyster bed near Galway and cost the members a shilling a dozen; muffins were sent from London. The cellar was of a corresponding degree of excellence, particularly with regard to champagne, which yet for some reason was cheaper here than in London clubs. There were plenty of comfortable bedrooms, for which the charge was three shillings and sixpence a night, so that the Club was a meeting place for gentlemen from all over the country, who before luncheon would congregate in the lofty hall with its staircase of elaborately carved stonework, its big game trophies and its blazing fire. The amenities of the Club included two private pews for the use of members in the nearby St Anne's Church of Ireland Church; the Club also had its own Masonic Lodge, drawn exclusively from members.

It was a cheerful and friendly club; members were expected to talk to one another whether they were acquainted or not. Percy La Touche, Maria's sporting son, once carried this tradition of sociability so far as to draw the attention of a crusty old member to a pretty servant girl who could be seen cleaning the windows of a house across the street. 'I say,' he remarked brightly, 'there's a pretty girl for you.'

Having elicited no response he repeated his observation.

Whereupon the older member subjected him to a long and stinging rebuke. 'Young man, I heard your remark perfectly well, as you intended me to do. I gather from it that you are one of those who go through life seeking the destruction of servants. One day a pretty housemaid will doubtless become an inmate of your home. The inevitable will happen, and then the girl will be discharged without a character.'[19]

The friendly atmosphere of the Kildare Street Club was due not a little to the fact that it was very exclusive. Members were at ease with one another, since they almost all belonged to the same Ascendancy world; if everybody did not actually know everybody else, at least everybody knew who everybody else was. Of the seven or eight hundred members, who paid a subscription of £10 a year, all but about eighty came from well-known Ascendancy families, the eighty consisting mainly of people connected with the Ascendancy, together with a sprinkling of eminent judges who may have come from a somewhat different background. Those members whose families were engaged in business were either of impeccable landed gentry stock, such as the wine merchant George Brooke of Summerton, or else had been assimilated into the landowning aristocracy like Lord Ardilaun and his brother Edward Guinness and James Jameson of Windfield in County Galway whose fortune came from whiskey. By 1882 the Guinness clan was represented in the Club by five members; whereas James of Windfield was then the sole representative of the no less prolific Jamesons.

The Club offered hospitality to the reigning Viceroy and to visiting members of the British royal family who, together with their ADCs or equerries, could use it without paying any subscription. It also opened its doors to British army officers of the rank of major and above, and to officers of similar rank in the navy, who could become temporary members while stationed in Ireland. On the other hand there was a strictly-enforced rule that nobody living in or within twenty miles of Dublin could be introduced as a guest, which served to isolate the Club from the rest of Dublin life, from those other worlds that were so well represented at the Castle. Influences that might have helped to break down the political prejudices of its members were in this way effectively shut out. Although the Club was meant to be non-political, during the years following the Land War it was virtually impossible for an active Home Ruler to become a member. The young Sir Thomas Grattan Esmonde, a Catholic County Wexford baronet of ancient lineage, resigned from the Club after being elected to Parliament as a Home Ruler in 1885.

Even before 1880, there had been only two Home Rule MPs in the Club, one of them being the great territorial magnate King-Harman. Significantly, both were Protestants; none of their Catholic colleagues in the Home Rule party had then been a member, though one or two had been elected after ceasing to be Home Rulers, notably O'Conor Don, the senior representative of the last High Kings of Ireland. For a Catholic to be elected to the Kildare Street Club, his politics had to be as impeccable as his lineage.

The Catholics in the Club in the early 1880s were thus a highly respectable lot. They included, in addition to O'Conor Don, three Earls, Westmeath, Granard and Kenmare together with Viscount Gormanston, Count de la Poer and the Viceregal Chamberlain Colonel Dease; Ambrose More O'Ferrall of Balyna in County Kildare, whose father had been a member of the British Government; and the rich young Edward Martyn of Tulira in County Galway. In all, they numbered no more than about thirty, a much lower proportion than that of Catholics to Protestants among the Ascendancy as a whole. This is often cited as showing how anti-Catholic the Protestant Ascendancy could be, but it was really due to the Club's system of election, in which any ordinary member could blackball a candidate. It took a very few bigots to keep a Catholic out; so that most Catholics of landowning families, rather than risk being blackballed, joined the St Stephen's Green Club where the membership was largely drawn from Catholic Dublin.

— *2* —

While the Ascendancy had its bigots, such as Sir Henry Hervey Bruce of Downhill in County Derry for whom 'the words "Roman Catholic" . . . were of fearful import',[20] the general run of Protestants mixed easily with those of their class who were Catholics. People were aware that the religious difference existed; Catholics, in the company of Protestants, tended to 'shut up like a clam' when religion was mentioned;[21] but Catholicism on the whole constituted a social barrier only in border-line cases – a family that barely made the grade as gentry might have been accepted if Protestant, not if Catholic. To have refused to have known Catholics would have meant cutting oneself off from peers and Deputy-Lieutenants, not to mention the Viceregal courtiers – at Dublin Castle in the early 1880s, not only were the Chamberlain and the State Steward Catholics but also the Gentleman Usher and Ulster King of Arms.

The Catholic County Longford landowner, Edward Gerald More O'Ferrall of Lisard, who followed his cousin Ambrose into the Kildare Street Club in 1884, was on excellent terms with his Protestant neighbours the Edgeworths of Edgeworthstown, the Lefroys of Carrigglas and the Wilsons of Currygrane. Unlike some of his co-religionists, who played down their Catholicism in the belief that this would make them more acceptable to Protestants, he entertained large numbers of Catholic clergy at Lisard, including two Cardinals. Catholic clerics of sound political views were in fact received at Protestant country houses as well as at Catholic ones; thus Father Healy, the popular parish priest of Bray, would come to luncheon with Lady Alice Howard's mother Lady Wicklow. Father Healy was even invited to Viceregal Lodge; he would repay the hospitality of his Ascendancy friends by giving dinners at which the main course was invariably a boiled leg of mutton – the only thing his housekeeper could do, though she did it to a turn.

The Protestants of the Ascendancy were less tolerant when their own relations married Catholics or converted to Catholicism. 'Poor Fanny is in great trouble as Maud has turned Roman Catholic,' Lady Alice Howard wrote of a cousin in 1884.[22] And when Lady Ardilaun's brother, the Earl of Bantry, married a Catholic, another of his sisters, who had been very close to him, took it so badly that they fell out for good. But while mixed marriages were in general very much frowned upon, a certain number of them did take place and were perfectly happy: such as that of Michael Morris of Spiddal, County Galway – afterwards Lord Chief Justice of Ireland and Lord Killanin – a Catholic whose wife was a Protestant. With regard to conversions, Maria La Touche went so far as to say: 'There are people I would gladly see received into the Catholic Church because I think it would be good for their morals.'[23] When her husband fell under the influence of the preacher Charles Spurgeon and became a Baptist, she declared that she 'had far rather it had been the Archbishop of Canterbury or even Cardinal Manning', while feeling grateful to Spurgeon 'for rescuing the "Master" out of the blighting narrowness of a life entirely given to Sport'.[24]

Maria's reference to the Archbishop of Canterbury is an indication of her High Church distaste for the prevailing Evangelicalism of the Church of Ireland. Her distaste was shared by Mary Ponsonby, who in a novel which she wrote at about this time describes a church that is obviously the church at Kilcooley though it could be one of a thousand churches attended by the Protestant Ascendancy all over the country: 'a dismal barn-like building so cold and damp that even in summertime it struck a chill all through one. The floor is ill-paved, the plaster peeling off the walls, the cushions moth-eaten.'[25]

Lady Alice Howard was another who found church-going in Ireland depressing. 'Very dreary,' was her comment on a Sunday service in 1882. 'Such a dull old parson and the church nearly empty.'[26] But while plenty of Ascendancy Protestants would have agreed with her and with Mary Ponsonby, there were those like Sir Henry Hervey Bruce who positively contributed to the gloom of the Sabbath. 'A Downhill Sunday in my grandfather's reign would have given even Calvin some hints in austerity for his government of Geneva,' Sir Henry's grandson was afterwards to recall.

> It was not so much the two-mile walk each way to church in all winds and weathers (a carriage on the Sabbath was of course unthinkable) and the stiff, uphill climb back; nor the ban on everything except hanging depressedly about waiting for the next religious exercise . . . No, it was something more than all this, something in the whole oppressive atmosphere of a Downhill Sunday, as if John Knox himself were of the house party.

Not content with the gruelling expedition to church, Sir Henry would summon his family and household to the dining room on Sunday evenings for further devotions. The servants sat along one side of the room, the family across the top, with Sir Henry presiding at the huge dining table in the pool of light cast by an oil lamp, 'his head bowed not in meditation but to facilitate a glance over his spectacles to check up on possible, but unlikely, defaulters'.[27] He would read an interminable sermon on a subject such as the Arian heresy, followed by lengthy extracts from the New Testament with Bentley's comments, their value somewhat diminished by the fact that he mixed up the comments with the text.

— *3* —

Life at Downhill, an eccentric palace built a century earlier by the celebrated Frederick Hervey, Earl of Bristol and Bishop of Derry, on a bare cliff top above the Atlantic, was, in the words of Sir Henry Hervey Bruce's grandson, 'a curious mixture of formality and happy-go-lucky Irishness'. Sir Henry, even when alone, would put on a white tie and tails for dinner, which was a stately occasion, with excellent wines and a glittering display of the Earl-Bishop's gold and silver plate on the table. But while the butler and footmen 'passed muster', the rest of the Downhill staff were old and comic. The so-called 'stable boy' was seventy; 'the coachman had come from Belfast for a weekend job some time in the 'sixties, naturally not bringing his wife with him, but, less naturally perhaps, never having gone back to fetch her. The head housemaid looked like an elderly caricature of Disraeli in his later days.'[28]

Though there were bedrooms enough in the main part of the house to accommodate the whole family plus a large shooting party, everybody except for Sir Henry and his wife was herded into a long corridor of cells known as the Curates' Wing. And while there were many noble apartments with Aubusson carpets and Venetian chairs emblazoned with the Earl-Bishop's coronet and mitre, the family was relegated to a small, low, shabbily-furnished room near the servants' quarters known as the Robbers' Cave, which was also the only place where smoking was allowed. Here they would sit hugger-mugger, sharing the smoke-laden atmosphere with a pack of wet and steaming retrievers and red setters.

With their army of loyal, if aged and grotesque retainers, the Hervey Bruces were more fortunate than some Ascendancy families at this time. 'I cannot bear new servants, especially footmen,' Maria La Touche complained when faced with the prospect of interviewing two prospective footmen and a butler at the same time as she was looking for a new cook. The upper servants in the grander Irish country houses tended to be English. This was not so much a reflection on the Irish as owing to the belief that each nation had its particular talents; thus the English were thought to make better butlers, footmen, cooks and lady's maids, the Irish better gamekeepers, ghillies and grooms. The La Touches were among those whose upper servants were English, but, as Maria lamented: 'the good ones won't come to Ireland. And the Master does not agree with me in preferring bad ones.'[29]

The Servant Problem affected Lady Wicklow and her daughters even more than it did the La Touches. In January 1883 they were having difficulty in finding a cook; in August of that year Lady Alice recorded that her mother was unable to go to church because 'the stable boy went off yesterday in a huff so she could not have the carriage'. In April 1884 Lady Alice and her mother went to Dublin to look for a footman but 'had no success'; a month later a new footman named Colin arrived from England on the mail boat, but on the day after his arrival Lady Alice was writing in her diary: 'Colin says the place won't suit him. Such a bore.' In September 1884 Lady Wicklow and her eldest daughter Lady Caroline went to Dublin 'to look at an under-footman'; in November 1885 a new butler and a new kitchenmaid came, but a footman whom they had engaged wrote to say that he had changed his mind. In July 1886, when Lady Alice was staying with friends in County Mayo, she heard from her mother that the new butler 'had got drunk and made a dreadful row and frightened them very much'. In January 1887 she went to Dublin to see another kitchenmaid; in September 1889 she went round all the agencies in a vain search for housemaids. A year later, Lady Wicklow was advertising for lady's maids.

Lady Wicklow and her daughters also had trouble with the men who worked on their farm. 'They have behaved too badly,' Lady Alice wrote in 1883 of the haymakers, who struck for higher wages. The farm, never a great success, seems to have been her own particular concern; accounts of Viceregal entertainments and country house visits in her diary are interspersed with records of the calving of cows.[30]

Lady Alice's other diary entries for this period include occasional pieces of gossip, such as the elopement of the daughter of rather grand county neighbours with 'a common stableman'.[31] There is also the odd reference to the Cripples' Home, which appears to have been one of the few charities in which she and her mother took an interest. On the whole, the ladies of the Ascendancy did not devote quite so much of their time to good works as did the wives and daughters of the English squirarchy; though by the 1880s an increasing number of ladies were working to encourage handicrafts and home industries as a means of improving the conditions of the country people. The Countess of Arran organized home industries near Castle Gore in County Mayo; Lady Clonbrock and Mrs Bagwell of Marlfield did the same in Counties Galway and Tipperary respectively. Mrs Hugh De Fellenberg Montgomery of Blessingbourne in County Tyrone started a copper-working class to enable the girls of the nearby village of Fivemiletown to supplement their livelihood by turning out articles of beaten copper. 'These efforts have been by no means without result,' the Duke of Abercorn, who took a keen interest in them, observed in a speech in 1888.

> But owing to various reasons – the competition of machinery, the lack of organized means of discovering and procuring regular markets, want of system, lack of funds, often, I fear, an absence of business-like habits and punctuality on the part of the workers themselves . . . the results, as a whole, have not been commensurate with even very moderate expectations.[32]

Of more frequent occurrence than good works in Lady Alice Howard's diary are the tennis parties which she and her mother and sisters gave during the summer months, sometimes for as many as seventy-five people. Lawn tennis was becoming increasingly popular with the younger generation; Mary Langrishe, the daughter of a County Kilkenny baronet, won the Irish Lawn Tennis Championship in 1879 at the early age of fourteen; she won it again in 1883 and 1886. Her brother Hercules, a handsome and dashing young man known to everybody as Herky, won a tennis tournament on the same day as he won a famous bicycle race. Bicycling was all the rage in the 1880s, like the game of rounders, of which Maria La Touche wrote in 1885: 'British matrons racing round and round in a wet meadow, while barristers, majors and others fling balls at them. Occasionally collisions and "ladies of quality" may be seen floundering on the grass with their – shoes – in the air!'[33]

To add to the gaiety of Irish country house life, particularly as far as the daughters were concerned, there was always a supply of officers from the depots of the Irish regiments and from English cavalry and county regiments stationed in Ireland, as well as from the navy at Queenstown and elsewhere. Officers were very much in demand for dances, tennis parties and other social occasions; the Cork County Club was not alone among the clubs of the Ascendancy outside Dublin in opening its doors to them regardless of their rank.

With its fine classical club house in one of the principal thoroughfares of Cork city, the Cork County Club was very much a Kildare Street in miniature; the Viceroy and the General Commanding the Forces were honorary members and out of the two hundred or so gentlemen who belonged to the Club in 1884, no fewer than a hundred and fifty came from the landowning aristocracy of County Cork and the neighbouring counties. Lord Bandon was of course a member, and so

Colonel Robert Cosby of Stradbally on his bicycle.

was Lord Listowel, so too were Lord Fermoy and his brother Alexis Roche. Other members included Sir George Colthurst as well as the County Kerry baronet Sir John Godfrey, the wealthy Arthur Hugh Smith-Barry of Fota, the two Penrose-FitzGerald brothers and Robert Cole Bowen. While being, like the Kildare Street, for men only, the Cork County Club made a gesture to the ladies by giving a fancy dress ball. The tall, bearded figure of Charles More-Smyth of Ballynatray, Earl Mount Cashell's brother, was prominent among the dancers in the guise of a crusader; the dapper William Moore-Hodder of Hoddersfield looked elegant in the ruffles and hose of an Elizabethan.

Among the amusements of the Ascendancy, tennis, bicycling and fancy dress balls were, of course, very much subordinate to hunting and all other sports involving the horse. The young Herky Langrishe may have been a crack racing cyclist, but he was even more celebrated as a rider with the distinction of having won two races on the same day at the Kilkenny Hunt's point-to-point meeting. With the ending of the Land War, hunting – except for some of the more ephemeral packs, such as Mr Chute's hounds in Kerry – quickly revived. Although Lord Waterford chose to remain in exile in the Shires during the next few seasons – until a swinging Leicestershire gate injured his spine, confining him to a wheelchair for the rest of his life – the hitherto absent Lord Desart, having divorced his errant first wife and married a wealthy Jewish heiress in 1881, returned to Ireland, did up Desart Court and became Master of the Kilkenny Hunt.

Like hunting, the fashionable race meeting held by the Kildare Hunt each spring at Punchestown was abandoned in 1882 on account of the Land War, but in the following year it started up again in all its former glory. Among those responsible for its management were Lord Drogheda and Percy La Touche, Maria's son, who won laurels in many a steeplechase. Maria herself, being totally uninterested in sport, regarded Punchestown as an opportunity to get on with her gardening: 'All the County is concentrated in one spot, which causes total solitude to reign everywhere else . . . one may wear one's very worst clothes and have earth all over one's hands and tools sticking out of one's pockets, with a peaceful certainty that no visitors will come.'[34]

– 4 –

Among those who entertained in their own tents at Punchestown was Earlie Clonmell, whose sister, Lady Annette, was Percy La Touche's wife. Earlie used to go and stay with that other Punchestown luminary Lord Drogheda at Moore Abbey, which had the name for being a very cold house; on one occasion he arrived bringing an exceptionally heavy trunk which, as the footmen were struggling to get it up the stairs, burst open and was found to be full of coal. Many Irish country houses were notorious for their coldness; but some, by the 1880s, already had central heating systems. When Lord Drogheda's neighbour, Dominick More O'Ferrall of Kildangan – a cousin of Ambrose and Edward – built himself a large new house to replace an older one that had been burnt in 1880, the total cost of £18,570 included £281 for heating apparatus. Peter Connellan, an uncle by marriage of Herky Langrishe, put a hot-air system into Coolmore, the house in County Kilkenny which he had built as a young man. To fuel it, he would order a shipload of coal – about 200 tons – from Wales each autumn, which would be conveyed in railway trucks to Thomastown, his nearest station, thence to Coolmore in farm carts.

The plumbing of Coolmore was less advanced than the heating; for many years after Peter Connellan's time his family made do with hip-baths, filled from large cans of hot and cold water which were hauled up two flights of stairs. Fixed baths were still something of a rarity in Irish country houses in the 1880s; the Morrises of

Spiddal were unusual in possessing one and would probably not have gone to the expense but for the fact that they had thirteen children who all needed bathing. Their bath, which was of noble proportions, was the first ever to be seen in Connemara; its advent aroused great interest – its journey along the road from Galway to Spiddal on a horse lorry was in the nature of a triumphal progress. After it had been installed, Mrs Morris invited one of the men from the place to come up and see it; he looked at it silently and then asked, in a critical tone: 'And will ye all get in together?'[35]

At Graiguenoe Park in County Tipperary, the home of Robert Cole Bowen's brother-in-law, Marshal Neville Clarke, the only taps were in the basement, supplied from an overhead tank into which the yard boy pumped rainwater from a storage tank underground, the rainwater being supplemented by water from the River Suir brought up in a cart. In contrast to houses like Graiguenoe, Lord Mayo's newly-built Palmerstown was so well plumbed as to have a bath cased in with 'best French-polished Honduras mahogany' together with three water-closets on each of the two principal floors and others on the top floor and off the back stairs.[36] Though many still had to make the matutinal pilgrimage through wet laurels as Mrs Herbert of Cahirnane had been obliged to do in the early years of her marriage, water-closets were by now fairly common. At Carton, the great house of the Dukes of Leinster in County Kildare, there was one of which the identity was proclaimed to all the world by the words 'Water Closet' inscribed on its door in full, in letters of gold complete with full stop. In a turret of Glenarm Castle, the Earl of Antrim's ancestral home in the Antrim Glens, there was a water-closet still in use which dated from when the castle was rebuilt in Regency times. Pakenham Hall, the Earl of Longford's house in County Westmeath, had possessed water-closets and a bathroom since the beginning of the century and a hot-water central heating system since the 1860s.

– *5* –

Life for the grander Ascendancy families was given an added dimension by visits to London; they took part not only in the Dublin Castle season in February and March but also in the London season in May, June and July. By the 1880s, travel between England and Ireland was very comfortable, at any rate for those who were good sailors. Aboard the fast, four-funnelled mail steamers, Ascendancy passengers were treated rather like club members by the stewards who knew most of them by name; when the ship reached Kingstown, as Dun Laoghaire was called in those days, they were able to sleep on in their cabins, rising at a civilized hour to disembark and walk a few steps along the waterfront to the Royal St George Yacht Club – which was then to all intents and purposes a marine extension of the Kildare Street – for breakfast.

When Lady Ardilaun travelled to London, the old head coachman went three or four days before her, with a carriage and pair and a groom. The second coachman drove her to Kingstown from St Anne's, the Italianate palace on the northern shores of Dublin Bay where she and her husband spent as much time as they did at Ashford Castle. On arriving at the mail boat, she was met by her husband's agent, who took her to the cabins which had been engaged for her and for her maid; they were full of flowers from her own garden. A footman who had come from St Anne's on the box of her carriage travelled in the ship and when they arrived at Holyhead he took her and her maid to a reserved compartment on the train; at each stop, Chester, Crewe and so on, he would appear at the window in case anything was needed. At Euston, the head coachman would be waiting to drive her to her house in Carlton House Terrace.

Lady Wicklow and her daughters did not travel in quite such style when they went on their annual jaunt to London during the season, though they took three servants with them to help in their house in Lowndes Street. If the crossing from Kingstown had been rough, Lady Wicklow herself and Lady Caroline would stay the night in the hotel at Holyhead while the more robust Ladies Loulie and Alice went straight through to London on the train. While in London, they mostly saw friends from Ireland: the Rosses, the Listowels, the Courtowns, the Carysforts, not to mention the Powerscourts who lived within walking distance from them in County Wicklow. And when the season was over, and they had made the return journey to Holyhead and across the Irish Sea, Lady Alice was always glad to be back in Ireland. 'Everything looks so green and beautiful,' she wrote on arriving at her home in County Wicklow after one London season. A day later, she was lamenting: 'Rained all day, too horrid, and the hay looks wretched.'[37]

Celtic Unionism

— I —

In the Spring of 1885, the Prince and Princess of Wales paid a visit to Ireland. They spent some days in Dublin where the Kildare Street and Sackville Street Clubs held a joint ball in their honour. They stayed with the Abercorns at Barons Court in County Tyrone and at Convamore in County Cork with the Listowels; Lord Waterford gave a luncheon for them at Curraghmore to which sixty people were invited. At Convamore a beacon blazed on top of the old castle near the entrance to the demesne to welcome the royal guests; but the village boys stood by the side of the road shouting 'oop de Maddy!' – up the Mahdi – in allusion to the Sudanese leader who had recently outraged British public opinion by causing the death of General Gordon. This was a foretaste of the hostile reception given to the Prince and Princess by the Nationalists of Cork city a couple of days later, when they were booed and pelted with onions.

By 1885 the Nationalist movement was fast gaining strength, and in an attempt to resist it the Ascendancy, hitherto divided between Conservatives and Whigs or Liberals, closed its political ranks. On 1 May, four days after the Prince and Princess left Ireland, the Irish Loyal and Patriotic Union was founded; among its most active members were Lord Longford, Arthur MacMorrough Kavanagh and Lord Castletown, the former Barnie FitzPatrick who succeeded his father in 1883. The immediate object of the new association was to fight the forthcoming general election on the single issue of maintaining the Union between Ireland and Great Britain. By the autumn of that year, when the election took place, sufficient funds had been raised to support Unionist candidates in most Irish constituencies outside Ulster, where the Unionist forces were as yet unorganized. In Ulster, opposition to Nationalism had so far come from the Orange Order, which was essentially working-class in character though there were some Ascendancy figures among its leaders, such as Derry Rossmore who in 1883 had led an army of seven thousand Orangemen to confront a Nationalist assembly of five thousand at Roslea in County Fermanagh. Surprisingly, no one was hurt, though at one stage in the proceedings the local RM threatened to arrest the incorrigible Derry, who afterwards criticized the Liberal Government so outspokenly in the papers that he was removed from the Commission of the Peace.

Despite the efforts of the Loyal and Patriotic Union, the 1885 Election was a great Nationalist victory, though on the other side of the Irish Sea the swing was towards the Conservatives, who came back into power. At the same time as the Home Rulers triumphed at the polls, the agricultural depression, which had abated during the past three or four years, returned with a vengeance; the weather was bad once again and prices fell to even lower levels than in 1879. The result was a new agrarian agitation, known as the Plan of Campaign and led, like the previous one, by Parnell; it was better organized than the Land War, but less widespread.

At the instigation of the National League, which had taken the place of the Land League, the tenants of certain estates demanded rent reductions beyond those fixed by the Government – in some cases as much as 30 per cent or even more. The same tactics were employed as in the previous agitation: no rent at all was paid if the tenants' demands were refused, and those who took the holdings of tenants evicted for non-payment of rent were boycotted. The agitation was at its worst in 1886 and might have become really violent but for the Home Rule Bill which Gladstone, who had returned to power in February, introduced without success in April; this somehow served to defuse the situation, though most of the Ascendancy regarded it as 'diabolical.'[1]

One of the first landlords to be attacked in this year was the Knight of Glin, who though not particularly well off had actually carried out improvements on his tenants' farms with money he had borrowed for the purpose. He had, however, evicted certain tenants, which led to a 'monster meeting' of the local branch of the National League being held at Glin on 7 March, to which contingents came from many parts of West Limerick and North Cork, some of them headed by brass bands. Inflammatory speeches were made, criticizing the Knight and declaring a boycott of those who had taken the place of the evicted tenants. A few hours after the meeting, outrages were committed on the farms of two of these men; the Knight made the most of them, in order to discredit the League, though the League condemned them and offered a reward of £100 for the discovery and conviction of the culprits. This gesture did not satisfy the Knight and there were bitter exchanges in the press between him and the League's supporters. On 13 March the pro-League *Munster News* wrote of him: 'It does not read well to find the representative of an old Irish family, who have lived at peace with priests and people, adopting a style and language more becoming some of the Cromwellian gang who cursed our country, to rob its people and persecute their creed.'[2]

In November, the League attacked the most notorious absentee landlord of his generation, the Marquess of Clanricarde. Safe in his rooms in London, Clanricarde ordered that all the tenants of his County Galway estate who did not pay their rent should be evicted without mercy, but the tenants resisted eviction and held out for some days against the military. All kinds of outrages took place: Clanricarde's unfortunate agent was assassinated when driving to church by the side of his wife; his successor went about, in the words of a contemporary journalist, 'surrounded by an armed guard the like of which is not to be seen on this side of Texas'.[3] The resultant publicity brought landlordism still further into disrepute, though landlords insisted with reason that Clanricarde was by no means typical. He was a strange, solitary character, pathologically mean though enormously rich; he dressed like a tramp and was alleged to have been personally malodorous. Many stories are told of his meanness, perhaps the best of them being that he asked for the rent of his rooms in London to be reduced. Like that notorious landlord of nineteenth-century Scotland, the Duke of Sutherland, he was, except in his dealings with his tenants, a liberal of advanced views; just as Sutherland admired Garibaldi, so did Clanricarde have a great admiration for Cavour, whom he had known as a young diplomat.

In 1887 the luckless Lady Kingston was once again singled out for attack; her tenants demanded a reduction of 20 per cent, which would have left her and her husband with not enough to live on and to meet the outgoings of her heavily-mortgaged estate after interest on the mortgage had been paid. Her husband Willie Webber agreed to make the reduction if the Church of Ireland, which held the mortgage, would agree to a corresponding reduction in interest; but the Church showed itself to be no more accommodating in this respect than any other creditor. So the reduction was refused and rents were withheld; writs for eviction were served on a number of tenants who barricaded their houses. The tenants' cause was espoused by the Nationalist MP William O'Brien and by John Mandeville, the brother of a Mitchelstown solicitor who was a kinsman of an Ascendancy family in County Tipperary. In the late summer of 1887 O'Brien and Mandeville were summoned before a special court charged with inciting the tenants to resist eviction, which the Conservatives, who had returned to power in August 1886, had made into a punishable offence. This led to a protest meeting on 9 September in the square outside the gates of Mitchelstown Castle, such as there had been on more than one occasion during the Land War; it was attended by several MPs, including Radicals from England. A large crowd confronted the police, who having retreated into their barracks under a barrage of stones and blackthorn sticks, fired two volleys, killing two and seriously wounding twenty. The so-called

Lord Doneraile, who died of rabies.

'Mitchelstown Massacre' embarrassed the Conservative Government as well as prolonging Lady Kingston's troubles by several months; the Church of Ireland moved to put the Mitchelstown estate into Chancery, though it agreed to appoint her husband as the receiver. Eventually, after negotiations between Webber, the tenants and the Church, a settlement was reached, and as in the Land War, all tenants evicted from the estate during the dispute were given back their holdings.

Lady Kingston's troubles were overshadowed by the terrible fate of her neighbour Viscount Doneraile, a popular hunting man whose beautiful daughter Clare was the wife of Barnie Castletown. Lord Doneraile had kept a pet fox; he used to take it with him when he went out driving in his carriage. On one of these drives, the fox suddenly bit Lord Doneraile and his coachman and was found to have rabies. Lord Doneraile and the coachman travelled to Paris to be treated by Pasteur; the coachman persevered with the treatment, Lord Doneraile grew bored with it and gave it up. In due course he developed the disease and on 26 August 1887, a fortnight before the Mitchelstown Massacre, he died a frightful death. 'There were such crowds of the country people,' Percy La Touche reported of his funeral. 'In these times it is not so common for *them* to show feelings and sympathise with those above them.'[4]

It was the National League's policy to attack landlords like Lady Kingston whose circumstances made it likely that they would accept whatever rent they were offered; if they went bankrupt that was so much the better as far as the League was concerned, for the tenants might then have been able to buy their holdings at knock-down prices. When, in October 1887, the Earl of Granard, an impecunious County Longford landlord, was in trouble with the League, the local Nationalist MP, Tim Healy, in a speech to his constituents, paraphrased Voltaire by saying that he hoped to see Lord Granard's mortgagee 'squeezing him out as you would squeeze out a lemon or an orange, and when they throw away the skin I hope to see you give it a kick and send it to its proper place'.[5] Lord Granard's mortgagee was, however, the Catholic Church, which had obliged this pious Catholic convert peer with a loan, so that when the League tried to stop his rents it brought down upon itself episcopal wrath.

Another of the League's victims was Charles Talbot-Ponsonby, a distant kinsman of Lord Bessborough and of the Ponsonbys of Kilcooley, who owned a large but not very remunerative estate in the south-east of County Cork. By the beginning of 1889 he was at the end of his tether; he had lost almost £25,000 in rent, and owed about £5000 to his solicitors. He was about to sell his estate for a miserable ten years' purchase when his neighbour Arthur Hugh Smith-Barry organized a syndicate of wealthy landowners in Ireland and England which bought it off him for twice as much. The rich and popular Smith-Barry was the leading spirit in the Cork Defence Union, which had been founded in 1885 under the presidency of Lord Bandon and with Sir George Colthurst and James Penrose-FitzGerald on the committee, to protect landlords and tenants against the National League. Now, as he acted on behalf of the syndicate which had taken the place of Talbot-Ponsonby, the League found him a formidable opponent. When the tenants of Talbot-Ponsonby's former estate paid no rent, it mattered little to Smith-Barry and his associates; they simply evicted the tenants and planned to turn the estate into a vast cattle and sheep ranch. The evicted tenants had to be supported for two years at the expense of the League; they then gave in and were reinstated in their holdings. This episode did much to break the Plan of Campaign, which had more or less petered out by the end of 1890. By then it was opposed not only by the Ascendancy but also by the artisans of Dublin and Cork who saw the reductions in the landlords' incomes as being bad for trade. At a meeting of the Dublin Trades Council in 1889 the Plan of Campaign was denounced for having adversely affected the market for hunting boots.

Although the Plan of Campaign ended with a theoretical victory for the landlords, in fact it marked a further stage in their economic decline. A new Land

The fall in Colonel Robert Cosby's rents did not prevent him from keeping a coach and four, seen here outside his home, Stradbally Hall. Two footmen stand on the steps.

Act, passed by the Government in 1887, brought further rent reductions by the Government Commissioners; in County Clare rents were cut by half, while in the more prosperous parts of the country there were plenty of landlords like Colonel Robert Cosby of Stradbally Hall in Queen's County whose rents were down by 40 per cent on the official valuation made earlier in the century. And on many estates the landlords or their agents had trouble in collecting even these reduced amounts.

As a way out of their difficulties, the landlords could now sell their tenanted farms to the tenants at a price fixed by the Government which financed the transaction. This was known as land purchase and had been brought in by the Conservatives in 1885 in an Act named after Lord Ashbourne, the Lord Chancellor of Ireland, who had drafted it, land purchase having been tentatively introduced by Gladstone in his Land Act of 1870. At the time when the Ashbourne Act was passed, most of the Ascendancy regarded land purchase as 'confiscation',[6] though there were a few landlords who favoured it, notably Barnie Castletown, while a certain amount of land had been sold to tenants since 1885, including about forty farms on the Mitchelstown estate. As the continuing agricultural depression made Irish land progressively less attractive as an investment, the Ascendancy's attitude to land purchase began to change.

From the social point of view, the Plan of Campaign naturally served more than ever to alienate landlords from their tenants, though there were plenty of estates where the old good feelings survived this second land agitation, just as they had survived the first. One such estate was Ballinamona in County Waterford, where Captain and Mrs Robert Carew, following the birth of their son and heir in 1888, entertained their tenants annually to a 'feast and sports' lasting two days, to celebrate the child's birthday. 'Everyone felt at home, and the abundance of good fare provided made all genial and happy,' a local newspaper reported of this celebration in 1891, when the prizes for the tug o'war, the donkey races and the other events were distributed by the three-year-old Master Carew himself.[7]

− *2* −

Undaunted by the overwhelming electoral successes of Home Rule, the Ascendancy, during the late 1880s and 1890s, threw itself heart and soul into the Unionist cause. Lady Alice Howard attended 'Loyal and Patriotic' concerts and also a great Unionist rally at which Father Healy, the parish priest of Bray, was present. The Unionists made the most of the fact that there were plenty of Catholics from outside the Ascendancy in their ranks. When the Countess of Aberdeen, whose husband was the Viceroy at the time of Gladstone's first Home Rule bill, observed brightly to Lord Chief Justice Morris at a Dublin Castle dinner party, 'I suppose everyone but yourself is a Home Ruler here tonight,' the staunchly Catholic Lord Chief Justice replied, with his strong brogue: 'Not at all, Your Excellency. Barring yourself and the waiters, there's not a Home Ruler in the room.'[8]

Since the British Liberal Party was committed to Home Rule, the Irish Unionists had to campaign against the Liberals in Britain. Barnie Castletown went to Birmingham to address a rally of 17,000 people; William Henry Mahon, the son of a County Galway baronet, attended an anti-Home Rule meeting at Sheffield. Edith Somerville of Drishane in West Cork and her friend Violet Martin of Ross in County Galway − known already to the reading public as Somerville and Ross − went to canvass in an election in East Anglia; it was a proud moment for the two young writers when they saw themselves referred to in a Radical poster as 'Irish locusts'.[9]

In the summer of 1892, a year before Gladstone's second Home Rule Bill was thrown out by the House of Lords, a great Unionist Convention was held in Dublin. The delegates filled two halls; in the larger of the two, the chairman, Lord Fingall, was supported on the platform by more than a hundred other notabilities, including the Duke of Leinster, Lords Mayo, Dunsany, Emly, Ventry, Massy and Cloncurry, Colonel Cosby of Stradbally and Major Barton of Straffan, Colonel Dease (the Viceregal Chamberlain) and Walter MacMorrough Kavanagh, son of the limbless Arthur. In the balconies sat a bevy of ladies, who 'not only lent a pleasing grace to the proceedings but took a lively interest in all that went on'. Before the speeches began, 'an orchestral band played a capital selection of music in a spirited manner. "God Bless the Prince of Wales" was loudly cheered; so, too, was "Rule Britannia", but the enthusiasm was simply unbounded when the strains of the National Anthem fell on the ear.'[10]

A few days before the Dublin Convention, the Ulster Unionists had held a Convention in Belfast, presided over by the Duke of Abercorn who concluded his speech with the words: 'Men of the North, once more I say we will not have Home Rule.'[11] After a slow start, the Unionist movement in Ulster was by now getting up steam and becoming increasingly independent of the movement in the rest of Ireland. Since the Ulster Unionists returned no fewer than sixteen MPs compared with the two who were all that the Unionists of the three southern provinces were able to muster, it was inevitable that the tactics of the two organizations should differ. And while in the rest of Ireland the Unionists emphasized the non-sectarian character of the movement, in Ulster the chief card which the Unionists played in opposing Home Rule was the extreme Protestant one. Ulster Unionism was closely linked with the Orange Order, though some of the Ulster Unionist leaders were not Orangemen, notably such Ascendancy figures as the Duke of Abercorn and Hugh de Fellenberg Montgomery. Montgomery, who attended the Convention in Dublin and always advocated a close cooperation between Ulster and the other Irish provinces, had been an outspoken critic of what he called 'Protestant bigotry' and the 'public, conspicuous and noisy gatherings' of the Orangemen.[12] In 1893 he felt so strongly about Home Rule as to allow the local Orangemen to celebrate the Twelfth of July in a field opposite Blessingbourne, his family home in County Tyrone; though he took the precaution of insisting that they should only drink lemonade and soda water.

Among the leaders of Ulster Unionism who came from the Ascendancy, by far the most influential was the Marquess of Londonderry. Or perhaps the real leader was Lady Londonderry, the proud and handsome Theresa, who is said to have found in political intrigue an escape from domestic unhappiness; though the celebrated story of how her husband never spoke to her except in public after learning from another lady, whose lover she had stolen, that she had been unfaithful to him is not strictly accurate.

Lord Londonderry was enormously rich, for in addition to his Ulster estates he had land and coal mines in the north of England. He and Theresa were unusual among the Ascendancy in having reigned at Dublin Castle; their Viceroyalty, which lasted from 1886 to 1889, had been a brilliant one, though Lord Londonderry's craze for getting through dinner as quickly as possible was unpopular with their guests, whose plates were often whisked away before they had a chance of eating anything. The Londonderrys' Viceroyalty was also remembered for the occasions when Lord Londonderry's younger brother, who was almost his double, stationed himself in a strategic position in the Throne Room so that the débutantes, mistaking him for the Viceroy, would offer him their cheeks to kiss.

As hostess of Mount Stewart, the Londonderrys' classical mansion overlooking Strangford Lough in County Down, as well as of their English country seat and of Londonderry House, their London palace in Park Lane, Theresa Londonderry was able to enlist powerful support for the Ulster Unionist cause. Once, when Daisy Fingall came to stay at Mount Stewart, Theresa told her that among the other guests there would be 'a clever young lawyer from Dublin who may be useful'.

Presently the door at the end of the room opened and a face appeared. 'Oh, my

The hall at Mount Stewart.

dear, what an awful face!' Daisy exclaimed under her breath to Theresa, who went to the door to greet the new arrival. She brought him back to introduce him. 'Mr Carson . . . Lady Fingall says you have an awful face.'[13]

Lord Londonderry's cousin, the Earl of Antrim, a man of powerful build and voice who was a throw-back to Sorley Buie and all the other mighty chiefs from whom he was descended, dealt with the problem of Home Rule in a simpler way. He held one meeting to discuss the matter, at which he produced a large revolver and placed it on the table before him. 'Anyone mentioning Home Rule will be shot!' he announced. Silence prevailed and after a while the meeting broke up.[14]

$-3-$

An active member of the Irish Unionist Alliance was Joseph Pike, who came of a wealthy Cork business family and moved in the best County Cork Ascendancy circles, being something of a social climber; he was a friend of both Lord Bandon and Sir George Colthurst, he was a Deputy-Lieutenant of the county, and a trustee of the Cork County Club. Living as he did only a short distance down river from Cork city, he would play cards in the Club almost every afternoon. The stakes were absurdly low; the most he ever lost at poker or nap was £14 which he could certainly afford to pay, even though he was personally not particularly well off, the family money being in the hands of his formidable widowed mother.

In the summer of 1893 a young member of the Club thought he saw Pike cheating; his suspicions were confirmed by other members who watched him subsequently. These members decided to follow the procedure adopted with such unfortunate consequences at Tranby Croft a couple of years earlier, namely to hush the matter up on condition that the accused man promised never to play cards again. Pike was accordingly approached through a friend, who did not, however, tell him in so many words that he was accused of cheating but simply expressed the hope that he would give up playing cards. Pike did in fact refrain from playing for several months, after which he played on one occasion with two of his accusers, possibly in order to vindicate himself. Meanwhile people were talking, particularly the wives, who started taking sides. Pike was cut by his next door neighbour, Colonel Robert Spotiswoode, a retired officer whose military career had suffered through his having inadvertently drowned a squadron of cavalry while leading it across a river in India. He and Pike had hitherto been on such friendly terms that they made a footpath linking their respective demesnes.

Through Spotiswoode, the story reached another of the Club's trustees,

Joseph Pike.

Richard Pigott Beamish, a Cork brewer who came of landed Ascendancy stock and was, like Pike, a DL. Beamish officiously decided to have the affair investigated by the Club committee, even though a promise had been given that it would be hushed up. He wrote a letter about it to Richard Longfield of Longueville, an important North Cork landowner who was also a trustee.

At this stage Sir George Colthurst stepped in. He believed passionately in Pike's innocence and told him that his only hope was to sue Beamish for libel. Pike was reluctant to bring an action for fear of antagonizing his mother, who was a strict Quaker with a horror of cards; but the old lady rallied to her son's support.

The case, which opened in Dublin on 8 May 1894, was a major social event: the court was packed with Ascendancy, a special place being reserved for the ladies; the Judge had provided seats for his own friends on the Bench. The witnesses included Lord Bandon and Sir George Colthurst. Pike's counsel, John Atkinson QC, moved in County Cork Ascendancy circles and therefore knew all the witnesses; in stating his case to the jury he was not only able to predict what the witnesses for the defence would say, but also to imitate the way in which each of them would say it. When each of the defence witnesses came into the box and spoke exactly as Atkinson had predicted, the jurymen could not restrain their laughter. The Judge joined in the fun and when Beamish's counsel remarked that Colthurst, in giving evidence for Pike, had won the admiration of the ladies, he asked jocularly: 'Were you jealous?' Colthurst's eloquence on behalf of his friend gave rise to jokes in court about his family's ownership of the Blarney Stone.

On 23 May the jury retired after a summing-up which was very much in Pike's favour. It was a blazing hot day: the court, more than ever crowded, was stifling; Mrs Pike, who had sat beside her husband throughout the action, could stand it no longer and left. After an hour and a half the jury returned and gave a verdict that the allegations made against Pike were not true. There was a tremendous burst of applause; hats were waved and Colthurst rushed up to his friend and shook him by the hand. Pike's good name was cleared, though the Judge also acquitted Beamish of having acted through malice. Neither Pike, nor Beamish, nor any of the other protagonists resigned from the Cork County Club; but Spotiswoode blocked the footpath between his demesne and Pike's by building a wall so massive that it would have stood up to heavy shelling.

$$- \, 4 \, -$$

The Cork Card Case afforded the Ascendancy entertainment at a time when the entertainments at Dublin Castle were being boycotted by the Unionists who regarded the Viceroy, Lord Houghton, as a traitor because of the Home Rule policy of his Government. But while the Unionists refused to meet Lord Houghton officially, the rich and handsome young widower Viceroy was entertained privately in some of the grander country houses. The Duchess of Leinster, who was a relation of his, invited him to Carton. 'I receive you as cousin, not as Viceroy,' she said as he came in. And she did not give him a curtsy.[15]

Hermione Leinster was one of the most beautiful and talented young women of her time. During her nine years of unhappy marriage to the shy and rather dull Duke, and in her brief widowhood before she died of consumption at the age of thirty-one, she found consolation in making a wonderful garden, in music, painting and sculpture and in a small and devoted coterie of friends that included Daisy Fingall. On arriving at Carton to stay with her, Daisy would find her amidst the baroque splendours of the white and gold saloon. 'She would have been sitting at her grand piano perhaps, playing, and would take her lovely hands from the keys as I came in and smile, that smile of hers that always seemed to light a room. The windows of that room looked out over the formal garden to the park and the

Another page from Clare Castletown's scrapbook, recording a house party at Carton in May 1893, with photographs of Hermione Leinster and her husband as well as of the house. The signatures include those of Lord and Lady Ardilaun.

Dublin and Wicklow mountains were always blue against the sky.' At night, after she had undressed, Hermione would come to Daisy's room 'with her lovely brown hair loose about her shoulders and sit talking by the fire, turning her feet up to the flames. That is how I know that she had beautiful feet'.[16]

Another of Hermione's friends was the writer Emily Lawless, sister of Lord Cloncurry, a County Kildare peer noted for his luxuriant mauve beard which had been turned that colour by some patent restorative; hostesses would complain that when he stayed in their houses he left mauve stains on the bedsheets*. A staunch Unionist, Emily Lawless loved Ireland passionately; her novels, such as *Grania* and *Maelcho*, and her poems are full of an intense national feeling. She always longed for the rocky desolation of the Burren of north County Clare. For her, as for

* See illustration on page 120.

her cousin, Barnie Castletown, and others of their background at this time, Unionism was in no way incompatible with the bourgeoning Celtic revival. Barnie, while always willing to speak on a Unionist platform, would at times don a saffron kilt and was reputed to believe in the 'little people'. He was also keenly interested in the revival of the Irish language, which was making progress since the founding of the Gaelic League in 1893 by Douglas Hyde, who was himself of the Ascendancy.

If Emily Lawless saw the regeneration of Ireland in romantic terms, her younger brother's friend, Horace Plunkett, saw it in terms of 'better farming, better business, better living', to use the phrase that was to become his slogan. A younger brother of Lord Dunsany, Plunkett had ranched in Wyoming, but had returned to Ireland to look after the Dunsany estate in County Meath during the absence of his father and of his elder brother; he also felt obliged to help his widowed sister Mary Ponsonby who was managing Kilcooley while her sons grew up. The Dunsanys were kinsmen of the Fingalls; Dunsany Castle and the Fingalls' castle of Killeen, both of them medieval though altered at various times, stood within walking distance of each other. Although the Fingalls had remained Catholic whereas the Dunsanys had conformed to Protestantism in the eighteenth century, the two families had always been on very friendly terms. When Horace Plunkett, who was a bachelor, was living alone at Dunsany, he would spend many evenings at Killeen with Fingall and Daisy, talking in the old upstairs library about his dream, which was to save Ireland by cooperation. Daisy's mind would wander and Fingall would snore; but then he would wake up and say: 'You should not give the Irish anything that they do not ask for.'[17]

It was Horace Plunkett's misfortune that he did not appreciate the wisdom of this remark. He was more English than Irish in temperament and felt it right to interfere in people's lives if he thought it was for their good. He had little imagination. But he was prepared to work unceasingly for his dream, and he was able to inspire others to work as hard as he did. Throughout the 1890s, he toured the country trying to persuade the farmers to join in setting up cooperative creameries. In 1894 he founded the Irish Agricultural Organization Society, a union of local cooperatives. Such was the attraction of his personality that he was able to induce a remarkable cross-section of distinguished Irishmen to serve on his committee, not only Ascendancy figures like Lord Monteagle, Colonel Dease and Christopher La Touche, Percy's cousin who was managing director of the Guinness Brewery; but also the Catholic Bishop of Raphoe and the Jesuit Father Tom Finlay. And at a time when political feelings ran high, it was very much to his credit that his committee should also have included the Home Rule MP John Redmond, Plunkett being himself in Parliament as Unionist Member for South County Dublin, a constituency with a large Protestant vote.

After the general election of 1895, which was a victory for the Unionists – as the Conservatives were now known, in Britain as well as in Ireland – Plunkett was able to work closely with Arthur Balfour's brother Gerald, the new Chief Secretary, who during his five years in that office did all he could to better the lot of the Irish people. One of his measures, the setting up of a Department of Agriculture, was actually Plunkett's idea. Gerald Balfour's policy and that of his two immediate successors came to be known as 'Killing Home Rule by Kindness'; but while Balfour invented the phrase, he used it in the opposite sense to that in which it was afterwards used by journalists and others. What he said was that it would not be possible to kill Home Rule by kindness. In this he was proved right, and while his policy failed to win over the Nationalists, certain aspects of it found little favour with the Ascendancy, in particular his Local Government Act which introduced democratically-elected County Councils in place of the old Grand Juries – those pleasant Ascendancy gatherings that had hitherto settled the affairs of each county. Maria La Touche expressed the prevailing Ascendancy view of local government when she wrote of it: 'Giving us Local Government is very like giving Nursery Government to the two youngest and most quarrelsome of the babies.'[18]

– 5 –

Although there were plenty of Irish landowners in the 1890s who took no interest at all in farming, there were others such as Colonel James Connellan of Coolmore in County Kilkenny who farmed extensively and progressively. Colonel Connellan founded the Kilkenny Agricultural Society and was one of the first people in Ireland to use basic slag; he sent the daughter of his farm steward as a dairy student to the Munster Institute in Cork which taught the methods advocated by Horace Plunkett. Among the larger landlords who farmed well was Lord Antrim; he would go to Scotland to buy cattle which he would bring back on the Stranraer to Larne steamer, driving the beasts home himself along the coast road from Larne to Glenarm.

All too many of the Ascendancy who farmed had as little success as Lady Alice Howard. 'Crawford took the pig to the fair and only got £2-10 for it; he said cattle were terribly down,' she recorded in her diary in 1896. Three years later she and her sisters tried to auction their hay, but none of it was sold – 'such a disappointment'. Eventually they sold it privately for a price that would not pay for the hay-making. Lady Alice was more successful growing violets; in 1896 she picked seventy-one bunches and sent them to the market.[19]

The Ladies Howard, now in late middle age and having lost their mother in 1892, continued their round of gaiety. In 1896 Lady Alice stayed at 80 St Stephen's Green with the Guinnesses, who were now Lord and Lady Iveagh, and attended her host's Investiture as a Knight of St Patrick; on another evening during her stay she went to a ball given by Lady Ashbourne, the wife of the Irish Lord Chancellor, whose parties had become a feature of the Castle season. Three years later Lady Alice was again at Number 80 when the Iveaghs gave a dinner for sixty including the Viceroy and Vicereine, Earl and Countess Cadogan; afterwards

Lord Iveagh in his Deputy-Lieutenant's uniform, wearing the ribbon and star of the order of St Patrick.

there was dancing to Gottleib's Band, which had been brought over specially from London.

In the autumn of 1897 Lady Alice stayed in County Cork with the Listowels at Convamore, a comfortable early Victorian mansion beautifully situated above the River Blackwater; the party went down the river in boats and had tea in the old castle, which was still stained with tar from the beacon lit in honour of the Prince of Wales twelve years earlier. Another autumn saw her nearer home staying with the Carysforts at Glenart, where the party included Lord Wolseley, the General Commanding the Forces in Ireland, as well as the Castletowns, Lord Cloncurry and Lord Monck. The Carysforts did everything in tremendous style, but many of the Irish found the atmosphere of Glenart a little oppressive. 'Our parties never seem to be quite a success, though we take so much trouble over them,' Lady Carysfort lamented to her sister in England.[20]

A garden party at Glenart: the clergy much in evidence.

Engaging new servants continued to be one of Lady Alice Howard's occupations: in 1896 and 1897 it was footmen, in 1898 a housemaid. The latter year saw Lady Alice riding a bicycle, though she was too old to take part in the bicycle polo which had become popular with the younger generation. One of its devotees was Lord Monck's son Charles, who also enjoyed roller-skating, then known as 'rinking'.[21]

– 6 –

In 1898 the Earl of Desart died and was succeeded by a younger brother, a distinguished lawyer who worked in London as Solicitor to the Treasury and Director of Public Prosecutions. Money was short and the new Lord Desart had to continue with his legal career, while planning to spend his summer holidays at

Desart Court, which was now in much the same state of neglect as when Maria La Touche came here some twenty years earlier, having been abandoned once again by his brother in 1886. But when he arrived at Desart for the first time after his succession, the dust and litter of thirteen years had been swept away by his wife and one of his daughters who had crossed over ahead of him and worked for a week with their own hands, helped by village girls. They had filled the pleasantly-faded eighteenth-century rooms with flowers picked from the overgrown borders; they had ordered scones for his breakfast.

Driving out from Kilkenny on a side-car, the new Lord Desart was greeted at Cuffe's Grange, a village near the corner of the Desart demesne, with a scroll of welcome in Irish; it was incorrectly written, but this mattered little as he could not read it. Then came a vociferous welcome from old Mary Welsh at the gate and then, as he drove up the avenue, the rain, which had been falling steadily, suddenly cleared and there was a gleam of sunlight. After many blessings and handshakes from the people who worked on the place, he went up the steps of the elegant Palladian house alone with his wife and daughter. The three of them passed through the hall, with its grained panelling and family portraits, through the drawing room, with its ceiling of rococo plasterwork, and out on to the terrace on the southern side. From here Lord Desart could survey his park and his woods, 'lovely and brilliant in the morning'. He stood silent for a while, then gave a sigh. 'I'm glad to be home,' he said, turning to his wife. But she had gone in to make the tea.[22]

Since the new Lord Desart had no son, his brother Otway Cuffe, a member of the Royal Household, was heir to the title and estate. Cuffe had hitherto lived outside Ireland; but he now returned to County Kilkenny having decided, like Horace Plunkett, to devote his life to helping the Irish people. To provide financial support for his cooperatives and other schemes, there was Ellen Lady Desart, the rich and philanthropic Jewess who was his eldest brother's widow. To lend moral support, there was his friend and mentor the writer Standish O'Grady, whom he brought to Kilkenny as editor of the local Unionist and Protestant weekly, the *Kilkenny Moderator*.

O'Grady, a cousin of Viscount Guillamore, was prominent in the Celtic revival; under his editorship, the *Moderator* was the first Irish newspaper of consequence to print a weekly Irish lesson and he started a Kilkenny branch of the Gaelic League with Cuffe as president. His real inspiration, however, came not from a remote Celtic past but from the eighteenth-century heyday of the Ascendancy, the Ireland of Swift, of Grattan, of Lord Charlemont's Volunteers. In one of his books he apostrophizes the Ascendancy leaders of his own time, contrasting their philistinism with the culture of their eighteenth-century forebears. 'Your ancestors who raised the noble classical buildings of Dublin loved a classical

Standish O'Grady, portrait
by John Butler Yeats.

quotation, but could one in twenty of you translate the most hackneyed Latin tag
in a newspaper? Christ save us all! You read nothing, you know nothing.'[23]

While being an outspoken critic of the Ascendancy, O'Grady was also its
champion. He urged the Ascendancy leaders to 'reshape themselves in a heroic
mould' so that they might once again become the real leaders of Ireland. Unless
this happened, he prophesied anarchy and civil war, 'which might end in a shabby,
sordid Irish Republic, ruled by corrupt politicians and the ignoble rich'. He saw
the situation in 1899 as analagous to that in 1782, when Lord Charlemont's
Volunteers had won concessions for Ireland in return for offering to defend the
Irish shores while England was at war with France. He now proposed that the
Ascendancy should take the lead in raising a new national army which could
defend Ireland and release the British garrison for service in South Africa, where
war was imminent. As the nucleus of this force, he collected recruits from the
Catholic and Protestants Boys' Brigades; they were drilled by Cuffe, who had
soldiered in his younger days and been an ADC to the Duke of Connaught.

To raise a new force of Irish Volunteers was not the only opportunity which

O'Grady held out to the Ascendancy. It had been revealed that, since 1880, Ireland had been grossly overtaxed; County Kilkenny alone had been made to pay £135,000 a year too much. O'Grady believed that by heading a crusade for financial justice, the Ascendancy could win back the popular vote. In fact, the Ascendancy had reacted quite strongly to this question of overtaxation. Barnie Castletown, who was one of O'Grady's admirers, made a speech threatening a new version of the Boston Tea Party. The Marquess of Ormonde became the head of the Kilkenny branch of the Financial Relations Committee which was to deal with the matter.

To O'Grady, Lord Ormonde was the obvious person to lead not only the financial crusade but the whole great Ascendancy renewal that he envisaged. As head of the great Anglo-Norman House of Butler, the 27th Hereditary Chief Butler of Ireland, Lord Ormonde was, historically speaking, one of the two most illustrious of Irish peers, the other being the Duke of Leinster, head of the FitzGeralds, who at that time was a schoolboy. Although by comparison with

Kilkenny Castle.

The Picture Gallery at Kilkenny Castle.

other Marquesses Lord Ormonde was not particularly rich – he was certainly nothing like as rich as the coal-owning Marquess of Londonderry – his prestige, which went far beyond the Irish Sea, made up for his comparative lack of money. The ancient city of Kilkenny was dominated by his ancestral castle, which rose, a vision of feudal grandeur, both genuine and nineteenth century, above the River Nore, the White Ensign flying proudly over the battlements when he was in residence, for he was a keen yachtsman and a leading member of the Royal Yacht Squadron. In and around Kilkenny, Lord and Lady Ormonde were like royalty; when they drove through the city in their open carriage, drawn by a pair of greys with a collar of bells, people would come out to watch them go past.

In April 1899 the Ormondes were visited by genuine royalty, the Duke and Duchess of York, the future George V and Queen Mary, who stayed five nights at Kilkenny Castle. The royal guests were taken on a water picnic from Thomastown, further down the river, in two of the local fishing-boats bolted together to make a kind of catamaran, painted bright green and filled with cushions, the fishermen who manned the boats being smartly dressed up as sailors. Country people lined the banks; a youth from the Coolmore farm stood stolidly, gazing at the royal party with his cap on. Colonel Connellan's fourteen-year-old daughter Marguerite shouted furiously to him to take it off, but he replied: 'Them's no Kings or Queens, they have no crowns on their heads.'[24]

Visit of the Duke and Duchess of York to Kilkenny Castle, April 1899. Lord Ormonde stands in the middle between the Duke and Lord Frederick FitzGerald. Lord de Vesci is at the extreme left of the back row, Lord Ava at the extreme right. Lady Ormonde sits third from the left, between the Duchess of York and Lady de Vesci. To the right of the Duchess sit the Ormondes' two daughters, Lady Beatrice and Lady Constance Butler.

The Duke and Duchess of York were photographed, together with the Ormondes and their two beautiful daughters, Viscount and Viscountess de Vesci, Lord Dufferin's handsome eldest son the Earl of Ava, Lord Frederick FitzGerald and other members of the house party, in the great picture gallery of Kilkenny Castle, a room a hundred and twenty feet long with a lofty glazed and timbered roof, its crimson walls hung closely with paintings including portraits by Holbein, Van Dyck, Lely and Kneller. Because the kitchen was immediately beneath it, the Ormondes used this vast gallery for breakfast and luncheon in preference to the dining room. When one of their menservants married their cook, they allowed them to celebrate in the picture gallery and to have a group photograph taken here, just like the photograph of the royal party.

Lord Ormonde, a simple, straightforward character whose passion, next to yachting and the sea, was woodcock shooting, would not have fancied the epic role in which O'Grady had cast him. He was even inclined to neglect the Financial Relations Committee, thereby incurring a rebuke from the disappointed O'Grady in the pages of the *Moderator* which he naturally regarded as an impertinence. To make matters worse between O'Grady and the head of the House of Butler, a row broke out between Lord Ormonde and the Desarts over the late Lord Desart's former agent, who was Colonel of the Kilkenny Militia. It had been discovered on Lord Desart's death that this man had appropriated £6000 of his money, but the money had been repaid by the Colonel's family and the matter hushed up.

Then, in order to clear his name, the Colonel claimed that the money had in fact been a racing debt which the late Lord Desart had owed him. Ellen Desart rallied to the defence of her late husband's memory and wrote a letter, which O'Grady printed in the *Moderator*, calling the Colonel a 'thief'. The new Lord Desart and Otway Cuffe demanded that the Colonel should no longer be allowed to command

Wedding group of Lord and Lady Ormonde's cook and one of their menservants in the Picture Gallery at Kilkenny Castle.

the Militia, and as Lord Ormonde had been one of those instrumental in maintaining him in his command, he was once again attacked by O'Grady in an editorial. Lord Ormonde retaliated by taking the Colonel as his ADC when he went to inspect the Protestant Boys' Brigade in the grounds of the Bishop's Palace. O'Grady printed an even more scathing editorial in which he declared that Lord Ormonde, the Bishop and, for full measure, Herky Langrishe, who was then Master of the Kilkenny Hunt, had 'betrayed the honour of the county'. He sent copies of the *Moderator* to the colonels of all the regiments on Salisbury Plain and also to the Duke of Connaught; he is said to have attempted to incite the Kilkenny Militia to mutiny.[25]

The Militia were then taking part in the great military manoeuvres of 1899, which were held in glorious summer weather on the borders of County Kilkenny and Queen's County. They lasted a fortnight and were a major social event; Lady de Vesci gave a dance for the young officers at Abbey Leix, having provided as many partners as she could by telegraphing for every girl she could think of to come and stay, but even so the girls were vastly outnumbered by the men. In those days there was a rule that no man could go into supper at a dance without a partner;

The coming-of-age of the Marquess of Waterford at Curraghmore in 1896. The young Lord Waterford stands towards the left of the group, behind the pony chair in which his invalid mother is sitting. One of his sisters, Lady Clodagh Beresford, stands at the extreme left, the other, Lady Susan, on the right, next to Lord Ormonde, who wears a buttonhole. Lord Waterford's grandparents, the Duke and Duchess of Beaufort, are in the middle.

so the hungry warriors, who had come straight from the manoeuvres in their uniforms and field boots, waited outside the supper room door and as each girl emerged with one man she was seized by another and taken in again. One of the girls, Lady Clodagh Beresford, sister of the new Lord Waterford who had recently come of age, reckoned that she ate about fifty suppers that night.[26]

The General Commanding the Forces, Lord Roberts, was present at the manoeuvres. One day, when he was watching the troops from a hill, a County Kilkenny lady, the widowed Lady Power of Kilfane, was brought up to him and introduced. She proceeded to introduce her two sons, the young baronet Sir John Power and his younger brother Derrick, telling him that they were both just about to go into the army. Lord Roberts was pleased to hear this; but said: 'I'm afraid they will not see much fighting unless they go out to India.'[27]

Two months later, the South African War broke out, but in Kilkenny it was overshadowed by the conflict between Lord Ormonde and the Desarts. The Bishop issued a writ for libel against O'Grady; further writs from Lord Ormonde and Herky Langrishe were reported to be on the way. Eventually O'Grady gave up his editorship of the *Moderator* and left Kilkenny in disgrace; the paper's former editor took over again and made peace with the House of Butler by inveighing against O'Grady's 'wanton, wicked and libellous attacks against one of the most exalted, popular and esteemed Peers of the Realm'. The controversial Colonel marched proudly at the head of the Kilkenny Militia when they set off, a thousand strong in their red tunics and spiked helmets, on their way to be trained in England for service in South Africa; but the departing regiment was followed by a straggling Kilkenny mob throwing stones and lumps of coal and screaming: 'Hurrah for Kruger and Lady Desart!'[28]

The South African War, which, from 1900 onwards, was conducted on the British side by a War Minister with an Ascendancy background – Lord Midleton's son St John Brodrick, a cousin of Lord Bandon – brought a fine response from the Ascendancy. Lord Dunraven, not far off sixty, went to South Africa with a battalion of Yeomanry which he had raised, only to be invalided home after a severe bout of dysentry. The fifty-one-year-old Barnie Castletown went out on Lord Roberts's staff; his wife Clare went with him. Lord Iveagh donated a hospital. The young Lord Wicklow, nephew of the Ladies Howard, went out with the Household Cavalry; the young Lord Waterford, with the South Irish Horse. The Knight of Glin, son of the Knight who had been troubled during the Plan of Campaign, went out with the Royal Irish Fusiliers. At one time during his service in South Africa, he and his brother officers used to bathe in a pool near their camp; a sentry was posted to prevent other ranks from bathing in the pool or seeing their officers 'in the buff'. One day the Knight decided to miss luncheon and have a bathe instead; but the sentry, imagining all the officers to be lunching, ordered him out of the pool at rifle-point. The Knight, standing naked in the shallows, shouted angrily: 'Can't you see I'm an officer?'[29]

So great was the response to the call to arms that many parts of Ireland suffered an acute shortage of men in the Ascendancy world. Edith Somerville and Violet Martin remembered a picnic held one summer during the war at which there were forty women and only two men; they themselves had managed to get out of it, but they had heard vivid accounts of its horrors from those less fortunate.

> The two men faced the position. Through smoke and bees they did their duty, carting back and forth the eighty cups of tea which the occasion demanded; but they said afterwards that more than patriotism barbed the regret that their country deemed them too old for active service.[30]

In addition to those who volunteered, there were, of course, the regular soldiers of Ascendancy birth who served in the war. To mention a very few, there was Field-Marshal Sir George White of White Hall in County Antrim who commanded during the Siege of Ladysmith; there was the commander of the Mafeking Relief Column, Colonel Bryan Mahon, of Belleville in County Galway; there were the two brothers John and Hubert Gough, sons of a General who won a VC in the Indian Mutiny and members of a great military family from Limerick, Galway and Tipperary.

Inevitably, some of those who went to the war did not come back. The handsome and brilliant Earl of Ava, eldest son of Lord Dufferin – who had received a Marquessate after being Viceroy of India – was severly wounded at Waggon Hill and died three days later. Lord Carbery's brother Cecil Evans-Freke also died of his wounds. Colonel William Aldworth, a kinsman of Clare Castletown, fell at Paardeberg; Lord Iveagh's cousin Colonel Eustace Guinness was killed at Bakenlaagte. Less than a year after that summer's day in Ireland when he met Lord Roberts, the young Sir John Power had been fatally wounded at Lindley. His brother Derrick, who succeeded to the baronetcy, died of typhoid in South Africa a few months before the war ended.

5

'George, George, the Bonus!'

— I —

Early on a June morning in one of the opening years of the new century, Daisy Fingall was in her room at the Chief Secretary's Lodge in Phoenix Park, where she was staying, just about to go to bed after a ball. A pebble hit her window; she looked out and saw her host, George Wyndham, standing on the path below, intensely good-looking and still young, though his hair and moustache were iron-grey. 'Be a sport,' he called up to her, 'come for a ride.' She flung off her ball dress and got into a riding skirt. Wyndham was waiting with the horses saddled; they rode out into the Park and galloped away across vast expanses of grass on which the dew was still grey. Suddenly they heard the sound of horses' hooves in pursuit, and the magic of their ride was broken by two mounted policemen trying desperately to keep the Chief Secretary in sight.

That dawn gallop could be an allegory of Wyndham's Chief-Secretaryship, Daisy as Erin by his side and his followers trying to keep up with him. As the member of the Government who was Ireland's actual ruler – the Viceroy being more in the nature of a figurehead – Wyndham was a knight-errant in a hurry. Though a Unionist and an English patrician, he was proud of being, through his mother, a great-grandson of the Irish patriot Lord Edward FitzGerald. He was in love with Ireland, there was so much he wanted to do for her and the time he had in which to do it depended on the vagaries of politics. He worked frenetically, chain-smoking, his hands restless, his features flushed, but with the fire of enthusiasm in his deep blue eyes.

What Wyndham most wanted to do for Ireland was to settle the land question; and this he succeeded in doing with a new land purchase act which was passed in 1903. Like the Ashbourne Act before it, the Wyndham Act enabled the landlords

George Wyndham.

to sell their tenanted farms to the tenants, the transaction being financed by the Government, but it was an improvement on the Ashbourne Act in that it gave the landlord an additional payment of 12 per cent known as the Bonus which came out of the British Treasury. The Bonus made all the difference to the landlords, for the price paid under both Acts depended on rents, which during the eighteen years since the Ashbourne Act had mostly been reduced. And it provided a useful capital sum for the landlords of heavily mortgaged estates, who might otherwise have been left with next to nothing after the sale of their tenanted land.

Though it was not compulsory to sell under the Wyndham Act, by 1914 three-quarters of the former tenants had bought their holdings. The former landlords kept only what they had occupied at the time of the sale, which in most cases consisted only of their house and the demesne surrounding it: perhaps two or three hundred acres including unproductive woodland and waste, though demesnes varied in size from under a hundred acres to over a thousand. Those who kept land in addition to their demesnes had either been fortunate enough to have a farm or two in hand when the tenanted farms were sold, or else owned outlying woods, mountains or bog. While the Wyndham Act was aimed at doing away with agricultural tenancies, it allowed landlords to continue to own tenanted houses in villages and towns, though these mostly brought in very low returns.

For most landowning families, the Wyndham Act was in the long term a disaster, though it provided a short-term solution to their financial problems. All too many of them were left with a demesne which was not a self-supporting unit; the money from the sale of the tenanted land was all too frequently lost through its being badly invested or spent as income when it should have been treated as capital. The fact that, in the case of an estate that was entailed, the Bonus was paid to the life owner meant that when an estate was heavily encumbered the expectations of the unfortunate heir went to paying off the mortgages, whereas the life owner had the Bonus to spend as he or she pleased. The story is told of how when Wyndham was walking through one of the gaming rooms at Monte Carlo a few years after the passing of his Act, he was greeted by an Irish peer of his acquaintance who pointed to the large pile of counters in front of him and said gratefully: 'George, George, the Bonus!'

At the time of the Wyndham Act, the Ascendancy was feeling the pinch after more than twenty years of reduced and uncertain rents. In many families economy reigned; Colonel Connellan told his twenty-year-old daughter Marguerite in 1904 that in future she could not have so many friends to stay in winter as the price of coal had just gone up to eighteen shillings a ton.[1] A couple of years earlier the young bride of another County Kilkenny landowner, on going to dine at Kilkenny Castle for the first time and seeing the liveried footmen, the priceless tapestries and the Ormonde gold plate in full display, was somewhat surprised when Lady

Group at Coolmore, County Kilkenny, at the turn of the century. Colonel Connellan is in the centre, below the steps; his daughter Marguerite is seated on the right.

Ormonde said to her: 'We are very poor.'[2] In fact, with the many commitments attendant on his great name, Lord Ormonde had none too much money to spare, particularly since, in addition to the castle and his London house, he kept a house at Cowes and a large yacht. When the yacht had to be sold, he felt more than ever insolvent.

Another Irish Marquess, the young Lord Headfort, having lived in very grand style for a couple of years after his marriage in 1901 to the Gaiety Girl Rosie Boote – the birth of their son and heir in 1902 was celebrated with a firework display which was long remembered – was obliged to shut up Headfort in County Meath and retire to a rented house in Hampshire. It was his wife who persuaded him to retrench in this way, for she was as strong-minded as she was beautiful and charming. When he married the delectable Rosie, Lord Headfort had to resign from the Life Guards, and he had some difficulty in getting her accepted in fashionable English society, but in Ascendancy circles in Ireland she was popular from the start, even though in addition to having been a Gaiety Girl she was a Catholic.

She was more fortunate than the petite and pretty Countess of Clancarty, formerly Belle Bilton of the Empire Theatre, who was never really accepted by the Ascendancy world. To relieve the tedium of life in her husband's rather austere mansion in County Galway she would drive into the nearby town of Ballinasloe and dazzle the inhabitants with the elegance of her turn-out. Unlike Rosie Headfort, she did nothing to curb her husband's extravagance; since 1895 he had been under the protection of the Irish bankruptcy court.

While Lord Clancarty had brought himself to the verge of bankruptcy, other leading lights of the Ascendancy in the Edwardian period were no less prodigal yet managed to keep financially afloat. Herky Langrishe, whose ancestral estate in County Kilkenny had been mortgaged seven times over, was able to support himself as a Master of Foxhounds, a yachtsman and a pioneer motorist by working his way through the £100,000 which his wife had been given by her father. As a first-class rider and shot, who was also highly intelligent and could be extremely entertaining, sometimes serious, sometimes playing the buffoon, he was one of the most popular men in Ireland; his popularity extended to England, where he knew everybody from King Edward VII downwards. Another pillar of the Edwardian Ascendancy who ran through a great deal of money was Lord Bandon, now in his fifties. His weakness was gambling; to pay for his losses he gradually despoiled Castle Bernard of its collection of Old Masters. He had copies made of the pictures as he sold them so that their disappearance went unnoticed.

During his long reign, Castle Bernard was one of the most hospitable of Irish country houses; and while he was, like Herky, an inveterate practical joker, he played his role as His Majesty's Lieutenant and a Knight of St Patrick with

Herky Langrishe.

Lord Bandon.   'Doty', Lady Bandon.

dignity. In County Cork, he and his wife Doty, who always dressed very grandly, were the undoubted King and Queen. As a sign of his standing in the popular estimation, the highest praise which a certain West Cork character could bestow on anyone was to say: 'Lord Bandon knows him well.'

'D'you know Paddy Mulligan? Ah, he's a great fellow . . . *Lord Bandon knows him well.*'

Things were done grandly in many Irish country houses at this time, even where there was not the liberality of a Castle Bernard. At Castle Bellingham in County Louth, Sir Henry Bellingham employed a man to do nothing else but rake the gravel, which was raked over immediately after anybody had walked on it. The Portland stone façades of Castlecoole, Earl Belmore's great classical house in County Fermanagh, were regularly washed by men suspended in bo'sun's chairs as though they were cleaning the side of a ship.[3] In most of the grander Irish country houses the groceries were ordered from London; they came once a week by rail and steamer in a crate, usually from the Army and Navy Stores. This would have been reasonable enough in the case of foodstuffs unobtainable in Ireland, but the bacon eaten at Castle Park near Limerick by the Delmege family and their guests had been exported from Limerick to London and then repatriated.[4]

Often the way in which a house was run depended not so much on money as on the quality of the servants. The Connellans of Coolmore, though only moderately well off, were fortunate in having Patrick Darcy, a perfect butler who had been with them for many years. Darcy also cleaned and filled the lamps and looked after the hunting kit of all the family. Marguerite Connellan once saw him washing her brother Peter's hunting boots in the kitchen yard late one evening and told him that it was much too late for him to be working, to which he replied that he did not mind what hours he worked 'so long as the Captain was the best turned out man at the Meet'.[5]

House parties were still the basis of Ascendancy entertaining, in spite of the price of coal; in 1902 no fewer than 147 people came to stay with Sir Algernon and Lady Coote at Ballyfin in Queen's County. In the following year, the number was down to 106; but in 1904 it rose to 161.[6] Sir Algernon Coote was the Premier Baronet of Ireland; Ballyfin was a classical house on a palatial scale. He received about £15,000 a year in rents, out of which he paid nearly £3000 in wages – the highest wage bill in the county. At the end of 1905 the *Leinster Express* published an account of the Christmas ritual when the hundred or so workmen on the Ballyfin estate were each given a present of 'substantial fare, in the shape of beef, etc.' as well as tobacco by Sir Algernon; at the same time as Lady Coote 'distributed many useful and suitable gifts of clothing, etc.' to their wives and families. 'Cheers were given for the generous donors by the recipients. Sir Algernon, in addressing the men, wished them a happy Christmas . . . he mentioned that he had been asked to join a Labour League, but he thought the best way to show his sympathy with the labourer was by giving plenty of employment (hear, hear).'[7]

Hunting and shooting were the chief reasons for country house parties during the winter months. Ladies were able to participate in the former sport and there were usually plenty of unattached men to keep them company in the hunting field, for the fathers of unmarried daughters were always willing to mount impecunious young officers from the local garrison; 'There's no such thing as a subaltern who can't afford to hunt' was the dictum of a certain Irish general.

The hunting season brought the hunt balls, of which one of the grandest was that held in the eighteenth-century Courthouse in Kilkenny. Three-quarters of the men present wore hunt coats; the girls were all in their best. At ten o'clock Lord and Lady Ormonde arrived like royalty, she wearing a tiara. They were greeted by Herky Langrishe, the Master of the Hunt, and his wife, who also wore a tiara, and escorted by them to a dais at one end of hall. Then the band, which was the most fashionable one in Ireland, conducted and led by a talented violinist named

Clarke-Barry, struck up; and the Ormondes and Langrishes opened the dancing with a quadrille. Afterwards there were Strauss waltzes and at midnight the Ormondes and Langrishes processed into supper in the Council Chamber, where they sat at a table at the far end of the room with a select party. At five, the band played John Peel with Herky blowing 'out of cover' on his hunting horn, and then came the National Anthem.[8]

When they were not hunting or shooting or dancing, country house guests played cards or engaged in practical jokes, as at Castle Bernard. There was also a certain amount of horse-play: at one house party Captain James Delmege of Castle Park picked up the notoriously fast Mrs Sadleir-Jackson, who had incurred his displeasure, and dumped her in a bath of cold water with all her clothes on; people said afterwards that her language heated the bath.[9] At her own house in County Cork, Mrs Sadleir-Jackson used to entertain her guests by sliding down the stairs on a tray, wearing pink tights. She also shocked the staid by her excessive use of make-up and by riding astride; when she did so for the first time at a hunt meet, the Master, by way of protest, took hounds home. Another lady who was regarded as fast was the novelist Dorothea Conyers, wife of a younger son of the Conyers family of Castletown Conyers in County Limerick: she shocked people by smoking a cigarette after dinner.

In summer there was tennis and, of course, cricket. Horace Plunkett's nephew, the young Lord Dunsany, had his own cricket ground at Dunsany Castle in County Meath, so had Lord Bandon at Castle Bernard; both provided lavish hospitality for visiting teams. Country houses closer to Cork city would entertain teams playing on the Mardyke ground, for the laying out of which Sir George Colthurst had been largely responsible. Once when W.G. Grace was playing here with a London County team against Cork County, he bullied the umpire into giving an unfair decision. He had not reckoned with Sir George Colthurst, who 'sallied onto the field and in vitriolic language told Grace just what he thought of his sportsmanship'. Grace tried to bluster it out, but Sir George was not going to be dictated to by anyone; and in the end 'the almost mythical hero of English cricket had to offer an unreserved apology'.[10] Another cricketing baronet who lived in County Cork was Sir Timothy O'Brien; he had the distinction of having played for England as well as for Ireland and is considered to have been the greatest cricketer who ever played for Na Shuler.

To hunting, shooting and cricket was added, in the early 1900s, the new sport of motoring. The second motor car to be seen in Ireland belonged to Herky Langrishe, who drove in motor races in England; in one race he took a pretty girl with him instead of a mechanic on the pretext that he needed her hat-pin for carrying out certain repairs. He succeeded in training a horse to a motor car. 'The process of training is extremely simple,' he wrote in 1903, 'the horse should be

One of Lord Iveagh's motor cars, with his second son, Ernest Guinness, at the wheel.

stood in a paddock and the motor vehicle driven round it in gradually decreasing circles.'[11] In that same year the Gordon Bennett motor race was held in County Kildare, not far from Harristown. 'That idiotic motor race,' wrote Maria La Touche, who was now nearly eighty; nevertheless she drove to the main road in her pony chair to watch the cars go by and quite enjoyed it. One of them stopped, and as she related in a letter: 'A truly beautiful young man . . . came up to the Irish witch (me), sitting in its chair, bowed, took off his cap and asked the way to Kildare.'[12] Her son Percy would have nothing to do with the race, regarding it as far too dangerous, but by 1905 he possessed a motor car of his own.

The Ladies Howard had ridden in the Iveaghs' motor car as far back as 1899, showing themselves to be very much in advance of the Ladies Bernard, Lord Bandon's three unmarried sisters, who were their close contemporaries. Although when young they had been known as the 'Wild Ladies Bernard' and had engaged in daredevil pranks like racing each other in carriages round a London square, now, in their early sixties, they would go neither in motor cars nor in lifts.

When King Edward VII and Queen Alexandra came to Ireland in 1903 on their coronation visit, they brought a motor car with them, which they used for touring the poorer areas of the West, known as the Congested Districts. In Connemara it broke down, but was got going again by the chauffeur of Horace Plunkett, who was

The royal carriage with King Edward VII and Queen Alexandra driving out through the gateway of Kilkenny Castle in 1904.

the proud owner of a De Dion Bouton. At the end of the tour the King made Plunkett a KCVO, which his friends thought hardly adequate in view of all that he had done for Irish agriculture.

That autumn there was an Irish section at a large exhibition in London. Daisy Fingall presided over one of the stalls, appropriately dressed in green Irish tweed. The King visited her stall and she sold him a cigar made from her own tobacco which she had grown at Killeen at the behest of Horace Plunkett who believed that tobacco-growing could be a valuable addition to Ireland's rural economy.

The King and Queen came to Ireland again in the following spring. They went to Punchestown and to an enormous dinner party given by the Iveaghs at 80 St Stephen's Green; they also stayed with the Ormondes at Kilkenny Castle, where baths with hot and cold running water had been installed in anticipation of their visit, there having hitherto only been hip baths. A reception to which people were invited from miles around was held in the picture gallery; the guests lined the walls on either side, leaving the way clear in the centre for the royal party to process to red and gold chairs of State at the far end. For some reason, the King and Queen were late, they were supposed to enter the gallery at nine-thirty, but it was ten-thirty and still they had not appeared. Then at last the King entered, Lady

Ormonde on his arm 'with a face of thunder',[13] followed by Lord Ormonde with the Queen. Behind them walked Herky Langrishe, imitating the King.

During the course of their Kilkenny visit, the King and Queen were supposed to be going to tea with the Langrishes at Knocktopher; new and rather dull carpets had been specially laid for the occasion, covering up the old William Morris ones. On the great day, Herky and his wife waited at the hall door with their eight-year-old son Terence rigged out in Little Lord Fauntleroy dress. But the King and Queen never came.[14]

— *2* —

The Ascendancy's connection with the Irish literary movement and the Celtic revival, which dated back to the pioneering days of Emily Lawless and Standish O'Grady, was stronger than ever by the beginning of the new century. George Moore and his friend Edward Martyn, a wealthy County Galway landowner, joined with Yeats in founding the Irish Literary Theatre. Martyn's Galway neighbour Augusta, Lady Gregory, was also closely involved with the Theatre and

Lady Gregory.

Yeats and George Moore (right) at Lady Gregory's home, Coole Park, County Galway.

became one of its directors when it was re-founded as the Abbey in 1904. John Millington Synge, the playwright who brought the Abbey immediate fame, was a grandson of John Synge of Glanmore Castle in County Wicklow.

Having lived out of Ireland since he was a young man, George Moore now returned; he preferred to live in Dublin than at Moore Hall, his ancestral home in County Mayo, which he lent to his brother Colonel Maurice Moore. Colonel Moore, like George Moore and Edward Martyn, was a member of the Gaelic League, and indeed, it was largely to the Colonel that George owed his own newly-found Gaelic enthusiasm. George had offered to pay for 'a nurse straight from Arran'[15] to teach the Colonel's children Irish, a gesture that was to be a source of contention between the two brothers, for the finding of a suitable Irish-speaking nurse proved more difficult than might have been supposed. One was unintelligible, others did not come up to the standards of cleanliness demanded by the Colonel's wife. 'I am in despair,' wrote the unfortunate Colonel in 1901. The quarrelsome George, who had made a will in the children's favour, immediately revoked it, and set a time limit of a year for them to speak Irish fluently. 'The first thing that concerns your children is to learn Irish,' he told his sister-in-law. 'Whether the nurses are dirty or ill-mannered are matters of no moment whatever.'[16] Eventually a satisfactory nurse was found, but there was further trouble when George, after his public renunciation of Catholicism in 1903, tried to have one of the Colonel's sons brought up as a Protestant.

At the same time as he was in conflict with his brother and sister-in-law, George Moore was quarrelling with his neighbours in Dublin. He offended the taste of the two sisters who lived next to him by painting his hall door green, they having particularly admired the five white hall doors in a row. They threatened legal action and he retaliated by rattling his stick against the area railings at midnight in order to rouse the dogs of the neighbourhood and disturb the sisters' sleep, but while he was doing so the sisters' dog bit him. He then accused the sisters' cat of threatening the life of a blackbird which sang in his garden and set a trap for it, but all he succeeded in catching was the blackbird. Another neighbour sided with the sisters and paid an Italian organ-grinder to play outside Moore's house during his working hours, and there was much mockery in the street when Moore gave a garden party at which an Irish language play was performed on a makeshift stage. He had, however, deliberately set out to annoy the non-Gaels of Dublin with this performance.[17]

The Irish cultural revival was not limited to literature and drama, but also extended to all the arts. In 1903 the Polish portrait painter Count Casimir Markievicz and his beautiful Irish wife Constance, herself a painter, came to live in a suburb of Dublin and they quickly helped to create what their future friend AE – the Irish poet and painter George Russell – called 'an art atmosphere.'[18] Soon

Constance Markievicz,
portrait by her husband,
Casimir Markievicz.

Lissadell.

Casimir and Constance were joining with AE to hold exhibitions of their pictures.

Constance Markievicz was the sister of a County Sligo baronet, Sir Josslyn Gore-Booth, who worked with Horace Plunkett in founding cooperative creameries. As girls, she and her poet-sister Eva had won the admiration of Yeats, who stayed several times with the Gore-Booths at Lissadell, their large and austere neo-classical house which stood among woods and glades, facing across the pale waters of Sligo Bay to the no less liquid blue of Knocknarea and the Ox Mountains. There is a story of how when Yeats stayed here for the first time, he appeared in the middle of the night to say that he had seen a ghost which he had not seen for twenty years.

Another of those who helped to create 'an art atmosphere' was Lady Gregory's nephew Hugh Lane. Having started life as the penniless son of a parson, he had become rich through buying French Impressionists when they were still largely unappreciated. He was now building up a collection of nineteenth-century and contemporary pictures for the city of Dublin, which in 1905 was exhibited in the National Musuem. The Director of the Museum was, however, hostile to Lane and alleged that one of his pictures, a Corot presented by the Prince of Wales, was a copy, and that Lane, as a dealer, was an interested party.

In an attempt to prove this allegation, he hung a photograph of a picture by a pupil of Corot at the entrance to the exhibition. There was an outcry and all kinds of insinuations went around, but the situation was saved by Lane's cousin John Shawe-Taylor of Castle Taylor in County Galway, who unscrewed the offending photograph under the eyes of the policeman on duty and carried it away. Before he could be prosecuted for stealing the Museum's property, he confessed his crime to the Viceroy over luncheon and received the Viceregal pardon. Shawe-Taylor was a handsome knight-errant rather like Wyndham, whom he had helped by initiating the conference which prepared the ground for the Wyndham Act.

Although most of the leaders of the literary and artistic revival had an Ascendancy background, the movement aroused all too little interest among the Ascendancy as a whole. Indeed it was suspect, because certain figures in it, notably Edward Martyn and Yeats's friend Maud Gonne, had been pro-Boer during the recent war; it was looked upon with even more disfavour after Maud Gonne and Martyn had helped to defeat the proposal that Dublin Corporation should present an address of welcome to the King when he visited Ireland in 1903. Martyn had become a Nationalist in 1899 and had immediately shown his colours by preventing 'God Save The Queen' from being played at a concert at Tulira Castle, his home in County Galway. Lord Clonbrock, the Lieutenant of the County, had demanded an explanation, and he had replied by resigning from being a DL and a

Lord Clonbrock and his family were all keen photographers. In 1899, the year of his controversy with Edward Martyn, he took this shot of his wife, his son Robin Dillon, and his daughters Ethel, Katherine and Edith Dillon, each with a camera.

JP. In 1905 Martyn became the first President of Sinn Fein, the organization founded by Arthur Griffith to pursue a more vigorous Nationalist policy than that of the Irish Parliamentary Party.

Not all the leaders of the movement had travelled as far along the Nationalist road as Martyn. Constance Markievicz, though at home in the world of the Gaelic League and the Abbey Theatre, frequented Dublin Castle. She and Casimir went to the ball given by that most glamorous of Viceregal couples, the Earl and Countess of Dudley, in 1905 at which everybody was bidden to come in Empire costume. In the same year she attended Lord Mayo's investiture as a Knight of St Patrick and featured in the picture which Casimir painted of the ceremony.

Another link between the Viceregal Court and the Gaels was Barnie Castletown, soon to become a Knight of St Patrick himself. A friend and admirer of Douglas Hyde, the founder of the Gaelic League, Barnie formed the Celtic Association to bring together the Celts of Ireland, Scotland, Cornwall, Brittany, the Isle of Man and, of course, Wales, where he was honoured by being made a Druid. To his friend of Oxford days, the diplomatist Sir Arthur Nicolson – whose wife was Lord Dufferin's sister-in-law and a staunch Ulster Unionist – he seemed more than a bit of a rebel.

In August 1905, the Nicolsons and their eighteen-year-old son Harold stayed with the Castletowns at Doneraile Court in County Cork*, which Clare Castletown had inherited from her father. Harold Nicolson recalls a hot, wet afternoon during that stay when he and his parents and their host and hostess sat peacefully in the conservatory which opened out of the end drawing room, 'inhaling the smell of the tube roses, listening to the rattle of the rain upon the glass roof, listening to the gentler tinkle of the fountain as it splashed among the ferns'. He also remembers going with Barnie to his study, a room associated with Clare's ancestress who was a woman Freemason, and being urged by him to read some cuttings from the Nationalist papers, as evidence of how badly the Irish were being governed. But 'when a step sounded in the passage, which Lord Castletown may have mistaken for my father's, he bundled the cuttings together and hid them rapidly in a drawer'.[19]

Barnie's politics, by this time, would have been rather the same as those of Lord Killanin, the son of the old Lord Chief Justice, who in 1900, a year before his father's death, was elected as MP for Galway. In Horace Plunkett's words, 'he ran as a Home Ruler who would call himself a Unionist so long as the Government behaved themselves'.[20] The idea of Home Rule was still repugnant to most of the Ascendancy, even though the Nationalist Party was now led by the moderate and statesmanlike John Redmond and the landlords' representatives had worked

* See illustration on page 284.

successfully with the Nationalists in the conference which prepared the ground for the Wyndham Act. Nevertheless, certain people were moving away from the rigid Unionism of the 1880s and early 1890s. Lord Dunraven, who, like Shawe-Taylor, played a prominent part in the land conference, was now a moderate Home Ruler, one of the prime movers in the scheme of devolution, a compromise between Union and Home Rule, which was put forward in the autumn of 1904 only to cause a furore that brought about the resignation of Wyndham. 'A trimmer, Sir,' Captain Delmege used to say contemptuously of Dunraven;[21] and all too many others in the Ascendancy would have been of the same opinion.

Horace Plunkett likewise lost popularity through being regarded as a trimmer, for while remaining a Unionist he became increasingly sympathetic towards Home Rule. His sympathies were shared by his friend and kinswoman Daisy Fingall, who in the fashionable Unionist circles which she frequented came to be known as the 'Sinn Fein Countess'. Nationalist sympathisers in the Ascendancy on the whole did not yet go so far as to make an overt break with Unionism, though there were a few Ascendancy figures who sat in Parliament as Nationalists or Home Rulers at various times during the 1890s and 1900s. They included Sir Thomas Grattan Esmonde and another baronet, Sir Walter Nugent from County Westmeath. Then there was the colourful Pierce O'Mahony of Kilmorna in County Kerry and Grange Con in County Wicklow who had fought for Bulgarian independence and changed his name from Mahony to O'Mahony in order to be more Irish. There was Walter MacMorrough Kavanagh, who had been on the platform at the Unionist Convention of 1892; there was Lord Fermoy's brother James Burke Roche,* whose younger brother Alexis was a friend of Plunkett and had ranched with him in Wyoming.

In 1899 Lord Emly, who as Gaston Monsell had been a Viceregal courtier and whose politics had hitherto been strongly Unionist, was elected to Limerick County Council not only as a Nationalist but also as a representative of Labour, and as a result of his Nationalist speeches he was removed from the Commission of the Peace. He was a slightly eccentric figure who went about the country on a bicycle, addressing meetings of labourers; for all his espousal of popular causes he was not popular in his locality. Like Edward Martyn and Daisy Fingall, Esmonde and Nugent, Lord Emly was a Catholic, whereas Dunraven, Horace Plunkett, Roche and MacMorrough Kavanagh were all Protestants, O'Mahony having started life as a Protestant and then become converted to Orthodoxy. From the Protestant Ascendancy also came Albinia Brodrick, a member of Sinn Fein. Albinia Brodrick's background was as socially exalted as it was impeccably Unionist: she was a daughter of Lord Midleton and a sister of St John Brodrick,

---

*He eventually succeeded his brother as Lord Fermoy. The Princess of Wales is his great-granddaughter.

Secretary of State for India in the Unionist government and before that, Secretary of State for War, and she was a cousin of Lord Bandon.

— *3* —

In December 1905 Balfour's Government fell and the decade of Unionist rule came to an end. The Liberals took office under Campbell-Bannerman and were confirmed in power by the subsequent electoral landslide. In Ireland, the Unionists' defeat marked the end of the Dudleys' brilliant Viceroyalty. Lord Dudley was enormously rich and had spent more than £50,000 a year over and above his official salary on such extravagances as hiring thirty-two black horses from London, all but four of which were used only twice yearly for the Viceregal state entry at Punchestown and the Horse Show. Lady Dudley, like her husband, was young, good-looking and charming; she had worked successfully to provide nurses for the country districts. The Ascendancy bade the Dudleys a sad farewell from the windows of the Kildare Street Club as they passed along Nassau Street in state on their way to the boat. The Club was crowded, ladies being allowed in for the occasion. Lady Alice Howard and her sister were there, having come with their neighbour the young Lady Powerscourt.

In place of the glamorous Dudleys came Lord and Lady Aberdeen, who had already reigned briefly at Dublin Castle in 1886. They were neither young nor glamorous; he was small of stature, bearded and fidgety, she was bulky and benevolent; unkind people called them Jumping Jack and Blowsy Bella. In fact they were an admirable pair, friendly, intelligent, philanthropic; but while as Liberals and avowed Home Rulers they were mistrusted by the Unionists, they failed to impress the Nationalists. The Ascendancy found the Viceregal Court lacking in dignity under their regime and rather too democratic. 'Very common lot,' was Lady Alice Howard's verdict on a dinner party at Dublin Castle when she and her sister Loulie stayed there during the Aberdeens' first season. On the following night, after a day spent shopping and interviewing a kitchenmaid, they attended another large Viceregal dinner, of which Lady Alice noted; 'Hardly a soul we knew.' Later that season, when the Aberdeens entertained their guests with Irish music and an Irish play, Lady Alice thought it was 'all too horrid and vulgar for words.'[22] To the Ladies Howard, as to the majority of Viceregal guests, who had little or no interest in the Celtic revival, the Aberdeens' desire to be more Irish than the Irish was rather tiresome. To Nationalist Ireland, it was a joke.

It was fashionable to sneer at the quality of the Aberdeens' hospitality, which was, in fact, perfectly adequate, even though Lord Aberdeen spent only about £6000 a year in addition to his official salary of £20,000, he and Lady Aberdeen preferring to spend their money on good works than on excessive display. The Castle balls were still very splendid, with all the colour and glitter of uniforms, the music of Clarke-Barry's band and the elaborate confections of Thévin, the Viceregal chef – for one St Patrick's Ball he produced a statue of St Patrick flanked by lions under an icing-sugar canopy. The more important ladies, however, were in constant dread of being invited to partner Lord Aberdeen, who as Governor-General of Canada had taken a great liking to the Canadian Polka, a dance of which nobody but he knew the steps. According to one of the younger guests, the lady thus honoured 'always had a "Heaven-help-me" look on her face' as the ADC led her up to His Excellency, who, after she had curtsyed, 'clasped her to the Star of the Thistle on his breast' and capered off with her in his favourite dance.[23]

Lord and Lady Aberdeen were a thoughtful pair, but they never really understood the Irish. When they visited the Protestant and Catholic Archbishops of Armagh, they somehow felt it would be tactless to let either prelate know of their visit to the other one. So having lunched at the Palace with the aged Protestant Archbishop Alexander and his unmarried daughter Nell who did hostess for him now that the hymn-writing Mrs Alexander was dead, the Viceroy and Vicereine suddenly took their leave without saying where they were going. They then drove round to the opposite side of Armagh city to have tea with the Catholic Archbishop, Cardinal Logue. To their great surprise, on arriving at the Cardinal's residence, they found Nell Alexander there, waiting to pour out the tea, having been asked by the Cardinal to come and do hostess for him.

— 4 —

By the early 1900s, the peers who had remained faithful to the Sackville Street Club were getting old. The Kildare Street was more than ever supreme, its commitee the innermost conclave of Ascendancy Ireland. Though there were always some changes in the membership of the Kildare Street Club Committee, a hard core of stalwarts remained on it year after year: they included the wealthy Lord Ardilaun and the mauve-bearded Lord Cloncurry; Lord Bandon's cousin and heir Percy Bernard; the Master of the Rolls Sir Andrew Porter and Christopher La Touche, a cousin of Percy La Touche who was himself on the Committee from time to time.

Normally, the business which came before this august body was not too troublesome. Gifts to the Club of pheasants and woodcock from Lord Ardilaun and of venison from Lord Cloncurry were acknowledged. A certain amount of time was devoted to the buying of champagne; it was decided to exchange the Pommery '98 for 1900. A naval man on the Committee, Captain George Poë, was asked to attend to the positioning of the ventilators in the Lower Lavatory. Permission was granted for a dinner party in honour of the Viceroy to be given in the Strangers' Room by Lord Langford, who was, however, to be reminded that people living within a twenty-mile radius of Dublin could not be brought into the Club as guests. Occasional complaints were looked into: Mr Hamilton-Stubber had been given a bad egg at breakfast, Mr Tighe doubted the freshness of his herrings. What looked like being more difficult to deal with was a complaint from the Coffee Room clerk that Lord Greville had used bad language; this peer from County Westmeath was alleged to have said: 'Damn your bloody eyes, do you think I am going to pay threepence for this rotten beef?' However, when called upon for an explanation, Lord Greville replied that there had been a misunderstanding: what he had actually said was that he would not pay for the beef because it was 'raw and bloody'.[24]

In 1899 the Committee had ordered Grove's *Dictionary of Music and Musicians* for the Club library on the suggestion of Edward Martyn. Although his home was in County Galway, Martin spent much of his time in Dublin and his stout, somewhat clerical figure was often to be seen in the Club, either writing standing up, as was his habit, at a tall desk specially provided for him by the Secretary, or sitting alone in the Coffee Room eating his way through a dinner that usually consisted of oysters if they were in season, a kipper and a huge steak with onions, washed down with quantities of strong tea. Martyn's tastes in food were rather similar to those of the old-fashioned Irish parish priest, and indeed, there was much of the priest about him. He was a devout Catholic and a natural celibate; in addition to his literary and political activities he helped to initiate the Irish stained glass movement and to improve Irish church music.

By openly sympathizing with the Boers, Martyn had made himself unpopular with many of his fellow-members, particularly with those who had fought in South Africa, or lost relations or friends there. He had received an anonymous note, written on a Kildare Street Club card, which said: 'Had you not better resign your membership here before you are expelled?'[25] But he had taken no notice and nothing happened. It was only after Martyn had written to the newspapers urging Irishmen not to welcome the King when he came on his visit in 1903 that the Committee had seen fit to ask him for an explanation. In his reply, Martyn had argued that his action had been political and that the Club was 'strictly non-political in its constitution'. The committee had replied that disrespect to the Sovereign could not just be called a political opinion. Martyn had insisted that it

Edward Martyn, portrait by Norman McLachlan.

could be, and there the matter had rested while the Committee consulted lawyers and took steps to have the rule which provided for the expulsion of members for conduct injurious to the Club tightened up. Attempts were made through Martyn's friends to persuade him to leave the Club of his own accord; Daisy Fingall, who was his cousin, said to him: 'Edward, how can you stay in a Club where you are so unpopular?' 'My dear Daisy' he said, 'it suits me. I like the food and anyhow I am not half as unpopular as Horace Plunkett.'[26]

What for the Committee was the last straw was when Martyn, in a speech which he made as President of Sinn Fein in November 1905, said: 'The Irishman who enters the army or navy of England deserves to be flogged.' Having ascertained from him that he had indeed spoken these words, the committee unanimously decided to call a special General Meeting to consider whether his conduct had been 'injurious to the character and interests of the Club'.[27] The Committee was bound to take a serious view of his remark, for it was once again not just a matter of politics; senior naval and military officers were honorary members of the Club – as indeed the King himself was – and would have found Martyn's remark highly offensive.

Whatever might be said about the Club having been non-political in theory and blatantly Unionist in practice, the fact remains that the Committee did not take action against Martyn because he was a Nationalist. It was certainly difficult, if not impossible, for Nationalists to join the Club – Nugent, O'Mahony, Roche and MacMorrough Kavanagh were none of them members, while Esmonde had resigned after becoming a Home Rule MP – but that is a reflection on the Club as a whole rather than on the Committee, which appears to have shown considerable forbearance in Martyn's case, ignoring his pro-Boer utterances and his refusal to play the National Anthem at Tulira in 1899. One suspects that some of the Committee members might have had a certain amount of sympathy for him. Christopher La Touche was known for his political toleration, as well as for his love of Irish literature. Lord Cloncurry was the brother of Emily Lawless; Lord Ardilaun was a patron of the arts and of scholarship.

The General Meeting to consider Martyn's conduct took place on 25 January 1906. Special luncheon arrangements had been made in anticipation of a large crowd, the Library being used to take the overflow from the Coffee Room. A resolution that Martyn's conduct had been 'injurious to the character and interests of the Club' – which if passed would, according to the rules, automatically bring about his expulsion – was put to the assembled members and voted on by ballot; the ballot box was sealed by Lord Ikerrin. The resolution was passed by 212 votes to 10.

Martyn was duly informed that he was no longer a member of the Club, but he would not accept this. On 27 January he visited the Club twice, refusing to leave when asked to; it took a letter from the Committee to keep him away. By now he had given notice of his intention to take legal action against the Club for wrongful expulsion, and in October, after consulting Sir Andrew Porter, who had recently given up being Master of the Rolls, the Committee decided unanimously to defend the action. Martyn continued to insist that he was still a member of the Club and in January 1907 paid his subscription as usual, only to have his £10 returned to him.

The case opened on 26 June in the Dublin High Court before the new Master of the Rolls. Counsel on both sides included some of the most eminent Irish lawyers of the day: among those acting for Martyn was the Nationalist MP Tim Healy, famous for his oratory and wit, while the Club's team was led by James Campbell, a prominent Unionist MP and a former Attorney-General for Ireland. Lords Cloncurry and Ikerrin, Sir Andrew Porter, Percy Bernard, Christopher La Touche and other Club members appeared as witnesses. Tennyson was quoted on freedom of speech in support of Martyn, but in the end the case was decided not on the rights or wrongs of his expulsion, but on the technicalities of what constituted a General Meeting. After a four-day hearing, the Master of the Rolls gave it as his judgement that the ballot which had expelled Martyn was not a proper General Meeting and that he was therefore still a member of the Club. He ordered the Club to pay most of the costs while reckoning that the Committee had been justified in acting as it did.

That evening, Martyn was back in the Club, enjoying his dinner; it is said that all the other members in the Coffee Room went up and shook hands with him. When Martyn once again paid his subscription for 1907, the Committee decided that it was only fair to refund him his 1906 subscription seeing that he had been excluded from the Club for most of that year. So the Secretary sent him back his £10, which he insisted on returning.[28]

'A doomed aristocracy'

— I —

In 1907 Hugh Lane obtained a commission for his friend, the young portrait painter William Orpen, to paint a picture of the Vere Foster family. Orpen, a cadet of a Kerry landowning family, was a prominent figure in the Irish artistic revival; in the words of a present-day writer, 'one of the great image-makers of what the outside world considered Irish between 1900 and 1930'.[1] He painted Unionist Ireland, he painted Nationalist Ireland, he painted literary and artistic Ireland; his sitters ranged from Yeats to Lord Iveagh, from Tim Healy to John Shawe-Taylor. Sir Vere Foster, a thirty-four-year-old baronet living at Glyde Court in County Louth, was the great-grandson of a British Minister to the United States and the great-nephew of the philanthropist and educationist Vere Foster, who as a young man worked among the Famine emigrants and in later life invented a copy-book used in every Irish National School. Sir Vere himself did little more than lead the life of a country gentleman, which made him unusual among Orpen's sitters who, if they were not political or literary or artistic, at any rate moved in fashionable society. Like many of the Ascendancy, he was a little eccentric, as was his good-looking wife, who had a passion for donkeys.

Orpen spent much of the summer of 1907 at Glyde, working on his picture. The house, Georgian with nineteenth-century Jacobean trimmings, was old-fashioned, though in the process of being done up; candles were the only form of lighting in Orpen's bedroom. Orpen also found the house very cold, though it was August. 'All seems strange here,' he told his wife in a letter. 'They seem like two children playing at being married.' Later he wrote: 'I feel years older than Sir Vere or Lady Foster and find myself giving them advice on how to manage their servants, etc., and children.'[2] The children consisted of two little girls, of whom

'The dead ptarmigan', a self-portrait of William Orpen in shooting garb.

Glyde Court.

the elder, aged nine, thought of herself as a boy, a fantasy that had originated in her mother's desire for a son and heir. For the picture, a large outdoor family group complete with donkey and dogs, she wore a knickerbocker suit of brown velvet, matching her father's coat which he wore with check breeches. Since he was meant to be out shooting, the donkey and the elder girl carrying a selection of dead game, the clothes worn by Lady Foster and the younger girl were a little too frilly.

'The picture goes on well,' Orpen reported to his wife. He explained how 'the two men' (Sir Vere and the elder girl) would sit to him one day, and 'the two women another. The dogs and donkey get in odd times, after tea mostly.'[3] Sometimes the donkey was led reluctantly into the drawing room, for as it rained almost every day of Orpen's visit there was little opportunity for painting out of doors. In August Lady Foster, who was pregnant, took to her bed for several days and Sir Vere went out shooting, leaving Orpen and the children to their own devices. 'Terrible games from 6 to 7, which nearly kill me – pillow fights etc.' Orpen complained to his wife. 'But I have to go through it.'[4] The children adored him and were amused by his habit of burning the toast at nursery tea and saying that he liked it that way.[5]

As a distraction from painting and amusing the children, Orpen sometimes went out with Sir Vere for half an hour's rat shooting before dinner. More diverting was the visit of Lady Massereene and Ferrard, whose husband, the son of the bibulous Lord Massereene, was Sir Vere's kinsman. She had big dark eyes, long lashes and sultry lips; she wore a skirt that came down only a little below the knee. 'She's very much in love with Sir Vere, I should imagine,' Orpen told his wife. 'Anyhow, she doesn't look at your humble.'[6]

During the earlier stages of the work, Sir Vere and Lady Foster had appeared to like the picture daily more and more. Later, they grew less satisfied with it and Orpen had difficulty in planning a subsequent visit to Glyde in order to get it finished. They decreed to go away for a few days at the only time he could manage, causing him to remark: 'It's wonderful how these people with nothing to do can't do anything!'[7]

— *2* —

Glyde was one of many Irish country houses to be done up at about this time. At Killeen, Daisy Fingall, on the advice of Hugh Lane – of whom her unartistic husband had remarked 'He is a good fellow, it is a pity he is like that' – painted the walls of the drawing room a soft stone colour and filled an alcove with famille rose and famille verte china. She turned the next room into a new library, with bookcases designed by Lane and made out of old mahogany by the famous Dublin cabinetmaker, Hicks; they cost nearly £1000, a very considerable sum in those days.[8] At Lisselane in County Cork, Reginald Bence-Jones also made a fine library by throwing together the existing library, another room and part of the original hall. 'And what do you call this grand room?' his formidable sister Carry, who was more than twenty years his senior, asked somewhat acidly when she came on a visit from England and saw it for the first time.

Reginald Bence-Jones was one of those landlords who had sold their tenanted land under the Wyndham Act and were enjoying a false prosperity. Another such landlord, but on a much larger scale, was the Marquess of Sligo, who had sold all but 3000 of the 100,000 acres which he had originally owned; he and Lady Sligo could afford to redecorate Westport House in County Mayo and to put in heating, electric light and as many as twelve bathrooms. Electric light was installed at Lisselane in 1907, at the same time as the new library was made, and at Kildangan, Dominick More O'Ferrall's house in County Kildare, in 1910; the plant and fittings cost him £687.

The scientific Lord Rosse had electricity at Birr Castle as far back as 1898, while the Bartons' house at Straffan had been lit by it since about 1900. Among the pioneers of electricity lower down the financial scale was Standish Barry of Leamlara in County Cork, who obtained his power from a water turbine situated immediately below the house; by pulling at a handle in his study he would open a valve which set the turbine going, and as an old servant of his proudly recalled many years later, 'in five minutes the entire house was alight'.[9] At bedtime he would close the valve, after which he and his family and guests had to make do with candles.

Oil lamps and candles continued to be the only source of lighting in most Irish country houses before 1914. Some people compromised and used gas: the young Sir Richard Levinge lit Knockdrin Castle in County Westmeath with 'Paterson's Acetylene'. Before 1900, Lord Dufferin, the Viceroy, had used acetylene gas at Clandeboye in County Down; it was stored in a gasometer which the staunchly Ulster Unionist house carpenter once struck with his adze in order to demonstrate to Lady Dufferin's young nephew Harold Nicolson the kind of assault he had wished to make upon Mr Gladstone. The vast metal drum had 'echoed with a horrible reverberation like the gong of doom'.[10] At Ballyfin, there were acetylene gas fires; Sir Algernon Coote had a dangerous habit of turning on the evil-smelling gas in his study, then searching for a match-box and then, when he had found one, throwing lighted matches at the fire until it exploded. His grandsons in the room next door would ask their step-grandmother what the noise was and were told: 'It's only Grandpa lighting his fire.'[11]

The Sligos with their twelve bathrooms were exceptional; Lord Langford with his compliment of four at Summerhill was unusually well equipped by the standards of the time – possibly they had been put in when he let the house to the Empress. The Bartons of Straffan, though they had electric light and other comforts, made do with a solitary bathroom down the nursery corridor. Captain Delmege put in the first bathroom at Castle Park about 1905 and Colonel Connellan converted a sewing room at Coolmore into a rather primitive one in 1910.

Killeen was yet another house which possessed only one bathroom, though it had nineteen bedrooms. A woman friend of Daisy Fingall's once called to see her on the morning of a hunting day and found her sitting in a hip-bath, naked but with her top hat and veil on and her coiffure beautifully done. 'You see, my dear,' she explained, 'Fingall is always most particular about my hair being well done when I go hunting, so I get my maid to do it in plenty of time before I have my bath.'

The spending spree to which Reginald Bence-Jones and his wife treated themselves on the proceeds of the Wyndham Act included the purchase of a magnificent Mercedes limousine, with silver flower vases in the passenger compartment; it came complete with a temporary chauffeur who taught the head coachman how to drive it. He proved more satisfactory than the chauffeur engaged for three months by Lord Mayo, who when driving his master in Wales in the spring of 1908 had two accidents. Writing to his agent in Ireland, Lord Mayo recounted what had happened. 'I was sitting alongside of him the whole time and he swerved across the road to avoid a beast, and just hit a telegraph post, and bent the wing of the car. That was Number One accident.' The second occurred going up a hill. 'I told him to go quite steadily, which he did not. There were two cows on the road; of course he ought to have slowed down. He hit one cow and knocked her down; she eventually got up and walked home, so the damage to the cow was not very serious. After this I cannot possibly trust myself to be driven by such a man.'[12]

Sir Henry Lynch-Blosse, son of the austere Sir Robert, had a more alarming experience when being driven in his motor shooting-brake by one of his coachmen, who, when ordered to go slower, pressed down the brake pedal on to the tail of a retriever. The dog retaliated by biting him in the leg whereupon he let go the pedal and the vehicle went careering down a hill, out of control. If Sir Henry thus endangered his own person, Lord Antrim was a menace to the public when he turned up at a horse-drawn funeral in his scarlet White's Steam Car; the hearse was upset in the ditch and the horses broke free and galloped away.

It was doubtless reports of incidents such as these which made the Ladies Bernard so determined never to ride in a motor. Their contemporary Ellen Letitia,

In August 1908, a few months after Lord Mayo's two motor accidents, another Irish peer, Lord Dunraven, sits proudly at the wheel of his Crossley, *Grisette*.

Madam O'Conor, widow of the O'Conor Don who died in 1906, shared their phobia; she would not even allow herself to be driven by one of her stepsons from the house to the gate lodge at Clonalis, the O'Conor Don family seat in County Roscommon. By contrast, the Ladies Howard became more motor-minded as they grew older. Thanks to the motor car of their nephew Ralph Wicklow they were able one year to do Punchestown from their own home, though on the first day, as Lady Alice recorded in her diary, 'something broke in the Motor so we had some stops.'[13] The septuagenarian Lord Massy, who lived not far from the Ladies Howard at Killakee in the Dublin Mountains, was another mid-Victorian who took readily to the new means of locomotion; his fleet included a motor charabanc for shooting parties.

For the Sligos, as for Reginald Bence-Jones and his wife, the Wyndham Act provided the wherewithal for ambitious gardening schemes. At Westport, the Sligos made formal gardens in the grand manner with balustraded terraces leading down to a lake. At Lisselane, the existing terrace above the river was greatly extended; the river was widened, a rose garden laid out, as well as a rock garden, a bog garden and an American garden. A pergola was constructed at the foot of the terrace, leading to a thatched summerhouse and an arbour inscribed with Dorothy Frances Gurney's lines:

One of Lord Massy's shooting parties at Killakee. Lord Massy, in a cloth cap, stands in front. The bearded figure at the right of the front row is Lord Cloncurry.

The Lisselane gardens in their Edwardian heyday.

The kiss of the sun for pardon
The song of the birds for mirth,
One is nearer God's heart in a garden
Than anywhere else on earth.

Here Mrs Bence-Jones, who was the leading spirit in all these schemes having a real talent for gardening, sat for her portrait wearing a shady hat. So impatient was she to get on with her plantings and layings-out that she came to dislike Sundays and holidays when the men were off work. On one such day some of her male guests undertook to erect the framework of a rustic arch for her, setting it proficiently in what they imagined to be cement. Several weeks later this was still soft and the head gardener was complaining about the disappearance of a sack of guano.

Mrs Bence-Jones crossing a bridge in one of her water gardens at Lisselane.

At the same time as the Lisselane gardens were growing apace, the young Richard Grove Annesley was gardening on an even grander scale at Annes Grove in the north of County Cork, while Arthur Hugh Smith-Barry, who had been raised to the peerage as Lord Barrymore in 1902, was continuing the planting of exotics on Fota Island in Cork Harbour which he had begun soon after coming into his inheritance half a century earlier. Lord Barrymore exchanged rare plants with friends in different parts of Ireland, including Lord Headfort who by 1907 was once again established at Headfort in County Meath; the improvement in his finances was due not to the Wyndham Act, for he still kept his tenanted land, but to his years of retrenchment in England and to the good management of his wife Rosie. Although the life at Headfort was now much simpler than it had been – the domestic staff of a butler, footman, cook and two or three maids was regarded as small for so large a house – Lord Headfort was able to embark on the planting of an immense arboretum.

He and Barrymore, Sligo, Annesley and Bence-Jones were only a few of the many Irish landowners of this period who were enthusiastic and knowledgeable gardeners. If the Ascendancy achieved nothing else in its declining years, at least it left Ireland with a legacy of great gardens which compare favourably with almost any in Europe in scale and variety of planting.

As well as gardening, many Irish landowners spent money obtained through the Wyndham Act on improving their home farms. With farming in the doldrums, this did not bring much in the way of returns apart from the honour and glory of breeding prize-winning stock. The 1900s were the great years of the county agricultural shows, which the Ascendancy was still able to run, even though now largely debarred from the running of the counties themselves.

— 3 —

May 1907 saw the opening of the Irish International Exhibition at Ballsbridge in Dublin by Lord Aberdeen. The Viceregal pair arrived in state; they processed to their places accompanied by a retinue that included Lords Ormonde, Mayo, Iveagh and Powerscourt while the orchestra played selections from *Tannhäuser*. Edward VII and Queen Alexandra were to visit the Exhibition in July, and while the King was in Dublin he was to invest Barnie Castletown as a Knight of St Patrick.

Four days before the royal yacht was due to steam into Dublin Bay, the diamond St Patrick Star and Badge worn by the Viceroy as Grand Master of the Order, together with other valuable insignia, were found to be missing. The door of the safe in the Office of Arms in Dublin Castle where they were kept was open and showed no sign of having been tampered with; the thief had obviously managed to get hold of the keys, which were in the custody of Sir Arthur Vicars, Ulster King of Arms. The missing Star and Badge, valued at £40,000 and the property of the Crown, were officially referred to as Crown Jewels which to the press and public made the crime appear even more sensational, as though crowns and sceptres had been stolen.

On greeting the Monarch at Kingstown, Lord Aberdeen was conscious that the Badge of the Order of St Patrick which he was wearing was being scrutinized. 'Is it not right, Sir?' he asked, fearing that he might not be wearing it correctly.

'Oh, yes,' said the King, 'but I was thinking of those jewels.'[14] He was obviously very angry about the theft, but out of consideration for Lord Aberdeen did not speak of it again during his visit except when the officials tried to pacify him with theories as to what might have happened.

'I don't want theories,' he snapped. 'I want my jewels!'[15]

The theft cast a shadow over the royal visit and poor Barnie's investiture was

King Edward VII speaking to Lord Aberdeen during his visit to Dublin at the time of the Crown Jewels scandal. In the carriage with the King are Queen Alexandra and Princess Victoria.

(*left*) Sir Arthur Vicars.

(*bottom left*) Barnie Castletown, wearing the ribbon and star of the Order of St Patrick.

(*bottom right*) Clare Castletown.

postponed; he was not invested until the following year and by the Viceroy instead of by the King.

The Government offered a reward of £1000; the Dublin Metropolitan Police and Scotland Yard began their investigations. But no clue of any significance was forthcoming. The wretched Vicars, who as Ulster King of Arms was responsible for the safety of the jewels, even went so far as to consult a medium; she told him, while in a trance, that they were to be found in a disused graveyard near Clonsilla, a village on the far side of Phoenix Park. Next morning Vicars drove out in search of the graveyard, which yielded nothing more than 'dank nettles and white laced cow parsley.'[16]

The King's anger in no way abated; he was determined that somebody should be punished for carelessness and began to press for Vicars's removal. Lord Aberdeen played for time; his natural kindness made him unwilling to see Vicars lose his job, which he had held for fifteen years to everyone's satisfaction. He may have been careless with keys, but he was devoted to heraldry. Towards the end of September the Viceroy was summoned to Balmoral for discussions on 'the unwelcome topic', as he called it;[17] and on his return to Ireland he reluctantly came to the conclusion that Vicars and the rest of the staff of the Office of Arms should be asked to resign.

Vicars would not resign, and demanded an inquiry. He had a vigorous champion in his elder half-brother Pierce O'Mahony, the friend of Bulgarian freedom and former Home Rule MP. There had been a coolness between the two half-brothers, O'Mahony as an ardent Nationalist having objected when Vicars made his son Pierce Mahony – who had not adopted the O' – a Herald, which meant that he was an official of the Viceregal Court. O'Mahony's sense of justice, however, brought him hurrying back from his Bulgarian retreat to rally to Vicars's cause. He wrote to the Government alleging that Vicars was being made a scapegoat; he drew up a petition calling for an inquiry and persuaded sixteen out of the twenty-one non-royal Knights of St Patrick to sign it, including Lords Ormonde, Waterford, Carysfort, Dunraven, Rosse, Bandon and Mayo.

The King was furious with the signatories, but agreed to the holding of a Commission of Inquiry, which found Vicars guilty of negligence. He was consequently dismissed and went to live at Kilmorna in County Kerry, one of the two country houses of O'Mahony, who generously allowed him to make his home there. O'Mahony continued to campaign on his behalf; he tried without success to enlist the support of the Nationalist leader, John Redmond, and even of the Sinn Fein leader, Arthur Griffith. The mystery of the jewels remained unsolved, giving rise to all manner of myths and wild speculations: they were said to have been stolen by Irish extremists to finance a future rebellion; they were also said to have been stolen by the Viceroy's highly respectable son Lord Haddo, who had been out of Ireland at the time of the theft. In 1908 an eccentric barrister went so far as to maintain that the culprit was Lord Aberdeen himself. Vicars's habit of giving very innocent drinks parties at the Office of Arms provided the basis for stories about orgies in Dublin Castle.

Perhaps the most likely solution to the mystery is that the theft was an 'inside job', carried out by one of Vicars's three Heralds, who frequently stayed in his house so would have had easy access to his keys. Of the three, Mahony is above suspicion; but one of the other two was a young man of extravagant tastes and doubtful character who some years later went to prison for fraud. That the police chose to ignore so obvious a suspect can be explained by his having frequented a clique of high-placed homosexuals who included Lord Ronald Gower, the uncle and close friend of the King's brother-in-law the Duke of Argyll. The theft of the jewels occurred only a couple of months after the homosexual scandal involving the Kaiser's friend Prince Eulenburg; it is possible that the King was determined at all costs to avoid a similar scandal in which his brother-in-law might have been involved.

$$- 4 -$$

If the medal of Wyndham Act prosperity was only gold-plated, it also had its reverse. Without tenanted land, Irish landlords were reduced to being, in the words of a present-day writer, 'merely rich men who lived in the countryside'[18] – and most of them were not even rich. They had already been to all intents and purposes excluded from local government; some of them managed to get on to the Board of Guardians, the Rural District Council or the County Council, but these bodies, except in Ulster, were dominated by Nationalist farmers, lawyers and shopkeepers. They were still in theory able to administer the law as JPs, but it was now customary for all the more serious cases to be tried by salaried RMs.

One former landlord who felt the anomaly of his position was the young Bryan Cooper of Markree Castle in County Sligo, no relation to the impoverished Coopers of County Limerick. The Coopers of Markree were genuinely rich, Bryan's grandfather having married an English heiress. One of them was probably the original 'rich man in his castle' of Mrs Alexander's hymn, which she is believed to have written with Markree in mind; certainly 'The purple-headed mountain, The river running by' is a precise description of the view from the vast nineteenth-century castle of the Coopers. Here in the summer of 1905 Bryan's coming-of-age was celebrated with illuminated addresses, a luncheon for employees, a fancy-dress ball for the County, theatricals and fireworks. It was a memorable occasion, yet to Bryan Cooper himself it all seemed a little false and empty. He had inherited a castle too big for his needs even in those spacious Edwardian days; he had inherited a beautiful demesne, some excellent salmon fishing and woodcock shooting and a fat portfolio of stocks and shares. But the 30,000 acres which were his birthright had been sold by his trustees.

He tried to make the best of his life in County Sligo, the days devoted to sport, the long winter evenings spent in rooms that were vast yet lacking in pictures and other works of art, though there was a very well-stocked library. It was a healthy outdoor life, but left him unfulfilled, like the hero of an autobiographical novel which he wrote a few years later. 'A man's life should have some responsibility in it, and to all intents and purposes Peter's had none.' The imaginary Peter's trustees had sold the greater part of his outlying property under the Wyndham Act. His only public duty was to walk once a month down to the Petty Sessions where 'he inflicted sixpenny fines on men who had neglected to paint their names on their carts, or been caught by nightfall without lamps.'[19]

Bryan Cooper solved his problems by going into Unionist politics. His chance came in 1910 when he was elected by a narrow majority as MP for Horace Plunkett's old constituency of South County Dublin; apart from the two Members for Dublin University he was the only Unionist to win a seat outside Ulster in the first general election of that year. Before the year was out, he had lost his seat in the subsequent general election, but at least he had established himself in the political world. Had he not succeeded in doing so, he might well have reverted to the life led by the majority of Edwardian Irish country gentlemen who hunted, shot and fished, played games and gardened, but otherwise did nothing in particular.

Such were the people whom the Church of Ireland Rector of Westport, James Hannay – better known as the novelist George A. Birmingham – had in mind when he wrote his two articles entitled 'A Doomed Aristocracy' which appeared in the *Westminster Gazette* early in 1909.

They just watch with peevish irritation the slipping of slate after slate from the roof of their castle of power . . . the saddest part of their ruin is that the class is not effete, worn out, incapable of doing things. The men and women who compose it are physically fine and beautiful. They have brains. They are virile still, strong, fit . . . capable of devotion to an idea, of sacrifice, of altruism. They are perishing because God has struck them blind – quite blind, so that they cannot see at all. They sit in their houses and grumble and complain day and night. Round them are old trophies. They add no new ones. Beside them on the shelves are their old books, good books, which represent the culture of their fathers. They themselves have bought no books since the year in which Gladstone passed the first of the Land Acts.

Some of this 'Doomed Aristocracy', during the years following the Wyndham Act, had reason to 'grumble and complain'. Though the Act was intended to put an end to agrarian unrest, in certain parts of the country it had the opposite effect, encouraging tenants to agitate in order to force landlords to sell them their holdings cheaply or to part with land they wished to retain. In 1908 Charles Neville Clarke of Graiguenoe Park in County Tipperary was boycotted because he refused to sell his home farm along with his tenanted land. No fewer than fourteen police had to be billeted in the house to protect him and his family, and since the local tradesmen had been prevailed upon not to supply him, provisions had to be sent each week from London to the nearby town of Thurles, whence they were brought to Graiguenoe under police escort. After all this had gone on for nearly a year, the shopkeepers began to feel the loss of the Graiguenoe custom and sent the parish priest to ask Mrs Clarke if she would persuade her husband to give up the farm. 'Father Tom,' she replied, 'you must know that I am a woman of enormous wealth. And I will spend every penny of it before Mr Clarke gives in.'[20] So instead,

Hilda Blennerhassett and her sisters, Nesta and Vera, forget the troubles of the Irish landlords on an idyllic day in 1904 at Caragh Lake, a few miles from their home in County Kerry.

the priest persuaded the ringleaders to lift the boycott and the dispute ended with no ill-feeling on either side.

Another landlord boycotted in 1908 was Walter Joyce of Corgary in County Galway who refused to sell his lands to the tenants on their own terms. Like the Clarkes, he held out resolutely and the agitation eventually collapsed. In the same county, an old lady of eighty had her servants scared away and her cattle driven off her land. Cattle-driving as a means of intimidation spread from the west to as far afield as County Carlow; the Liberal Chief Secretary Augustine Birrell incurred the contempt of landowners by telling them that they should protect their own property. As one of them wrote in 1907: 'I have 250 head of cattle, besides sheep, scattered over a large farm. How can I keep a private army ready to ward off the attacks of 100 men who may come at any time of the day or night?'[21]

It was just what had been prophesied before the passing of the Wyndham Act by Ascendancy diehards such as the Knight of Glin's niece, Miss Hilda Blennerhassett of Ballyseedy. In 1902 this youthful Cassandra from County Kerry had written the following verses, which may or may not be of her own composition, in her scrapbook:

> He was an Irish Landlord
> Loyal to King and true
> Fought in England's battles,
> Fought in the van right through.
>
> Now he is robbed and plundered,
> Turned out of house and land,
> All by the British Parliament
> Urged on by the rebel band.
>
> Alas for his faith and valour,
> Alas for the flag he bore
> Right to the front for England
> On many a distant shore.
>
> The man who shot the Landlord,
> The man with the blackened face,
> The man who houghed the cattle
> Is the man to take his place.
>
> Oh England think and ponder
> Before it is too late
> What would it be with Ireland
> Wholly a rebel State.

Without actually leading to boycotting or agrarian crime, the negotiations over the sale of land under the Wyndham Act often led to troublesome disputes between landlords and tenants. In 1909 Sir Algernon Coote had a disagreement with some of his tenants to whom he was by way of selling their holdings which ended in his calling off the sale.[22] Sometimes the quarrel was not with the tenants but with the government body which financed the deal, the Land Commission or the Congested Districts Board. The latter, having offered George Moore £40,000 for the tenanted lands of Moore Hall, infuriated him by trying to impose the condition that it should be able to give people grazing rights in his demesne. Eventually a sale was agreed which brought Moore £30,000 after the mortgages had been paid off. He kept Moore Hall and 500 acres; by then his brother the Colonel and his family had gone to live in Brussels and Moore himself, disillusioned with Ireland, had moved back to London so the house was closed up.

Moore Hall was one of several County Mayo houses abandoned by their families in the years before 1914. George Moore's cousin Colonel Llewellyn Blake gave Ballinafad, his ancestral home, to Catholic missionaries. At about the same time the trustees of Sir Henry Lynch-Blosse, who was in financial difficulties having, as a young man, borrowed heavily on his prospects, were obliged to sell most of the Athavallie estate including the house and demesne to the Congested Districts Board. The proceeds of the sale were held in trust for Sir Henry's younger brother, who was his heir; Sir Henry himself, as life tenant of the estate, obtained the Bonus, in this case £19,000. He got through it in a few months, living like a millionaire in Canada; he then went to end his days in the English seaside resort of Worthing.

In the neighbouring county of Galway, Tyrone House, the magnificent eighteenth-century mansion of the once-powerful St Georges on the shores of Galway Bay, had been abandoned in 1905 after the death of the ninety-six-year-old Honoria, widow of Christopher St George, though two of her daughters continued to own it jointly. Christopher St George had married very much beneath him; moreover Honoria was a Catholic and he a Protestant and in the days when mixed marriages were legally invalid unless performed by Protestant clergy they had been married by a Catholic priest. A Protestant marriage had followed, but not until after the birth of ten of their twelve children who were consequently illegitimate in the eyes of the law. Christopher, a celebrated sportsman and an MP, lived extravagantly and when he died in 1877 his estates were already depleted; the decline continued during the years that followed and the family came down in the world. Honoria and some of her children and grandchildren lived in various corners of the great house; the cooking was done over an open fire in a room on the top floor.

After the family had moved out, the house stood empty, a favourite haunt of

Tyrone House, County Galway.

trippers from the neighbouring towns, who were allowed to dance in the dining room. Most of the furniture had gone, though the lifesize marble statue of an eighteenth-century Lord St George dressed as a Roman emperor was still in its niche in the hall. In 1912 Violet Martin, whose own home, Ross, was not very far away, came here; she described the house in a letter to Edith Somerville. 'A great square cut stone house of three stories with an area, perfectly empty, and such ceilings, architecture, teak doors and chimneypieces as one sees in old houses in Dublin . . . It is on a long promontory by the sea.'[23]

Just as she was leaving, one of Honoria's daughters, who lived nearby in a little castle built by a St George a century earlier as a love-nest, drove up in her donkey-trap: 'a strange mixture of distinction and commonness, like her breeding, and it was very sad to see her at the door of that great house.'[24] The visit, which provided the inspiration for *The Big House of Inver* – written by Edith Somerville nine years after Violet Martin's death – gave Violet an exaggerated idea of the extent to which the St Georges had gone to seed. They were, she wrote, 'all illegitimate four times over',[25] having heard some garbled account of the invalid marriage. And she was under the impression that they had, for several generations, been in the habit of marrying local village girls, whereas before Honoria's time their wives had been consistently grand.

If the decline of the St Georges was due to past extravagance, the financial collapse of Lord Clancarty, head of another illustrious County Galway family that had known better days, was brought on by his own dissipations. In 1907, a few months after his wife, the former actress Belle Bilton, had died of cancer, he went bankrupt in Ireland with liabilities of £6500. Three years later he was made a bankrupt in England. The family estate was held by trustees, who paid him an annual allowance of £1000 at their discretion.

The year which saw Lord Clancarty's second bankruptcy also brought a financial crisis for Sir George Brooke, who had to sell Summerton, his hospitable house near Dublin – 'You'll have no difficulty in finding the house, you can smell the roast beef at the lodge gates,' he used to tell prospective guests.[26] It was not that he was extravagant; it was simply that, over the years, he had paid more servants, fed more hunters, entertained more guests and educated more sons than his resources could stand, even though they were based not on a landed estate but on a flourishing family wine business.

The cost of educating his children was a factor in the Earl of Carrick's eventual decision to sell Mount Juliet, his family seat in County Kilkenny. Lord Carrick – who as Lord Ikerrin had been a witness in Edward Martyn's action against the Kildare Street Club – inherited the estate in 1909, by which time the house was let, for his father, on succeeding an eccentric kinsman in 1901, could not afford to modernize it after paying death duties. The tenant was General Sir Hugh

McCalmont, two of whose uncles had made vast fortunes in the City of London; his own family home was in County Antrim, but he preferred to live at Mount Juliet, where he and his wife entertained in style.

− 5 −

Two popular figures in North County Cork were the cricketing baronet Sir Timothy O'Brien* and Lord Fermoy's brother Alexis Roche. Both moved freely in fashionable sporting circles in England as well as in Ireland, though neither was particularly well off. Roche who in his younger days had ranched in Wyoming with his friend Horace Plunkett had supplemented his income since his return to Ireland by dealing in horses. In 1891 O'Brien had bought a horse on Roche's recommendation which he afterwards alleged to be unsound; such were his accusations that Roche had contemplated taking legal action. Instead, there was an abortive attempt to settle the affair by getting Lord Listowel to act as arbiter. There the matter had rested, with the two of them not on speaking terms and O'Brien continuing to cast aspersions on Roche's integrity.

On 7 March 1908 both Roche and O'Brien were out with the Duhallow Hunt. A large crowd of gentlemen and ladies were riding to covert, Roche and O'Brien among them. Suddenly O'Brien, who was in front, wheeled his horse round and began to abuse Roche in a voice raised for everyone to hear.

'You are a swindler. You are a liar. You are a thief, and you have been living by swindling for twenty years.'

O'Brien's friends gathered round him and begged him to apologize, but he said: 'I have waited for years for this opportunity to do this in your presence.' He went so far as to suggest that Roche had pocketed a sum of £120 which the Hunt had given him as 'fowl money' – to compensate farmers for losses in poultry caused by foxes.

Roche immediately served a writ for slander and the case came up at Cork Assizes in July before the greatest living Irish judge, the venerable Lord Chief Baron, Christopher Palles. Cork Courthouse was packed to capacity with the hunting world, including a large number of ladies: never had it 'presented a more fashionable aspect'.[27] The scene recalled the Pike card case, but that was in Dublin. As a link with that earlier trial, Roche's junior counsel was Cecil Atkinson,

* See illustration on page 167.

whose father had led for Pike, while O'Brien's leader, James Campbell, and also the second member of Roche's team, had been prominent in the more recent case of Edward Martyn versus the Kildare Street Club.

Leading for Roche was the Irish Solicitor-General, who during the first two days successfully disproved some of O'Brien's charges, including the matter of the fowl money and a story about Roche having sold an unsound horse to the Duchess of Sutherland. Far from being unsound, the horse had been so much to the Duchess's liking that she had commissioned a portrait of it, which now hung at Stafford House in London. Roche was examined and gave a good impression, also examined was a Duhallow follower who had witnessed O'Brien's outburst at close quarters. He told the court that he had feared that O'Brien was going to hit Roche, so had caught hold of his bridle and 'chucked him back'. 'The horse or Sir Timothy?' Campbell asked facetiously, raising a laugh.

The laughter was louder and there were cheers when the answer came: 'The horse. Sir Timothy had no bridle on that day.'[28]

On the third day of the trial there was a sensation. One of the jurors was called into the witness box where he revealed that he and O'Brien were close friends. Moreover, he told the court that O'Brien had sent him a message through the secretary of the Cork County Club to the effect that he would rather have an award of a farthing's damages to Roche than that the jury should fail to agree. This was nothing short of an attempt to interfere with the course of justice, though the Club Secretary, when called, tried to excuse O'Brien by saying that he had acted as he did because he suspected that the Lord Mayor of Cork, who sat on the Bench during the hearings, was canvassing the jurors against him. The Judge ordered O'Brien to appear before the Court of King's Bench in Dublin to show cause why he should not be imprisoned for contempt of court. The jury was discharged, which meant that the trial would have to begin all over again after O'Brien had purged his contempt.

O'Brien accordingly appeared before the Lord Chief Justice in the Court of King's Bench in November to apologize for his conduct. He assured the court that it had never occurred to him that he had acted with impropriety. The Solicitor-General, however, pointed out that if he had got his way over the farthing's damages, Roche would have been disgraced as well as having to pay costs. The Court fined O'Brien £300 and ordered him to pay all the costs incurred up till then.

The case between Roche and O'Brien finally reopened in Dublin before Mr Justice Kenny at the beginning of the following June, Roche having in the meantime suffered the loss of his wife. As in the abortive Cork trial, the allegations against Roche were demolished one by one, though counsel on Roche's side made the mistake of repeating some allegations against O'Brien that were likewise shown to be false, such as that a certain gentleman had refused to play cricket with him. It was also suggested that O'Brien, who was a Catholic, had made trouble for his local priest with the Bishop; this was denied by the Bishop himself, who appeared as a witness. Other witnesses ranged from Lord Listowel to Roche's former groom, who having been with him for fifteen years had left to go and work for O'Brien whom he had also left, giving as his reason that he did not like being paid his wages by the gardener. Much of O'Brien's case against Roche depended on the evidence of this 'thoroughly ungrateful servant', as the Judge described him in his summing-up.[29]

The case dragged on for nine days. The Judge in his summing-up said that 'of all the interesting cases that he had ever tried, the present was, perhaps, the most interesting. It was full not only of equine interest, but of human interest.' It seemed, he said, that O'Brien simply wanted to turn Roche out of County Cork, out of the Hunt and out of his home. He reminded the jury that if they found for O'Brien, Roche would 'go forth a bankrupt in credit, reputation and honour'. Whereas if they found for Roche, O'Brien would not be dishonoured 'but affected, perhaps, financially by the result of the verdict'.[30]

Having withdrawn at 5.30 in the afternoon, the jurors returned nearly two hours later, uncertain on a number of points. When these had been cleared up, they retired again and did not finally return until after 9 at night. They gave Roche a verdict for £5 damages. He was also awarded costs, so that while the damage done to his good name might not have been valued at very much, O'Brien's refusal to let bygones be bygones cost him a great deal of money.

– 6 –

St Patrick's Eve 1909, a day melancholy for Alexis Roche, for it was the day of his wife's death, saw Dublin Castle en fête for the Aberdeens' Irish Industries Ball. The dancing was preceded by a Grand Irish Industries Pageant formed by groups of ladies and gentlemen representing Flax and Linen, Shipbuilding, Minerals, Agriculture, Pottery, Tobacco, Toys and Soap, not to mention the Horse Industry. The Aberdeens were full of original ideas for Viceregal entertainments; there was one at which Miss Muriel Poë, the rather plain daughter of Captain Poë who had seen to the ventilators in the Lower Lavatory at the Club, appeared as the May Queen. She sat enthroned in a flowery arbour, attended by a bevy of girls and also by the Viceregal Pages, twin sons of the Comptroller, Lord Carrick: two

Lady Aberdeen dressed for her Irish Industries Ball.

'The Court of the May Queen'. Miss Muriel Poë enthroned in a flowery arbour attended by the viceregal pages, Viscount Ikerrin and Somerset Butler, twin sons of the Earl of Carrick.

angelic little boys in Van Dyck costume who at Castle functions generally spent their time concealed between the great double doors of the State Apartments, smoking. At Viceregal Lodge, the Aberdeens gave an open-air performance of Standish O'Grady's play, *Finn and his Companions,* with some of the cast sporting extravagantly-horned headgear.

The Aberdeens' finest hour came in 1911, when King George V and Queen Mary, within a month of their coronation – at which O'Conor Don had borne the Standard of Ireland – visited Dublin. They stayed not at Viceregal Lodge but at Dublin Castle, which had been renovated and replumbed and given a new State Dining Room in anticipation of their visit. The Lodge had likewise been added to and replumbed; henceforth one of the attractions of staying in either Viceregal residence would be the hot water – it was possible to get a really hot bath even at three in the morning after a ball.

This time, all went well; no disaster, like the theft of the Crown Jewels, occurred to mar the royal visit. Lady Aberdeen, assisted by the wives of the Lieutenants of Counties, had organized an address of welcome to the newly-crowned Queen from the 'Women of Ireland'; reproductions of their signatures, 165,000 in number and headed by that of Daisy Fingall, filled six volumes. A deputation presented them to Her Majesty in the Castle drawing room, while Lady Aberdeen read out the actual message from the Irish women together with an explanation of the Celtic allegorical design on its St Patrick's blue morocco cover.

> To the four-voiced Wind they commit their message. The strong, dark wind from the North; the mild, white wind from the South; the sad, brown wind from the West; the fresh, red wind from the East – all mingle their breath, and in unison blow Justice, Love, Mercy and Courage in a golden shower of hope on the jewelled crown of Queen Mary.[31]

Despite the success of the 1911 royal visit, the Aberdeens were no more popular now than at the beginning of their reign. They tried so hard, but always seemed to rub people up the wrong way, whether through thoughtlessness or sheer bad luck. Thus, when Lady Alice Howard went to a meeting of Lady Aberdeen's campaign against tuberculosis, Lady Aberdeen arrived half an hour late. The campaign itself, though well-meant, did not add to her popularity, for her somewhat tactless methods of publicity gave the impression to the outside world that everyone in Ireland was consumptive.

According to the writer of an article entitled 'The Irish Social Ladder' which appeared in the society magazine *Irish Life* in 1912, the Dublin Castle season had by then become a 'dead letter'. 'The kindly, well-intentioned Scotch nobleman who fills the position of top rung perhaps scarcely realises the extent to which he is jeopardising the Dublin Season.'[32] In so far as this was true, it was mainly on account of his politics. The long-drawn-out crisis over Home Rule had already begun; feelings ran so high that most of the Irish peers and peeresses and other grandees, being Unionists, boycotted the entertainments of the Liberal Viceroy. People from the official, professional and business worlds of Dublin remained faithful to the Castle; but the shortage of lords and ladies caused some of them to complain that the parties there were now 'sadly mixed'.[33]

7

The shadow of Home Rule

— I —

So badly did the Liberals fare at the polls in 1910 that from now on they could only stay in power with the help of the Irish Nationalists. The price of the Nationalists' support was Home Rule, which could no longer be thrown out by the Lords after the Parliament Act of 1911 had deprived them of their veto. Asquith accordingly introduced a Home Rule bill into the Commons in April 1912, casting gloom over Punchestown; there were no cheers for the Aberdeens as they drove on to the course in their procession of State carriages. But for Asquith's inconsiderate timing, that Punchestown would have been a good one; there were house parties at Powerscourt, Harristown, Shelton, Straffan and many other great houses in Kildare, Wicklow and Dublin. The Bandons stayed with Percy and Lady Annette La Touche at Harristown; and the Iveaghs' party included Lord and Lady Midleton, Daisy Fingall and her daughter Mary, Lord Londonderry and Lord Charles Beresford, now a distinguished Admiral and MP for Portsmouth.

Charlie Beresford had spent Easter with the Londonderrys at Mount Stewart, where the house party included Carson and Bonar Law, another of Theresa Londonderry's protégés who was now Leader of the Unionist Opposition in Parliament. Bonar Law and Beresford were among the seventy MPs for English, Scottish and Welsh constituencies who showed their solidarity with the Ulster Unionists at a demonstration held at the Balmoral show grounds outside Belfast on Easter Tuesday, when no fewer than a hundred thousand men marched past the platform. There had been another great rally in the previous September at Craigavon, the home of Carson's lieutenant, the wealthy distiller Captain James Craig. A committee was making plans for a provisional government for Ulster so that the Province could secede from the rest of Ireland if a Home Rule parliament

A house party at 80 St Stephen's Green. Lord Iveagh, the host, sits on the ground in front of Lord Ormonde; Lady Iveagh sits in the front row, in profile, with Lady Waterford on her right; the Duke of Abercorn sits on the extreme right, leaning on his stick. The Ormondes' unmarried daughter, Lady Constance Butler, stands behind Lady Waterford, with her sister, Lady Beatrice Pole-Carew, above her to the right. To the right of Lady Beatrice is Lord Kitchener, and then, at a slightly lower level, the Duchess of Abercorn, Lady Ormonde, Lady Kenmare, Lady Hamilton, Lord Kenmare and Lord Duncannon. At the extreme left of the back row is the Duke of Leinster's younger brother, Lord Desmond FitzGerald; the two ladies in the middle of the back row are Lady Phyllis Hamilton and Theresa Londonderry. Lord Hamilton, who after succeeding his father as Duke of Abercorn was to become the first Governor of Northern Ireland, is at the extreme right of the back row.

Lord Charles Beresford, now an admiral and an MP, with his brother, Lord Marcus, who trained the King's horses.

were established. Money was pouring into Carson's Unionist Defence Fund.

In the rest of Ireland, opposition to Home Rule was no less determined, though it lacked the popular backing which made it so formidable in Ulster; outside the Ascendancy it was largely confined to Protestants and to the most prosperous of the Catholic urban middle classes. Anti-Home Rule meetings were held up and down the country. Andrew Jameson of the distilling family, one of the leaders of the Southern Unionists, lent the Ladies Howard his motor to take them to a meeting in Wicklow town which was being chaired by their nephew Ralph Wicklow; the hall was crowded, despite bad weather. While the Unionists of the South naturally felt a bond with their fellow-Unionists in Ulster – Violet Martin travelled north to Coleraine in September to watch the Ulstermen* signing their 'Solemn League and Covenant' against Home Rule – the Protestant sectarianism which was the Ulster Unionists' chief weapon was causing them increasing disquiet. Lord Ormonde, speaking from a platform draped with Union Jacks to a gathering of more than a thousand in the picture gallery of Kilkenny Castle in

---

* For simplicity's sake, the word 'Ulstermen' is used from now on to denote 'Ulster Unionists', though this is not, strictly speaking, correct, since there were plenty of Ulstermen who were not Unionists.

October, assured his audience that neither he nor those beside him on the platform – who included the Catholic Lord Kenmare as well as Protestants such as Lord Desart, Lord Midleton and himself – would have been there had the meeting been 'in the slightest degree of a sectarian character', a statement greeted with cries of 'Hear, hear'.[1] At an anti-Home Rule meeting held at Killadoon, the home of the Protestant County Kildare landowner Henry Clements, great annoyance was caused when the local Church of Ireland clergyman made a speech hostile to Catholics; the situation was saved by the principal speaker, Bernard Shaw's kinsman Sir Frederick Shaw of Bushy Park, who stood up and said that the Catholic and Protestant Churches were like two billiard balls; you could hit whichever one you liked and get as far with either.[2]

Considering that so many of the Southern Unionists were moderates, like Henry Clements or Lord Ormonde and his friends on the Kilkenny Castle platform, it may seem surprising that they were opposed to so moderate a measure as Asquith's Home Rule bill, which only gave Ireland a very limited autonomy with wide powers reserved to the Imperial Parliament. A passage by the playwright Lennox Robinson – a clergyman's son who grew up on the fringes of the Ascendancy in County Cork – conveys how the average reasonably broad-minded Unionist landowner of 1912 felt about Irish Nationalism.

> The Nationalist Member is without principles, a rebel, an instigator of cattle-drives and terrorism of various sorts; this talk about Home Rule is rot – but dangerous rot; the Board of Guardians is notoriously effete and corrupt, such men put in charge of the country would bankrupt it in ten years. At all costs the English connexion must be maintained, any alternative spells disaster. And as to this new craze for Gaelic![3]

Nevertheless, the number of recruits to the ranks of Home Rule from among the Ascendancy was slowly but steadily growing. There was Lord Granard, whose social position was of the most exalted, for he was Master of the Horse to the King; having been given this post in 1907 by Campbell-Bannerman as one of the few younger Liberal peers who knew something about horses. Since then his family fortunes, which had been at a low ebb when he inherited as a schoolboy in 1889, had been spectacularly restored by his marriage to an American heiress. There was Winston Churchill's cousin Shane Leslie, eldest grandson of Sir John Leslie of Glaslough in County Monaghan, a young Catholic convert of literary talent who in 1910 had stood for Derry city as a Nationalist against the Duke of Abercorn's son and heir, losing by a mere fifty-seven votes. There was Lord Monteagle's daughter Mary Spring-Rice.

For Sir Josslyn Gore-Booth's sister, Constance Markievicz, Home Rule was now far too moderate. The St Patrick's Ball of 1908 had been her last appearance at the Castle; an acquaintance had afterwards remarked that he had not seen her at the Castle lately and she had replied: 'No, I want to blow it up.'[4] Ten days after her last Castle ball she had joined Sinn Fein; she had since become a devoted disciple of the Socialist Republican James Connolly. When George V and Queen Mary were in Dublin, she had publicly demonstrated her extreme Nationalism by attempting to burn a Union Jack in the street. The actual burning had not been a great success; there had been a tug o'war with the police pulling at one end of the flag, and Constance, the other end tied round her waist, being pulled by a Nationalist crowd. When she had finally got hold of the flag it would not burn, even though a boy obligingly brought her some paraffin.

— 2 —

Under the shadow of Home Rule, Ascendancy life went on the same as ever. The Horse Show of 1912 was accompanied by the usual round of gaieties; the new General Commanding the Forces, Sir Arthur Paget, and his wife gave a ball at their official residence in the Royal Hospital, Kilmainham, at which Lady

Dublin Horse Show, 1912. Lord Powerscourt with an Indian visitor, the Maharaja of Alwar.

Kilteragh, Sir Horace Plunkett's house in the Dublin Mountains.

Ormonde, Lady Granard, Lady Iveagh and other great ladies were present, all 'wearing their most resplendent jewels.'[5] Since the Pagets occupied a high official position, their house guests, who included Lady Ormonde and her daughter Lady Constance Butler, had to attend the dance which the Aberdeens gave at Viceregal Lodge; but most of the fashionable world preferred to go to a dance given on the same night by a foreign visitor, Baron Francis de Tuyll, at the Café Cairo.

People who no longer wished to take part in the Castle season still came up to Dublin for private entertainments, such as the bal poudré given earlier in 1912 by Mrs Duckett of Duckett's Grove for her daughter. Mrs Duckett was unusual among the county gentry in possessing a Dublin house, to which she had recently added a 'spacious ballroom of octagonal form'; this, for the ball, was 'profusely decorated with white lilies, azaleas and standard Dorothy Perkins rose trees.'[6]

If the house of any one member of the Ascendancy at this time came near to being the centre of Dublin life, it was Kilteragh, the large villa at Foxrock between the Dublin Mountains and the sea which Horace Plunkett had built for himself to the design of a Swedish architect. It was fan-shaped, to catch the sun; Plunkett's own bedroom was on the roof and open to the elements and could be turned to face whichever way he fancied by means of a handle reached from his bed. The house was always full of guests; people would come out from Dublin for luncheon or dinner; people came from other parts of the country; 'everyone interesting or interested who visited Ireland' came here.[7] The talk was nearly always about Ireland and the way in which the country should in future be governed. Plunkett now realized that some form of self-government was inevitable; his dream was that the new Irish constitution should be signed on the stoep outside his windows, which he had copied from the one at Groote Schuur, Cecil Rhodes's house near Cape Town.

What was happening in Dublin did not really affect the social life of the Ascendancy as a whole, which continued to be based on local events such as Tramore Races, Lough Derg Regatta or the Annual Cork Industrial Exhibition which in 1912 was opened by Lady Bandon in the presence of a large gathering of county ladies. During that same summer, there was an even more fashionable gathering at the Annual Flower Show and Fête at Knocklofty near Clonmel, the home of Lord and Lady Donoughmore, who had a house party for the occasion as did their neighbours the Duchess of St Albans and the Bagwells of Marlfield. In North Cork, there was Mallow Lawn Tennis Tournament, at which the General Commanding the Forces and Lord and Lady Listowel were present; the tennis-playing girls, who were partnered by young officers from the local garrison, included the daughters of Sir Timothy O'Brien.

Tennis in the summer months provided the daughters of the Ascendancy with as good an opportunity of meeting and attracting young men as hunting did in the winter. 'The girls there were all in short, exceedingly tight white dresses' Lady Talbot de Malahide reported of a County Dublin tennis party in the summer of 1913. 'Nothing of the human form was left to the imagination.'[8] They were as bad as Joan Grubb, the young daughter of a Tipperary County family, who followed the example of Mrs Sadleir-Jackson and rode astride. As an alternative to tennis,

Miss Joan Grubb riding astride.

mixed hockey was becoming increasingly popular. At various country houses in County Kilkenny, notably Kilmurry, home of the watercolourist, Miss Mildred Butler, and her sister, it became customary for mixed hockey matches to be followed by dances. The teams would retire upstairs for hot baths and to enable the girls to change into something more alluring; they would then dance to the piano until about eight o'clock, with tea, sandwiches and scones for refreshments.

The chief Ascendancy game was, of course, cricket, in which girls could not participate except by looking decorative among the spectators, having tea with the teams and perhaps dancing with them in the evenings during country house cricket weeks. Cricket in Ireland continued to flourish, the rising stars from the younger generation being Lady Gregory's artist son Robert, Thomas Jameson and two sons of cricketing fathers, George Colthurst and Bob Fowler, son of Captain Robert Fowler of Rahinston in County Meath. As a boy at Eton in 1910, Bob Fowler had been the hero of 'Fowler's Match', the most famous Eton and Harrow match ever played, snatching victory from the Harrow team – which included Thomas Jameson and also Harold Alexander from County Tyrone, a younger brother of the Earl of Caledon – by taking eight wickets for nine runs. Such was his instant fame that a congratulatory telegram addressed to his mother as 'Mrs Fowler, London' was delivered to her that same evening.[9]

Among the patrons of Irish cricket, Lord Bandon and Horace Plunkett's nephew Lord Dunsany – who was now making a name for himself as a poet and playwright – had been joined in 1907 by the wealthy bachelor Stanley Cochrane, son of a baronet whose family fortunes were founded on the manufacture of mineral waters. At Woodbrook, his country house a few miles outside Dublin in County Wicklow, he had made a ground regardless of expense; he would bring over the best English, Australian and South African teams to play here against his own eleven.

Alongside his cricket ground, Stanley Cochrane had built himself a private concert hall, where he would sing accompanied by professionals brought over specially from England. In 1913 Lady Alice Howard, who was a near neighbour of his, went to a concert at Woodbrook given by the London Symphony Orchestra. Concerts, if not up to Woodbrook standards, were organized by the Ascendancy all over the country. When the Duke and Duchess of Connaught stayed at Bessborough, the great Palladian house of the Earl and Countess of Bessborough in County Kilkenny, they were treated to an amateur concert in which Marguerite Connelan sang 'The Mountains of Mourne'. She was meant to sing it with bare feet but forgot and sang in her bedroom slippers. Bessborough was also one of the many Irish country houses which went in for amateur theatricals. The Bessboroughs' eldest son, Vere, Lord Duncannon, acted well and had a talent for producing plays; but he brought over a professional producer from London when

A house party at Bessborough in honour of the Duke and Duchess of Connaught,
who sit in the front row with Lord and Lady Bessborough; Princess Patricia on the
extreme left and the Duchess on the extreme right. Behind the Duke stands the
Bessboroughs' daughter, Lady Oranmore and Browne, with her sisters, Lady Irene
Congreve and Lady Gweneth Ponsonby standing at either end of the middle row;
their eldest brother, Lord Duncannon, stands at the extreme right, and another
brother, Bertie Ponsonby, is second from the right in the back row. Norman Leslie,
younger brother of Shane, is second from the left in the back row; next to him is
Marguerite Connellan. At the extreme right of the back row is Lord Iveagh's
youngest son, Walter Guinness, who was to become Lord Moyne and was
assassinated in Cairo towards the end of World War II. His wife, Lady Evelyn
Guinness, is third from the left in the middle row. In the same row, on the right of
Lady Oranmore and Browne, is Harry Goodhart-Rendel, who was to become a
distinguished architect.

he put on *The Merchant of Venice* with his sister Lady Gweneth Ponsonby as a very
beautiful Portia and Marguerite Connellan as Jessica.

Lord and Lady Bessborough and their family were only at their Irish home for
eight weeks in the summer and four weeks at Christmas, but they made the most of
their time there; as well as producing plays and acting in them, Lord Duncannon
and his brothers hunted their own pack of hounds; there was also shooting and a
continual house party. In fact, when the family was at home, Bessborough was the
smartest house in the county. Kilkenny Castle was grander, but the Ormondes'
entertainments were less sophisticated. In about 1912 they gave a children's

The Merchant of Venice at Bessborough. Lord Duncannon, as Bassanio, on the left.

Lord and Lady Ormonde, as their granddaughters remember them.

Flower Ball for their grandchildren, John, Marye and Victoria Pole-Carew; the girls had to come dressed as flowers and the boys as vegetables.

The young Pole-Carews spent a great deal of time with their grandparents at the castle. They had a schoolroom at the top of one of the round towers; they slept in the range that ran along the street, above the porter's lodge, where, surprisingly, their grandfather's uniforms were kept, looked after by the old porter. Their grandparents slept in the same part of the castle as they did; for Lord Ormonde, with his simple tastes, preferred the rather poky rooms on this side to the more spacious accommodation elsewhere.

Looking back after many years, the two granddaughters remembered the characteristic and not unpleasant smell of the central heating, coming up through gratings in the stone entrance passage of the castle, and the smell of pot-pourri in the corridors upstairs. They had memories of breakfast and luncheon in the great picture gallery, vast quantities of food that was good except for the lumpy breakfast porridge, of the epergne on the luncheon table with its little baskets full of sugared petals of lavender, lilac and violet which came from France. They had memories of tea, when their grandfather, who like so many men of his generation disliked tea as a beverage, would drink whiskey and soda. They had memories of their grandfather himself, with his bright blue eyes, his thick white hair, his slightly droopy moustache and his pipe shaped like the head of a woodcock, for next to yachting, woodcock shooting was Lord Ormonde's great passion.

Outside the castle, they remembered peacocks and fantail pigeons, doves and a golden pheasant, Chinese geese on the pond in the park, an expanse of pasture and trees that rose in a gentle slope from the open side of the castle courtyard. Here their grandmother kept a Jersey herd. Apart from the carriage horses in the stables across the street, the livestock on the place also included donkeys and pigs kept by their Aunt Constance.[10] Lady Constance Butler, the Ormondes' unmarried daughter, was a young woman of rather farouche beauty and modern ideas; she was interested in medicine and worked for the great surgeon Sir Arbuthnot Lane. She had her own flat in London, she drove herself around in her own motor car.

Lady Constance was not the only young woman in County Kilkenny who drove a car; Marguerite Connellan had learnt to drive her father's Ford in 1911, when she was twenty-six. Now that motors had become quite common and also fairly reliable, young people had the best of the old world and the new: they could drive to dances, shoots or tennis parties a long way off and return home the same evening; on the other hand, if they did not fancy driving both ways in the one day, there were as many hospitable country houses ready to put them up as there had been in the days of horses. Going to stay in a strange house could, however, be a little alarming for the young, particularly if it was a very grand one. The first time Marguerite and her soldier brother Peter were asked to stay at Bessborough they tried to think of excuses for not going, fearing that it would be much too smart for them, although Peter had been a friend of the two younger Ponsonby boys at Harrow.

In 1913 the twenty-two-year-old Irish Guards subaltern Edward Stafford-King-Harman and his younger brother Cecil went to stay for the first time at Lissadell in County Sligo. They went there by train from Rockingham, their home in the neighbouring county of Roscommon; it was not far, yet they somehow managed to arrive a little late at the rather severe neo-classical house of the Gore-Booths. Then Edward unfortunately mistook their host, Sir Josslyn Gore-Booth, for the butler and handed him his hat and coat, which did not help matters with Sir Josslyn who was already rather cross with them for being late. It was, he said, nearly dinner time.

The two young men changed as quickly as they could, but when they came down they found no one in the drawing room and feared that the party must have already gone in to dinner. But the dining room was empty, peopled only by the strange, elongated, larger than life-sized portraits of members of the family and retainers painted on the pilasters by Sir Josslyn's brother-in-law, Casimir Markievicz. Here, in modern suits, but with the timeless faces of Russion ikons, were images of Sir Josslyn's younger brother, of Markievicz himself, of the forester and the gamekeeper and also of the real butler, the grey-bearded Kilgallon, who had accompanied Sir Josslyn's father on a voyage to the Arctic in his yacht and saved his life by shooting a menacing bear which now stood stuffed and grinning in the hall.

At last the party came down and dinner was served. Afterwards there was a ball, and Edward and his brother did not get to bed until very late. They had barely gone to sleep when Kilgallon woke them and said gruffly: 'You must get up, you've got to go.'

'Go?' the two brothers asked in sleepy astonishment, noticing that it was only just after six. 'We've been asked to stay for three days.'

'You've got to go, those are my orders.'

There was nothing for it but to get up and get dressed. At seven, without any breakfast or even a cup of tea, the two unfortunate young men were bundled into the carriage and driven into Sligo town to catch the eight o'clock train. They arrived back at Boyle, the town at the entrance to the Rockingham demesne, with no car ordered to meet them, so they had to walk up the two miles of avenue to the house. They felt very offended with the Gore-Booths, only to learn through a neighbour that the Gore-Booths were very offended with *them*. Eventually the mystery was cleared up: the Gore-Booths had indeed expected them to stay for three days, but the wretched Kilgallon had taken it into his head to get rid of them after barely a night.[11]

The beautiful José Metcalfe, whom Lord Carbery married less than two months after he came of age.

Another house at which there was a ball in 1913 was Castle Freke on the West Cork coast, a castellated mansion recently restored and modernized after a fire. It was the home of Doty Bandon's young cousin Lord Carbery, who came of age that year; he had succeeded to his title and estates when he was only six, his father having died young of tuberculosis. It is said that his mother, who was English and wrote romantic books about the Irish in a cottage by the lake in the Castle Freke demesne, was foolish enough to make him believe that he, too, was doomed to an early death; this has been given as the reason why he grew up to be a reckless daredevil. He loved fast cars and the sea; he once swam out so far from the shore that his uncle, who was with him, was certain he was drowned. Not satisfied with swimming and sailing and driving fast, he learnt to fly. He brought his aeroplane to Castle Freke and took the old head gardener up for a flight, scaring him by looping the loop.

For all his dash and his good looks, there was a sinister side to John Carbery's nature. A large canvas of the Carbery Hunt hung in the Castle Freke hall; he shot out the eyes of the figures in it. This may have been merely devilment and a sign of his contempt for all tradition, but he also disliked animals and was cruel to horses and cats. Less than two months after he came of age, he married an English girl of outstanding beauty. Her friends had tried to prevent the marriage, telling her of his cruelty; but she had said: 'I'd rather be miserable with John than happy with anybody else.'[12]

John Carbery sometimes kept his yacht in Castlehaven, an inlet about ten miles westwards along the coast from Castle Freke. Here, at the head of the little harbour, was the village of Castletownshend which was unusual among Irish villages in being inhabited by the Ascendancy. A community had grown out of the ramifications of the two local landed families, the Somervilles and the Townshends, who were themselves vaguely related. Drishane, the weather-slated Georgian house of the Somervilles, stood in its demesne at the upper end of the village; the Castle, seat of the Townshends, was at the bottom of the hill by the water's edge, the tower of the Church of Ireland parish church rising from among the trees above its battlements. Some time in the second half of the nineteenth century Sir Joscelyn Coghill, a County Dublin baronet who was a brother-in-law of the reigning Somerville, had settled here; his son Sir Egerton now lived at Glen Barrahane, a house standing in grounds carved out of the Drishane demesne, while Sir Joscelyn's surviving brother, the Indian Mutiny veteran, Colonel Kendal Coghill, lived down by the harbour in a house called Cosheen, which he had remodelled in bogus Tudor. At Red House lived two nephews of Sir Joscelyn, Colonel Edmund Aylmer and his brother Percy, who came of an ancient County Kildare family. Yet another nephew, Major Henry Chavasse, who was also related to the Townshends through his wife, had recently come to live at Seafield.

Edith Somerville, at a meet of the West Carbery Hunt.

To add to the community, there were various Somervilles and Townshends living about the place, in addition to those reigning at Drishane and the Castle. The best-known resident member of the Somerville clan was, of course, Edith; whose bachelor brother was the present owner of Drishane. Their sister, to complicate matters, was the wife of Sir Egerton Coghill.

The inhabitants of Castletownshend also included a few people from outside the charmed cousinhood, but of impeccable Ascendancy background, such as Major Nathaniel Barton, a kinsman of the Bartons of Straffan, and old Miss Sandes, whose family had been of consequence in County Kerry since the time of Cromwell. As well as the permanent residents, there were summer visitors from other parts of Ireland or from Britain who rented houses and became temporary members of the community; in about 1913 a house was shared by two English couples who caused great scandal by exchanging wives.

In winter, Castletownshend occupied itself by hunting with the West Carbery, the pack immortalized by Somerville and Ross and of which Edith had herself been Master. In summer, there was yachting; the annual Castletownshend Regatta was known popularly as 'Calves', since it was acclaimed as Cowes in miniature. Its leading light was the octogenarian Colonel Coghill, a keen yachtsman who had recently also become an enthusiastic motorist. He had learnt to drive at about the age of eighty, acquiring a car which he described with gusto to

Major Chavasse as 'a ripper'.[13] Since he expected everybody to get out of his way, he constituted no small menace on the roads.

While differing from most of the Ascendancy in being High Church rather than Low, the inhabitants of Castletownshend were true to form in their strong service tradition. The fact that people like them preferred to serve the Empire as soldiers, sailors and administrators rather than serve Ireland was blamed by Canon Hannay for their growing isolation from the Irish people as a whole. They were, he wrote, 'dazzled with England's greatness and the prospect of Imperial power'.[14] But it was only natural that a life of adventure in far-off lands where sport was both plentiful and cheap should have been more attractive to a young sprig of the Ascendancy than working as a civil servant in Dublin Castle. And some of the Ascendancy did in fact make their careers in Ireland. At the time when Hannay was writing, the most influential Irish civil servant was Sir Henry Robinson, a cousin of Herky Langrishe and a son-in-law of Sir Robert Lynch-Blosse. His son Christopher, in 1912, became one of the many Irish RMs who were of Ascendancy background, another being Francis Henn of Paradise Hill in County Clare. As yet another example of a son of the Ascendancy – and an elder son at that – making his career in Ireland at this time there was Henry Bowen, who worked as a lawyer in Dublin, compiling a monumental work on land purchase, only going to Bowen's Court in the vacations. Moreover, people like Sir Henry Robinson were not necessarily any more in touch with the Ireland outside the Ascendancy world than those who followed 'an Imperial career'; the latter, when abroad, made friends with other Irishmen serving the Empire whose background may have been very different from their own.

Hannay, like Standish O'Grady, looked back with nostalgia to the eighteenth-century golden age of the Ascendancy, when, as he wrote, 'the younger brother of this great lord or that held a deanery or a bishopric in the Church' and 'the son of the squire succeeded to the family living . . . Now all this is changed. It is a rare thing to find an intimate connexion between the castle and the rectory.'[15] Here again, he was ignoring the obvious. The Church of the eighteenth and early nineteenth centuries, with its tithes and ample endowments, offered the younger sons of the Ascendancy a lucrative career; the present disestablished and impoverished Church did not, while affording scope for Ascendancy influence on the Synod. And while the pious Victorians had taken Holy Orders regardless of worldly considerations, the Edwardians were less noted for their piety. For an ever-increasing number of Ascendancy Protestants, church-going was now a bore, though not perhaps to quite such an extent as it was for Lord Mayo's unmarried sister, Lady Florence Bourke, who when attending the church near her family home in County Kildare would relieve the tedium of the sermon by jabbing the people in front of her with a hatpin.[16]

− *3* −

The Home Rule bill passed its third reading in the Commons in January 1913 but was defeated by the Lords whose delaying power enabled them to hold it up for another year. In the same month the Ulster Volunteer Force was formally established to provide a military backing for the provisional government which the Ulster Unionists planned to set up. The raising of this force had already begun; it was being done quite legally, for the law allowed magistrates to authorize military operations in defence of the constitution. Landowners enlisted in the ranks alongside farmers, shopkeepers, labourers and mill-hands; they invited the Volunteers to drill in their demesnes as an alternative to the Orange Halls: Lord Dufferin's uncle Colonel Gawin Rowan-Hamilton had them drilling in the courtyard of his castle in County Down. The force was as yet by no means fully armed, though a certain quantity of rifles and ammunition had already been smuggled into the Province. The words of command were often unconventional –

The Killyleagh volunteers drilling in the courtyard of Killyleagh Castle, seat of Colonel Rowan-Hamilton, in 1913.

one officer would halt his men by shouting 'Whoa'.[17] But the men who were joining the Ulster Volunteers were young, fit and easy to train; above all, they were determined.

During the summer of 1913, while the Ulstermen drilled and trained, the Ascendancy in the South had other things to think about. In June, County Cork was shocked when Captain Jack Longfield lost his life through driving his car off the road and into a tree; it was one of Ireland's first motoring fatalities, perhaps the very first where the victim was of the Ascendancy. In July, a week or so after the Home Rule bill had once again been passed by the Commons and rejected by the Lords, the Ladies Howard – whose ages now ranged from sixty-seven to seventy-six – gave one of their most successful garden parties, with music provided by Clarke-Barry's band. The day was fine and more than a hundred of their friends came from far and near, while no fewer than forty-nine servants were given tea in the yard, for in addition to the household staff there were visiting chauffeurs and footmen as well as outside helpers.

August, the month in which Lord Kenmare's great red brick mansion at Killarney was accidentally burnt down, was also the month of Marguerite Connellan's engagement. Her fiancé, Dick Solly-Flood, a soldier like her brother Peter, came of an old and distinguished County Kilkenny family, but he only had his captain's pay of about £200 a year. Though she had about the same, her father reckoned that they could not afford to marry while continuing to hunt and enjoy themselves in all the other ways to which they were accustomed, so that they would have to wait until Dick obtained a staff appointment. Meanwhile, as a distraction, she was asked to go and stay at the Palace at Armagh and do hostess for Archbishop Crozier, Alexander's successor, who having formerly been in Kilkenny as Bishop of Ossory was an old family friend. She went north in September; while she was there she watched Carson reviewing the Volunteers at a rally addressed by one of the principal English champions of Ulster Unionism, F.E. Smith. She found it all very disturbing.[18]

Towards the end of September the Ulster Unionist Council met with Lord Londonderry in the chair and formally set up a provisional government for Ulster which would take over if Home Rule became law. Before the meeting, Carson had begged Londonderry not to involve himself and his family in what was nothing short of an open threat of rebellion against the will of Parliament. 'They can do little to me,' he said. 'But you have great possessions, a great title . . . You have to consider also the future of your son Charley. The Government, when they grow vindictive, as they will, may strike at you – and him.' With tears in his eyes, Londonderry replied: 'My dear Edward, if I was to lose everything in the world, I would go with you to the end.'[19]

The Government's reaction was to consider the possibility of a compromise

A house party of Ulster Unionist leaders at Craigavon. Sir Edward and Lady Carson stand together in the middle, flanked by Theresa Londonderry and their host, Captain James Craig. Mrs Craig sits in front of her husband next to Bonar Law, who has the Craigs' daughter Aileen on his knee. Sitting on Bonar Law's right is Lord Londonderry.

whereby Ulster would be excluded from Home Rule. The Southern Unionists, who hoped to put off Home Rule for as long as possible and, in alliance with the Ulstermen, to obtain adequate safeguards when it finally came, were dismayed at the prospect of being left to the tender mercies of a Home Rule Parliament while Ulster was allowed to stay within the pale of the United Kingdom. The idea of Ulster being separated from the rest of Ireland was no more acceptable to the Nationalists, who in November 1913 formed their own military force, the Irish Volunteers, to support the establishment of Home Rule over the whole of Ireland against Ulster's threat to secede.

Towards the end of November a great Unionist meeting was held in Dublin at the Theatre Royal, with Carson and Bonar Law as the principal speakers. They made it clear that the Ulster leaders were bent on exclusion and could offer no assurances of their solidarity with their Southern brethren; all they could offer was sympathy. To the Southerners, this attitude of 'I'm all right, Jack' was a bitter disappointment; there were mutterings of 'Betrayal!' among the audience. To make matters worse, although Redmond had given orders that the meeting should not be molested, a hostile Dublin mob managed to invade the upper galleries and spat copiously upon the assembled Unionists in the stalls. There followed a sorry scene in the Kildare Street Club as crestfallen members and their wives came in with their coats and wraps covered with spittle, which the Club servants made heroic attempts to remove.

In the following March, the Government offered to amend the Home Rule bill to enable Ulster to opt out for six years. 'We do not want sentence of death with a stay of execution for six years,' was Carson's response to this proposal, which was immediately rejected.[20] The Government then planned to move troops into Ulster from the South to protect military depots against any sudden take-over by the Volunteers. This plan was misrepresented by Sir Arthur Paget, the General Commanding the Forces in Ireland, when he briefed his senior officers on 20 March; he gave them the impression that civil war was imminent and told them that they must either agree to take part in 'active operations' in Ulster or be dismissed the service. Those with an Ulster domicile would, however, be allowed to 'disappear'.

General Hubert Gough, commanding the Third Cavalry Brigade, decided immediately to resign his commission. He was a Southerner, his roots were in Tipperary and Limerick and he was a nephew of the Catholic Count de la Poer of Gurteen in County Waterford; the Nationalist Lord Emly was his uncle by marriage. But his feelings of kinship with the Ulstermen and of sympathy for their cause, however unhelpful their present attitude might have been, made the prospect of 'active operations' against them utterly repugnant to him.

Gough returned to the Curragh Camp with Paget's ultimatum and told his officers of his decision to send in his papers; fifty-seven of them resolved to follow his example. Faced by the so-called 'Curragh Mutiny', the Government did not order the troops to go north; Gough and his brother-officers were reinstated. For the time being, the only 'active operations' in Ulster were those of the Suffragettes, who in that March of 1914 burnt Abbeylands, the family home of General McCalmont outside Belfast. The house was empty at the time, the General and his family having been living for some years in County Kilkenny.

A month after the Curragh affair, the Ulster Unionists defied the ban on the importation of arms into Ireland and landed a shipload of 35,000 rifles bought in Germany, complete with five million rounds of ammunition, at Larne in County Antrim. The operation was carried out under the cover of darkness and with military precision; the arms were unloaded into a fleet of several hundred motor cars, many of them lent by the gentry, and distributed throughout the Province. Anyone in the South or in Britain who might hitherto not have been inclined to take the Ulster Volunteers seriously certainly had to take them seriously now.

The Government continued with their plan to amend the Home Rule bill as proposed in March, and in June an amending bill was introduced into the Lords. While it was being debated, the London season was in full swing; Theresa Londonderry was bringing out Bonar Law's débutante daughter Isabel. Theresa's influence over the Leader of the Opposition was a source of unease to some of his political colleagues; Londonderry House had become the 'the social hub of the Unionist Party'.[21] As a widower and a stranger to the fashionable world, Bonar Law was only too pleased to let the capable Theresa entertain on his behalf, but it meant that his party became more than ever identified with Ulster Unionism, particularly as his own roots were in Ulster.

While Isabel Law danced under Theresa's chaperonage, the Ulster Volunteers, now properly armed, continued to drill. The as yet unarmed Irish Volunteers were drilling too, in Leinster, Munster and Connaught as well as in the more Nationalist counties of Ulster such as Monaghan. A story is told of how Shane Leslie, slipping quietly out of the house at Glaslough one evening on his way to inspect the local regiment of Irish Volunteers, met his father going out to review his own regiment of Ulster Volunteers.

Ireland seemed close to civil war, yet this cast no damper on the week of celebrations in County Roscommon before the wedding of Edward Stafford-King-Harman and Olive Pakenham-Mahon. Still less were the festivities marred by the news of the murder of an Austrian Archduke. The marriage would unite the two principal families of the county – the bridegroom owned Rockingham, with its Regency mansion and its magnificent demesne along the shores of Lough Key; the bride was heiress to Strokestown, a property almost as fine. Had it not been for the Wyndham Act, the couple would between them have stood to own something like 70,000 acres. Although the tenanted lands of Rockingham had nearly all been sold, the former tenants were invited to the celebrations and entertained in a huge marquee outside the house; there was a tug o' war between the men from the plains and the men from the Curlew Mountains. Such was the betting on this event that even more drink was consumed than was provided by the generous young host; some of the guests are said to have been in so permanent a state of inebriation that they remained at Rockingham for nearly the whole week.[22] The wedding itself, on 4 July, took place not in County Roscommon but at the Guards' Chapel in London.

While Edward and Olive were setting off on their honeymoon, Marguerite Connellan was busy with the preparations for her own wedding, which was to be on 8 August at the Church of Ireland Cathedral in Kilkenny. Archbishop Crozier of Armagh was coming south to perform the ceremony; there were to be five bridesmaids. Armed with a cheque for £200 from her father, she went to London to buy her trousseau. Since her mother was dead, it fell to her to make the arrangements for the wedding breakfast, which was to be at Coolmore. She engaged a well-known Dublin firm of caterers whose quotation was half-a-crown a head, which was to include the waiters as well as the crockery and glass. The wine would be extra.

Marguerite was too taken up with plans for her wedding to think much about the threat of civil war. The Ladies Howard, who had no such preoccupations, do not appear to have been much concerned about it either, judging from Lady Alice's diary, in which her only reference to Ulster is a mention of how their butler went up to Belfast for the day on 13 July to celebrate the Twelfth, which this year was on a Sunday. He and other members of the County Wicklow Orange Lodges travelled north in a special train.

For the Ladies Howard, Ulster and Home Rule paled into insignificance compared with the fact that they now possessed a motor of their own. They did not, however, take the opportunity of showing it off among the motor cars that converged on Woodbrook on 18 July for a flying display given by Lord Carbery, preferring to watch the flying from a bench outside a neighbouring country house. Stanley Cochrane had lent his cricket ground for the occasion; it was like a garden party, with music from the band of the West Kent Regiment and the ladies in their summer dresses. The afternoon was fine, except for a few banks of cloud; the mountains were blue, the sea sparkled. Lord and Lady Powerscourt were among the many fashionable people present.

Punctually at three-thirty, Lord Carbery appeared, wearing neither helmet nor goggles, and was cheered as he climbed into his Morane-Soulnier monoplane. To the crackle of his engine, the dashing young peer got off the ground and, in the words of the *Irish Times*, 'pirouetted in mid-air as friskily as schoolboys playing leap-frog'.

'Lord Carbery is himself not much more than a schoolboy,' the paper went on to inform its readers. 'In fact, as he dismounted from his monoplane after looping the loop, a lady was heard to remark: "Oh, he's frightfully young".'

After giving joy-rides to several people – one of whom turned out to be 'rather weighty', obliging him to come down in a field – he took off again and headed in the direction of the Sugar Loaf Mountain. When there had been no sign of him for some time, people began to get worried. His wife, the beautiful José Carbery, gazed anxiously into the sky from the veranda of the cricket pavilion. But then his plane reappeared and landed safely; it was just that he had paid a visit to Powerscourt, Lord and Lady Powerscourt having returned home in time to receive him. Before the display ended, José, wearing 'a tight-fitting dark cap', went up in the plane with her husband. 'Although looking a trifle pale, she evidently enjoyed the prospect of looping the loop.'[23]

During the week following John Carbery's display, an attempt was made to

John Carbery speaks to his wife, José, across the fuselage of his aeroplane.

settle the Irish question by negotiation. A conference of political leaders, representing the Ulster Unionists and the Nationalists, as well as the British Government and Opposition, was held at Buckingham Palace by invitation of the King, who had long been urging his ministers to take more positive steps to break the deadlock. The Southern Unionists were not officially represented – a sign of how they were now more than ever politically out on a limb. However, the elder statesman Lord Lansdowne, who with Bonar Law represented the Opposition, was himself a leading Southern Unionist; his chief interests were in England, but he was an Irishman and a landowner in West Cork and Kerry, which he regarded as his real home. After four days of discussions, the Buckingham Palace Conference broke up, unable to agree as to how much of Ulster was to be excluded from Home Rule. While the Speaker of the House of Commons, who had presided over the conference, was waiting in an anteroom to say goodbye to the King, he picked up an evening paper and read of Austria's ultimatum to Serbia.[24]

On the Sunday after the conference broke up, the Nationalists, following the example of the Ulstermen, landed arms at Howth on the northern side of Dublin Bay. The operation had been planned in London by a largely Ascendancy group that included Mary Spring-Rice, Erskine Childers – a cousin of the Bartons – and the distinguished former consular official Sir Roger Casement, whose roots were in Ulster and whose cousin-in-law, Mrs John Casement, had lent her motor for the gun-running at Larne. The arms were safely distributed, though as they were being conveyed into Dublin there was a clash between the Irish Volunteers and the military with a tragic sequel when the soldiers were stoned by the crowd and opened fire, killing three people and wounding thirty-two.

The actual landing of the guns took place in broad daylight and there was little of the secrecy that had surrounded the gun-running in the North. The twenty-year-old Stuart Bellingham of the Castle Bellingham family, who kept a boat at Howth, heard when the guns were arriving and went along and helped with the unloading. He had the distinction of having also helped to unload the guns at Larne; his godfather, Andrew Jameson, who was a friend of Carson, had motored him north on what promised to be something of an adventure.

On that Sunday, while the rifles were being unloaded at Howth, a search was going on at Pierce O'Mahony's home in County Wicklow, Grange Con, for O'Mahony's son Pierce Mahony, the former Herald, who had been missing since the previous afternoon. He had planned to row across the lake to have tea with neighbours on the other side; he had set off, taking a gun and cartridges with him, hoping to get some waterfowl on the way. But he had not turned up at the neighbours' house and the boat had not been taken out. Eventually his body was found lying in the water near the boathouse with the gun beside it. He had been shot through the heart, both barrels having been fired. The inquest called it an accident; people inevitably believed that he had been murdered because he knew too much about the theft of the Crown Jewels.

Marguerite Connellan continued with the preparations for her wedding. Each day brought a fresh crop of presents; by now there were nearly four hundred, the most spectacular being a diamond and fire opal pendant from the Bessboroughs and a diamond ornament from the Donoughmores. The Coolmore staff gave a Royal Worcester dinner service with her fiancé Dick's crest on it in gold; it had been chosen by an aunt of Marguerite's at Goode's in London. Dick's cousin, Major Hanford-Flood of Flood Hall, was lending them his Daimler, complete with chauffeur, for their honeymoon, which was to be in Kerry. Dick himself would not be over from England, where he was stationed, until just before the wedding, but her brother Peter, whose regiment was also in England, arrived on the morning of 1 August. He and Marguerite were very close and they were both in high spirits at being together again.

Later that morning, while she was arranging flowers, Peter came into the room and put his arm round her. 'I'm afraid, darling, I have bad news. I have just had a telegram recalling me and must go back tonight as the whole regiment has been ordered to join a division being mobilized at Harrow.'

She 'felt sick with dread'. For the past week or so, she had been conscious that what was happening in Europe might lead to war; the fear of civil war in Ireland had receded into the background. Now war seemed inevitable.

Peter consoled her by telling her that Dick, at any rate, being at present with the Territorials, would not be affected by the crisis, and that he himself, with luck, might be able to get back in time for the wedding, which was still a week off; at least he could come over for the day. He went to have a sleep, and then Marguerite drove him to Thomastown station where she had gone to meet him only a few hours earlier. She watched the train steam out, her brother waving to her through the window.

Marguerite drove sadly home, trying to convince herself that everything would still be all right. Three nights later she was awoken by gravel thrown at her window, which was only a few feet above the ground. She leant out and somebody handed her a telegram. Opening it by the light of her bedside candle, she read: 'Wedding must be postponed. War declared. Leave cancelled. Dick.'[25]

Next day, while Colonel Connellan was busy writing several hundred ha'penny postcards to put off the wedding guests, a pony trap set out from Bowen's Court in County Cork taking Henry Bowen and his fifteen-year-old daughter Elizabeth to a garden party at Mitchelstown Castle. Bowen's Court was fairly isolated and the newspaper had not yet come; nobody in the house had so far as much as mentioned the international situation, not at any rate in Elizabeth's hearing. For the past few days her one concern had been whether the rain would stop in time for the garden

The Long Gallery at Mitchelstown Castle.

party. Today, though the sky was overcast and there was a cold wind blowing, it was not actually raining.

They stopped in a village and Henry went into the post office. After a minute he emerged and stood framed in the doorway. He cleared his throat and said: 'England has declared war on Germany.' He added, as he climbed back into the trap: 'I suppose it could not be helped.'

'Then can't we go to the garden party?' was all Elizabeth could say.

But they carried on to Mitchelstown and were greeted in the long gallery of the Castle by Willie Webber, whose wife Lady Kingston was now dead. He was no longer young and preferred to stay indoors, but the guests were expected to go outside. As Elizabeth Bowen afterwards recalled:

Wind raced round the Castle terraces, naked under the Galtees; grit blew into the ices; the band clung with some trouble to its exposed place. The tremendous news certainly made that party, which might have been rather flat. Almost everyone said they wondered if they really ought to have come, but they *had* come – rightly: this was a time to gather . . . For miles round, each isolated big house had disgorged its talker, this first day of the war. The tension of months, of years – outlying tension of Europe, inner tension of Ireland – broke in a spate of words.[26]

8

Terrible beauties

— *1* —

If the sons of the Ascendancy were 'dazzled with England's greatness and the prospect of Imperial power', as Canon Hannay accused them of being, they were at any rate true to their principles and ready to fight and if necessary to die for England and the Empire; those not already in the army or navy lost no time in joining up. Men like Lord Bandon, Barnie Castletown and Colonel Connellan who were too old for active service made speeches at recruiting meetings while their womenfolk threw themselves heart and soul into war work. The Ladies Howard went to their first Ambulance Lecture at Bray Town Hall less than a week after the outbreak of hostilities – 'crowds of women and very confusing'.[1] Three days later they were busy making shirts for the troops.

Lady Rosse set up an organization at Birr Castle for sending parcels to prisoners of war from Irish regiments. Lady Ormonde, dressed as a nurse, presided over knitting classes in the Kilkenny Castle dining room. Lady Talbot de Malahide – whose home, Malahide Castle on the north County Dublin coast, was now surrounded by tethered airships, used for patrolling the Irish Sea – became Acting President of the Red Cross for her county. Feeling that the job called for some proficiency in public speaking, she went into Dublin to Mrs D'Esterre's lectures on this art, which were also attended by Daisy Fingall and her daughters.

The setting up of the Red Cross was the occasion for one of the last, but by no means the least, of Lady Aberdeen's *faux pas*. She wrote a letter to the editor of the Nationalist *Freeman's Journal* alleging that there was 'a bit of a plot amongst the Unionists to capture the Red Cross Society in Ireland'. The letter was not meant to be published, but it somehow found its way into the columns of another newspaper; the Unionists in the Red Cross naturally resented her suggestion that they were 'guilty of the use of a great public calamity for political purposes'.[2]

One way in which the ladies of the Ascendancy helped the wounded was by collecting sphagnum moss, which was renowned for its healing properties and used in hospitals for dressing wounds. Mrs Ralph Coote, Sir Algernon's daughter-in-law, put her children on to collecting it in the mountains behind Ballyfin. Another way was to grow herbs required for medical purposes, which Mrs Bence-Jones did at Lisselane. She did it by remote control, for she and her husband preferred to do their war work in London rather than in Ireland. Their two sons, the younger of whom was only seventeen at the time, went straight into the army the moment war was declared; Lisselane, like many Irish country houses, was closed for the duration. Few if any country houses in Ireland during the Great War were requisitioned; Sir Vere and Lady Foster were asked if they would lend Glyde for 'a Belgian family of position'[3] consisting of four adults and five children together with their servants, but they do not appear to have been keen on the idea, though willing to offer some hospitality to Belgian refugees.

Bertram Barton of Straffan helped the Allied cause by converting his Sizaire-Berwick saloon, which he had originally kept at the family wine château near Bordeaux, into an ambulance. Though nearer sixty than fifty on the outbreak of war, he drove it himself, even to Verdun. Another fine car which became an ambulance was the Lisselane Mercedes, though Reginald Bence-Jones did not follow Barton's example and drive it himself. When the Dowager Lady de Vesci, who now lived in Surrey, put her car at the disposal of the Red Cross, she handed over her chauffeur as well. She hoped this would exempt him from call-up, to which he was liable as he was working for her in England, though he came from Abbey Leix. But he was taken by the army all the same and sent to East Africa, where he died immediately of dysentry.

Though there was no conscription in Ireland, the Ladies Howard forced their coachman, who had been with them for years, to go over to England and enlist. 'Oh Ralph, we had to stand on the platform to make sure that he went off,' they afterwards told their nephew.[4] The man managed to find some employment in England, being, of course, far too old for the army. His colleague, Wiggins the chauffeur, had no fear of being packed off to England in this way, for he was quite indispensible. For the Ladies Howard, 'the Motor' had assumed an almost mystical significance.

While the Ladies Howard were sewing shirts and learning about first aid, their neighbour Lord Powerscourt, before rejoining his regiment, the Irish Guards, was drilling and organizing the Irish Volunteers.* He was one of a number of Southern Unionists who gave their support to the Nationalist Volunteers during those early

---

* The Duchess of York is his great-granddaughter. See illustration on page 143.

John Redmond and Sir Timothy O'Brien (right) inspecting the Irish Volunteers soon after the outbreak of the Great War.

days of the war; others included Fingall and Bryan Cooper. The Home Rule controversy had been shelved for the duration; the Nationalist leader John Redmond had pledged Ireland's support for the war effort in his Commons speech of 3 August. 'Your speech has united Ireland,' Bryan Cooper had telegraphed to him two days later, and indeed, with Redmond addressing recruiting meetings organized by prominent Unionists, and Lord Bandon and the Nationalist Lord Mayor of Cork acting together as patrons of the Cork Volunteer Training Corps, it really did seem as though Ireland's differences had been forgotten. They were more than ever forgotten among the tens of thousands of Irishmen who went to the Front, where, in Bryan Cooper's words, 'the bond of common service and common sacrifice proved so strong and enduring that Catholic and Protestant, Unionist and Nationalist, lived and fought and died side by side like brothers'.[5]

Redmond's wholehearted support of the war effort, while it won him the trust and gratitude of the Unionists, alienated the extreme Nationalists among his followers. In September 1914 the Volunteers split, one half remaining under Redmond's control and participating in the war; the other half anti-British and trying to discourage recruiting. This was not the only anti-British para-military force in Ireland then: there was also the militant side of the Trade Union movement, the Irish Citizen Army, which had grown out of the Great Dublin Strike of 1913. The socialist republican James Connolly was at its head; but it had been originally organized by a retired British army officer, Captain James White of

White Hall in County Antrim, son of the defender of Ladysmith. Another of Connolly's principal lieutenants in the Citizen Army was Constance Markievicz, who was to be seen marching through the streets of Dublin in a dark green uniform with a wide hat turned up at one side. She and Casimir had by now parted company; he had returned to his home in the Ukraine.

The Ascendancy became more than ever conscious of the war as the casualty lists began to come in. Even if one's own family was spared the dreaded telegram, one read almost daily in the newspapers of the death of somebody one knew – or of a close relation of somebody one knew. Maurice Dease, great-nephew of the former Viceregal Chamberlain, was killed at Mons on 23 August, winning a posthumous VC, as did James Brooke in October, three weeks after his cousin, Sir George Brooke's son and heir, was fatally wounded. October also saw the death in action of Shane Leslie's dashing younger brother Norman.* An amorous escapade in Egypt had brought Norman Leslie the distinction of being the last serving officer in the British army to have fought a duel; he was his mother's favourite and had been the heir to Glaslough since Shane was disinherited for turning Catholic. 'Some will live and many will die, but count the loss not,' he had written to a friend before going into battle. 'It is better far to go out with honour than survive with shame.'6 His attitude was shared by many sons of the Ascendancy – a fatalism, a death-wish even, as though they knew that their world in Ireland was dying and saw little point in surviving it.

On 21 October the former Marguerite Connellan – she and Dick Solly-Flood had been married quietly in England in September – heard that her brother Peter had been killed at Armentières, where Norman Leslie fell. She had not seen him since she waved goodbye to him at Thomastown station on 1 August. Lord Monck's son, Charles, was killed on the same day as Peter.

By the end of October the war had claimed Sir Richard Levinge of Knockdrin Castle in County Westmeath, so lovable a personality that his cousin Lord Dunsany was told afterwards by a local: 'Sure, when Sir Richard was killed, the old people round Knockdrin all cried themselves sick.'7 In November the realities of war were brought home to the Ladies Howard, for that month saw the death of the new Duke of Abercorn's brother, Lord John Hamilton, whose sister was married to their nephew Ralph. Edward Stafford-King-Harman, the bridegroom of July, was killed on the same day, as was Lord O'Neill's son and heir.

Towards the end of the year Norman Leslie's mother paid a visit to the widowed Lady Caledon, whose demesne marched with Glaslough on the Tyrone side of the county boundary. She belonged more to the eighteenth century than to 1914, driving about the county in a high-sprung barouche with postilions. On arriving at

*He appears in the illustration on page 147.

Caledon, Mrs Leslie was told by the butler that three of Lady Caledon's four sons – including Harold, her favourite, whom she called Tubby – had been reported missing. But Lady Caledon, when she saw her, appeared to have lost none of her usual composure. In the event, all three missing sons turned out to be safe.[8]

In February 1915 the Aberdeens' long reign came to an end. After nearly ten years they had become an institution; people were in the end quite sad to see them go. Their departure was seen as being not just the end of a reign but the passing of the Viceregal office, which seemed likely to be abolished when the inevitable changes in the government of Ireland came in after the war. The Viceroy in wartime was a mere shadow of his peacetime self: the Viceregal splendours of Dublin Castle were already a thing of the past. There were now hospital beds in the State Apartments.

Crowds lined the streets of Dublin to watch the Aberdeens go by on their way to the boat. But there were no cheers, no waving handkerchiefs, nor yet a sorrowful or a hostile silence. There were just roars of laughter. For when, preceded by the mounted escort and by her husband and his staff also on horseback, Lady Aberdeen came into sight in her open carriage with postilions, she was seen to be sitting bolt upright, one hand holding a Kodak high above her head, the other pressing a rubber bulb at the end of a long red tube as she took snapshots without being able to see what she was taking.

The new Viceroy, Lord Wimborne, a first cousin of Winston Churchill, had little to be said for him except that he and his wife were young and smart and he was enormously rich. As a notorious lecher he was always in danger of being involved in some scandal, while the rather flashy state which the Wimbornes saw fit to keep up at Viceregal Lodge did not strike the right note in wartime. They had gold plate and powdered footmen and Lady Wimborne tried to introduce the so-called 'Spanish curtsy', with a stamp of the heels and a flourish of the fan.

The new regime might have been worse but for Lord Basil Blackwood, a younger son of the former Viceroy of India, Lord Dufferin, who having been grievously wounded at the Front now came to Dublin as Wimborne's Private Secretary. Lord Basil was one of the most attractive personalities of his time, a hero out of the pages of his friend John Buchan. He had inherited much of the reputation of his distinguished father. As an Ulsterman who in temperament came close to the Southern Unionists while sympathizing with the Nationalist point of view, he was just the person to prevent the Viceroy from inadvertently giving offence to one or other of the various shades of Irish public opinion. 'One shudders to think of His Ex. unchaperoned by him,' Lady Cynthia Asquith, the Prime Minister's daughter-in-law, wrote in her diary, having described Wimborne himself as 'very easy – just a fairly frank bounder'.[9]

A month after the Aberdeens left, their one-time Vice-Chamberlain, Captain

Lord Wimborne inspecting the guard of honour at Dublin Castle on his arrival as Viceroy.

Robert Bowen-Colthurst – a kinsman both of Sir George Colthurst and the Bowens of Bowen's Court – was killed; he was one of nine former members of their staff who fell in the war. The casualties continued; Lord De Freyne and his younger half-brother, George French, were killed on the same day in May 1915, the month in which Hugh Lane went down in the *Lusitania*, the month in which those two reputedly fast ladies Dorothea Conyers and the former Joan Grubb both lost their husbands and Lord Carbery his uncle. The latter was a Yeomanry Colonel in his forties, not as old as Lord Longford, who went to the war as a Brigadier-General of Yeomanry aged fifty. He was among the thousands who died that summer in Gallipoli.

September saw the death of Peter Connellan's friend Myles Ponsonby and of Dermot Browne, the second of Lord Kenmare's three sons. Dermot was the white hope of his parents; their eldest son Lord Castlerosse showing a tendency to dissipation and their youngest being rather dull. It was much the same with the three sons of the late Duke of Leinster and the beautiful Duchess Hermione: the young Duke was mentally unstable, the youngest brother a spendthrift, the second brother, Lord Desmond FitzGerald,* was brilliant. In March 1916 on the Western Front, an unexploded bomb fell at his feet. A chaplain standing next to him picked it up and it went off, maiming the priest and killing Lord Desmond.

'Nearly everyone I know in the army has been killed,' the Gaelic enthusiast, Douglas Hyde, lamented in the late summer of 1915. 'Poor Lord De Freyne and his brother were shot the same day and buried in one grave . . . All the gentry have suffered. *Noblesse oblige*.'[10] Hyde was particularly concerned about the death of Lord De Freyne and his brother, for he lived near French Park, their home in County Roscommon.

At the time when the two brothers were killed, their kinsman Field-Marshal Sir John French was Supreme Commander of the British Expeditionary Force in France. French's Chief of Staff, General Sir Henry Wilson, also came from the Ascendancy. His family home was in County Longford and he was the younger brother of James Mackay Wilson, a prominent Southern Unionist. Among other Generals with an Ascendancy background, there was Sir Stanley Maude, soon to command the Mesopotamian Expedition, who was a cousin of Captain Anthony Maude of Belgard Castle in County Dublin. There was Sir Bryan Mahon of Mafeking fame, who now commanded a Division in Gallipoli. And there was Gough of the Curragh affair, who by 1915 had risen to commanding a Division in France. His brother John had also risen to being a General, but had died of wounds at the beginning of the year.

Of Great War Admirals, the most celebrated, Beatty, came from County Wexford and was related to the Longfield clan of County Cork. From County Tipperary came Sir Sackville Carden, who commanded the naval force in the Dardanelles until obliged to resign in March 1915 owing to illness; his successor, Sir John de Robeck, came from County Kildare and was a cousin of Lord Cloncurry. Then there was Lord Longford's cousin, Sir William Pakenham, who took command of a Battle Cruiser Fleet in 1916.

— *2* —

As people got used to the idea of being at war and those who had not actually suffered bereavement grew hardened to the casualties, Ascendancy life settled down again to its normal pattern. Food was plentiful, though some people deliberately ate less flour, meat and sugar to set a good example. Lady Gregory's two small granddaughters were only allowed jam *or* butter, not both together, 'to

* He appears in the illustration on page 140.

Bernard Shaw, when staying with Lady Gregory at Coole.

help the troops'.[11] When Bernard Shaw came to stay he shocked the girls by putting butter on one side of his bread and jam on the other side.

For those landowners who farmed, the war was a time of prosperity, with rising cattle prices. Hunting carried on, even when the Master was away at the Front; so did shooting, fishing and racing. The war naturally brought its vexations; the troops encamped in the demesne of Clandeboye, Lord Dufferin's family home in County Down, cut down trees without asking the permission of his mother, the former Vicereine of India, who was living there at the time.

The great increase in the military during the war had its disadvantages, but these were outweighed by the advantage of a plentiful supply of officers to take the place of men away at the Front as partners for dances and tennis. There was not the shortage of men there had been during the South African War. To officers stationed in Ireland, the hospitality of the country houses seemed boundless. Some people also put up officers from the Dominions who were on leave. The septuagenarian Richard Longfield – head of the great Longfield clan of County Cork – and his wife usually had two Australian officers staying with them at Longueville, their family home near Mallow, along with the numerous relations who frequented that spacious Georgian house. The house was still lit by oil lamps, but the Australians were generally much impressed by the luxury – the butler, the vast quantities of food, the fires blazing in every room – as well as by the formality, for the Longfields naturally still dressed for dinner, which was of seven or eight courses.

If an officer had the bad luck to be stationed in a place where the local landowner and his family were away, he usually managed to get himself invited to shoot or fish in his demesne, which made up for the lack of entertainment in the Big House. General Edward Montagu-Stuart-Wortley, an English grandee who had rented his castle in Hampshire to the Kaiser in 1907, went to fish on the Blackwater at Convamore one day during the war, invited by the absent Lord Listowel. When, having put in to eat his sandwiches, he was back in the boat being poled out into midstream by the ghillie, he suddenly realized that he had left his gold drinking-flask on the bank.

'I'm afraid we'll have to go back and get my flask,' he told the ghillie apologetically. 'It's rather valuable, it was given to me by the Kaiser.'

'You must be a spy,' said the ghillie.

− *3* −

Towards the end of April 1916 Lord and Lady Donoughmore, who were now living mostly in England on account of their wartime activities, crossed over to Dublin for his Investiture as a Knight of St Patrick. The ceremony, at which Lord Powerscourt – back from Gallipoli – and Lord Midleton were also invested, took

Fishing on the Blackwater at Convamore in pre-war days.

place privately at Viceregal Lodge. During the Viceroy's speech, when he was congratulating himself on the success with which he was governing Ireland, Lord Donoughmore winked over his head at his friend Maurice Headlam, an Englishman in the Irish Civil Service. They both knew that Sinn Fein was becoming increasingly active and had even staged a 'trial attack' on Dublin Castle which the authorities had seen fit to hush up.

The Donoughmores, together with Headlam and Captain Anthony Maude, spent the following weekend, which was Easter, at Knocklofty. It was a bit of a picnic, for the house was mostly under dust-sheets, but they enjoyed the fishing and the peace and quiet of the Suir Valley. They all four of them left on the Monday, taking the Dublin train from Clonmel.

At Thurles the train stopped longer than usual. They sat in their compartment playing bridge, the windows closed and fogged up, for it was raining hard. Then somebody came and told them that there was a rebellion in Dublin and that the train would go no further. Nobody seemed to know what had happened. The Donoughmores, who were on their way back to England, decided to take the next train south, hoping to get the boat at Rosslare. Maude, who was anxious to rejoin his wife and children at their home near Dublin, hired a car and set off with Headlam through the heavy rain, stopping to buy provisions in case his family were without food. By the time they reached the Curragh it was eleven at night so he decided to knock up Captain Harry Greer, the manager of the National Stud, and ask him to give them a bed. They found the house locked and barricaded, but Greer looked out and, recognizing Maude, immediately invited them in.[12]

The Fingalls were spending Easter with Horace Plunkett at Kilteragh. On the Sunday, the Under-Secretary had come to luncheon, bringing sensational news: Sir Roger Casement, who had gone to Germany at the beginning of the war, had been landed by a German submarine on the Kerry coast and been picked up by the police. He was coming with German rifles for a Sinn Fein rising; now that he was safely under arrest and the arms ship scuttled, all was well. Next morning Fingall and some of the house party set off in Plunkett's car for Fairyhouse Races. Plunkett himself stayed behind and so did Daisy, who later that morning tried to telephone the Under-Secretary's wife. Having failed to get an answer she rang Dublin Castle and asked to speak to the Under-Secretary himself at his office. 'You can't,' said a voice. 'There is a rebellion on.'

Daisy hurried to the window and looked out on to the lawn where Plunkett and one of his male guests were playing 'old man's golf', for here it was not raining but sunny. 'Horace!' she shouted. 'There is a rebellion on in Dublin.'

'What nonsense! Someone is pulling your leg.' And he went on with his game.

She telephoned the Kildare Street Club and, speaking for Plunkett, asked the porter if there was a rebellion on in Dublin.

'Never heard a word of it.'

A few minutes later the telephone rang. It was the Club porter. 'Tell Sir Horace that there *is* a rebellion. They have taken the General Post Office and shot a policeman.'

Meanwhile at the races all kinds of rumours were going around: the rebels had seized Dublin, they held all the roads into the city. Fingall and his companions decided to leave, giving a lift to some young officers who wanted to get back to their barracks. They stopped at a country house not far from the course where the officers telephoned for orders and were told: 'Stay where you are until further instructions.' They did not realize that they were speaking to one of the rebels who by now held the Dublin telephone exchange. Even so, they happily ignored this message when Fingall proposed that they should try and get to Dublin nevertheless. The men of the party, including Fingall himself, were all in uniform, so they took the precaution of changing into civilian clothes borrowed from the lady of the house; they then set off under cover of darkness. Fingall knew the back roads and they reached Dublin without any hitch; the officers were able to get back to their barracks and Fingall returned safely to Kilteragh.[13]

Early on the Tuesday morning, Captain Maude and Maurice Headlam set off from the Curragh. They met a detachment of 17th Lancers on the road and asked the officer for news, but he could tell them nothing. Maude's home, Belgard Castle, was not much further on, and they reached it without difficulty. As they drove up the avenue, they saw, standing behind the closed gates of the courtyard, Maude's two schoolboy sons and his fourteen-year-old daughter, each holding one of their father's guns and ready to defend the house against the rebels.[14]

Lord Dunsany woke up at Dunsany Castle on the morning of that Tuesday, the third and final day of his Easter leave from the army, with no idea that anything unusual had happened. On coming down he began to hear rumours, and his son's French governess, who was by way of leaving by train that day, returned from the station saying that there were no trains running. This made him decide to drive into Dublin and offer his services to the military if indeed a rebellion had broken out.

He set off, chauffeur-driven and accompanied by a friend from Gallipoli who was staying with him; they reached GHQ where Dunsany was told to go to the assistance of an officer in the north-eastern part of Dublin. He was not, however, told which way to go, with the result that they drove straight into a rebel road-block on the quays near the Four Courts, which was one of the public buildings held by the insurgents. The car was fired upon and Dunsany and his chauffeur were both hit. A man came up and took Dunsany prisoner; noticing the bullet-hole in his face, he said: 'I am sorry.'

The insurgents carried Dunsany on a stretcher to the nearby Jervis Street

Hospital. His chauffeur was allowed to go to another hospital; his friend was marched off to be confined in the cellars of the Four Courts. In Jervis Street, which was in the thick of the fighting, Dunsany was nursed by a nun, who as the bullets whistled past the windows said with disdain: 'The nasty little things.'[15]

Across the river, the Kildare Street Club was also in the thick of the fighting. Rebel snipers were firing from the roofs of the houses between Kildare Street and Dawson Street; the troops were firing back at them from the Trinity College side of Nassau Street. Several members had been stranded in the Club since the previous day, among them Lord Fermoy and Herky Langrishe. Lord Fermoy was rash enough to stand in the big bay window overlooking the grounds of Trinity; a sentry on the roof of one of the College buildings thought he was directing the Sinn Fein fire and fired at him. He was unscathed, but there were three bullet holes in the window and one in the opposite wall of the room above the fireplace. When the officer commanding the guard realized what had happened, he sent an apology; the members responded by sending out page-boys with trays of tea and bread-and-butter for the soldiers.

Another peer who came under fire on that day was Lord Donoughmore. Having failed to get to Rosslare, he and his wife had spent the previous night at Knocklofty and today had driven up to Dublin, bringing their neighbours Mr and Mrs John Bagwell of Marlfield. As they drove down Harcourt Street on their way to the Club, they were stopped and informed that St Stephen's Green, which lay between them and their destination, was in rebel hands. They turned round and, going back along the street, they heard rifle fire. A bullet came in through the hood of the car, went through Mrs Bagwell's shoulder, through the upper part of her husband's arm, through Lord Donoughmore's great-coat, giving him a slight flesh wound, and out through the windscreen.[16]

At about the time when the Bagwells were wounded, the troops arrested Francis Sheehy-Skeffington, an Ulster Protestant who was an extreme Nationalist as well as a socialist, a feminist and a pacifist. While sympathizing with the insurgents, he had, during the past two days, adhered to his self-appointed non-combatant role of trying to prevent looting in the streets. He was taken to Portobello Barracks, where the officer in charge was Captain John Bowen-Colthurst, brother of Robert who was killed in the previous year. John Bowen-Colthurst had been posted to Dublin to recover from shell-shock; the events of the past two days had proved too much for his disordered mind. On hearing Sheehy-Skeffington's political convictions, he saw him as a dangerous rebel and had him summarily shot on the following day, together with two other prisoners. Bowen-Colthurst himself shot a man and two boys in the streets. In between his rampagings, he suffered remorse. After the shooting of Sheehy-Skeffington, he said that he had 'lost a brother in this way'.

Having shot the second boy he said, 'It's a terrible thing to shoot one's own countrymen, isn't it?'[17]

The Fingalls were still at Kilteragh, from where they could hear the explosions and see the smoke and flames rising from the city. From the rumours and garbled reports which continued to come in, Horace Plunkett and his guests were beginning to get some idea of what had happened and was happening. The insurgents consisted of part of the Citizen Army and part of that section of the Volunteers which had broken with Redmond. They had seized the General Post Office in Sackville Street, where the two principal leaders, James Connolly and the young schoolmaster Padraig Pearse, had proclaimed an Irish Republic. They also held the Four Courts and a few other vantage-points in the city, including the Royal College of Surgeons on St Stephen's Green, where Constance Markievicz, in dark green uniform, was second-in-command. Various people were claiming to have been shot at by her.

As the city was suffering from a shortage of food, Horace Plunkett organized a Food Committee. Each day he drove at speed through the Dublin streets to the Castle, where the civil servants were still at their desks and where the meetings of his Committee were held. On the Saturday, as he was driving through Merrion Square, a party of troops called on him to halt; being rather deaf he drove on. The military opened fire at him; they also shot at his nephew Tom Ponsonby of Kilcooley who had been following in another car and had got out and lain down in the road when the fusillade started. Plunkett suffered no injury but his companion in the front car was shot through the arm, while Ponsonby, whom the soldiers had mistaken for a rebel about to fire at them from behind the cars, was badly wounded.

Away from Dublin, the country was remarkably peaceful. Life went on as usual, except for the breakdown in communications and the food shortages. Lord and Lady Desart, who were at Desart when the Rising took place, were completely cut off from the outside world for over a fortnight.

By Saturday the insurgents, who were only a thousand strong, had reached the end of their tether, and that day the leaders in the Post Office negotiated terms of surrender with the military. Some of the rebels in the College of Surgeons wished to continue the fight on their own, but Constance Markievicz urged them to lay down their arms as Connolly had done. When an unarmed British soldier walked into the building and one of her comrades raised his revolver, she said: 'Don't, Joe, don't. It would be a great shame now.'[18] The officer who took the surrender of the College of Surgeons happened to be an Irishman, Captain Henry de Courcy-Wheeler from County Kildare, so small was the Ascendancy world that he was connected to Constance by marriage. He offered to take her in his car, but she preferred to march with her comrades. They went as prisoners to the Castle, where

Connolly, who was wounded and in great pain, lay beneath the gilded ceiling of one of the State Apartments which Lady Aberdeen had turned into hospital wards.

During the following week, people from the country started coming into Dublin once again. Mrs Ralph Coote, hearing that her soldier brother in Dublin was short of food, drove up from Ballyfin with a supply of chickens and eggs accompanied by her eight-year-old son, who broke off 'icicles' formed by molten lead in Sackville Street and collected them as trophies.[19] Percy La Touche and a neighbour drove up from County Kildare on Tuesday 2 May, taking revolvers with them just in case. 'The streets are full of troops, armoured motor cars, ambulances and machine guns,' La Touche reported in a letter to his old flame Clare Castletown, in which he also speculated as to when racing would start up again.[20]

He also told his 'dear Lady' that he had seen the General Commanding the Forces, Sir John Maxwell. 'Sir J. seems determined to put the rising down with a strong hand, if only the politicians will let him, and I believe a considerable number of rebels have been shot. Pearse was being tried by court martial yesterday and was probably shot this morning.'[21] He clearly approved of Maxwell's 'strong hand', as indeed did most of the Ascendancy, in whose eyes, as in those of public opinion in Britain, the execution of Pearse and Connolly and thirteen other leaders in the first two weeks of May was amply justified by the bloodshed and destruction of property they had caused, not to mention the 'stabbing in the back' of loyal Irishmen and British at a dark hour of the war. The liberal and humane Lord Powerscourt – who blamed the Rising on the 'tendency among some of the upper classes in Ireland' to despise the national movement, thereby allowing it to fall 'into the hands of unprincipled organizers',[22] felt so little compassion for the rebel leaders that he even wished to see Constance Markievicz shot, though he was a friend of her family. She was condemned to death along with the others, but in the event, like de Valera, she was reprieved and sent to prison in England.

In the Ascendancy world, the birth of that 'terrible beauty' of which Yeats sang passed unnoticed, overshadowed by that other terrible beauty born in the mud of Flanders and on the beaches of Gallipoli. Shane Leslie, who had joined in the efforts to get America to prevent the executions was one of the few who realized the danger of making martyrs.[23] People convinced themselves that ordinary decent Irishmen and Irishwomen had no sympathy at all for the rebels. At present, the prevailing mood of the Ascendancy was one of relief, even of self-congratulation. Basil Blackwood went so far as to maintain that what had happened had 'all been for the best . . . the complete exposure and collapse of a dangerous conspiracy'.[24] Blackwood helped to persuade the Prime Minister that Wimborne, as a figurehead, could not be held responsible for the bungling that had enabled the Rising to take place, so he was allowed to stay on as Viceroy. The blame fell on the

Chief Secretary, the scholarly Augustine Birrell, and on the Under-Secretary, both of whom had to go. For the Ascendancy, Birrell's departure was an added bonus; he was regarded as the arch 'wet', to use the word in its modern political sense.

— *4* —

Just as the Ascendancy was returning to wartime normal after the Rising, its social life was dealt a grievous blow by the introduction of petrol rationing. For the Ladies Howard, to have their enjoyment of the Motor curtailed by the 'tiresome order about petrol' was bad enough, but the filling in of the necessary forms seemed beyond their capabilities. They had to invite a neighbour to tea so that he could show them how it was done.[25]

The petrol shortage made it impossible for Sir Charles and Lady Barrington to take Doty Bandon to visit some disabled soldiers when she and her husband were

Sir Charles Barrington in his younger days, got up as 'The Deputy Warden of Glenstal Castle'.

staying with them at Glenstal Castle near Limerick in August 1916. However, the Bandons were able to hire a motor and go off on a jaunt to the west; they stayed with Lady Ardilaun at Ashford Castle on Lough Corrib. One evening the three of them went up the hill and had a picnic among the rocks at the top, from where there was a view to the Connemara Mountains. 'It is a wild fascinating country, with all its legends – Fin Varra the King of the Fairies who lives on the hill,' Doty wrote wistfully when they were back with the Barringtons in County Limerick. 'How it all rejoiced my poor gypsy heart, and now I have returned to civilization I am unhappy and dreading having to face a tea party in a few minutes.'[26]

Lady Ardilaun, childless and now a widow, lived alone at Ashford and at St Anne's on the northern shores of Dublin Bay where she gave garden parties to which all Dublin was invited – the business and professional worlds, the artistic and literary worlds, the military, the officials and the Trinity dons, as well as the Ascendancy. But while the gardens of St Anne's, for which she was herself largely responsible, gave pleasure to all manner of people, the great Italianate mansion, now that the large house parties, dinners and balls for which it was built were a thing of the past, had become something of a mausoleum. The wind whistled through the decayed winter garden – 'Listen! The wailing and crying never stops,' Lady Ardilaun used to say – and the rain came in through the leaky glass roof; if the downpour was heavy enough, it would put out the central heating boiler in the

St Anne's.

cellar below. The St Anne's central heating boiler was not very satisfactory at the best of times, not even with the help of the Guinness millions. In winter, the house was arctic; Lady Ardilaun had been obliged to retreat to the Shelbourne Hotel, together with her maid and her secretary, whenever she had a cold. She had now made comfortable winter quarters for herself out of two adjoining houses in St Stephen's Green, where she entertained when it was not the season for garden parties.

In about 1917 she invited a large and varied company here for tea and to listen to Yeats reciting his own poems. Her guests were standing about the drawing room chatting when the poet arrived and appeared framed in the doorway. Lady Ardilaun came forward to greet him and asked whether he would like tea before or after his recitation.

'I'll speak now.' Yeats, still standing in the doorway, paused while everybody hurriedly sat down. He then looked past everybody, as though he had seen a vision.

'I speak of the moon.'

And he spoke of the moon at length, in a slow, chanting voice. Nobody could understand a word.

When he had stopped, as abruptly as he had started, Lady Ardilaun asked him to recite *Innisfree*. He ignored her request.

'A verse to the moon.'

It only consisted of four lines, half spoken, half sung. Yeats then bowed, told Lady Ardilaun that he would not be staying to tea, and hurried away.

'Quite batty I suppose, poor fellow.'

The officer who put forward this supposition did so in tones redolent of the hunting field. There followed the rumble of an old and deaf peer.

'Couldn't catch it all, but there's no moon tonight.'[27]

Round the corner of St Stephen's Green from Lady Ardilaun's winter retreat, the palatial Number 80 was still occupied from time to time by her brother-in-law Lord Iveagh, now a widower, though like St Anne's, the house was no longer the setting for grand entertainments. But on 24 July there was an entertainment here which if it did not compare with the balls and dinners of former years for brilliance, was far more historic. This was the dinner given by Lord Iveagh to Lord Midleton, Lord Desart and other leading Southern Unionists on the night before the opening of the Irish Convention.

The Convention was a final attempt by the British Goverment to settle the Irish question without the exclusion of Ulster. The iniative for holding it came from the new Prime Minister, Lloyd George, who may have been as much motivated by the need to placate the Irish-Americans now that the United States had entered the war as by any special concern for Ireland – though Barnie Castletown believed that, as a Celt, he was particularly qualified to solve Ireland's problems. Whatever

The Irish Convention.

his motives, he chose an opportune moment when, as a result of the Easter Rising, the moderates, both Unionist and Nationalist, were more than ever anxious for a peaceful settlement.

There was a preponderance of Nationalists among the ninety-five representatives who met at Trinity College under the chairmanship of Horace Plunkett, for they included people like mayors and chairmen of county councils as well as MPs and peers. All political parties were represented, with the significant exception of Sinn Fein. The surviving Sinn Fein leaders had by now been released from prison, but refused to attend; they were, however, represented unofficially by the young Edward Lysaght, son of Sidney Royse Lysaght, a Clare and Cork landowner who was also a poet; but he resigned from the Convention before it ended. The Convention also had Catholic and Church of Ireland Archbishops and Bishops and the Presbyterian Moderator among its members, together with various other distinguished Irishmen such as the poet and artist AE.

The eleven Southern Unionists who dined at Number 80 on the eve of the Convention were very much in the minority, yet they were a strong team. Their leader, Lord Midleton, while being an Irish landowner and well-known in Ireland – though he lived principally in England – was influential in British political circles having, as St John Brodrick, been a cabinet minister at the turn of the century. To make up for Midleton's notorious obstinacy and shortage of tact, there was Lord Desart's talent for compromise and conciliation – he had served on the International Court of Arbitration at The Hague. The team also included Lord Mayo and Andrew Jameson.

Midleton and his colleagues originally hoped to work with the Ulster Unionists, who outnumbered them by nearly two to one, but even before the Convention opened the Ulstermen behaved towards them in a high-handed manner, making them leave Lord Iveagh's dinner early for a meeting and then keeping them waiting an hour. It became all too clear that, far from working to achieve a solution that did not entail partition, they had come to the Convention to frustrate any such settlement. So the Southern Unionists stayed on their own, doing their best to conciliate the Ulstermen while becoming increasingly in sympathy with the Nationalists. After two months had been wasted with windy oratory and unnecessary visits to Belfast and Cork, Lord Desart felt that the time had come for him and his colleagues to take the lead, so they put forward a scheme for a wide measure of self-government with safeguards for minorities.

The scheme met with the approval of the Nationalists, and when Carson had it put before him by Archbishop Crozier, who was prominent in the Convention, he said: 'You and I, Archbishop, must sacrifice all the popularity we have gained in Ulster to serve the passage of this measure.'[28] At a party in Dublin in January 1918 given by Lord Granard, whose hospitality did much to bring the various groups together, Carson said to Midleton: 'I think you may count on us.'[28] It looked as if the Southern Unionists, so long without any appreciable political influence, had solved the problem of Ulster and Home Rule – something which the mighty politicians of Nationalist Ireland, Ulster and Britain had failed to do. It was the Ascendancy's finest hour in its twilight years.

Ironically, the scheme was thwarted by a fatal blunder made by one of the Ascendancy – none other than Horace Plunkett, who as Chairman postponed the discussion on it until various committees had reported.[29] This gave the extremists on both sides time for second thoughts, which in the case of the Nationalists might have been dispelled had not John Redmond died on 6 March. The scheme also foundered on the rocks of Lloyd George's distrust and of his Government's ill-timed attempts to introduce conscription in Ireland.

The Convention ended with the Ulstermen as determined as ever to stay out of a Home Rule Ireland and with the Southern Unionists having come to terms with Home Rule. Not all Southern Unionists agreed with the 'Midletonites', as they came to be known, but an increasing number were adopting a Midletonite point of view. Unfortunately, the sort of Home Rule which the Midletonites were prepared to accept, while it might have been acceptable if established over the whole of Ireland, including Ulster, was already out of date in the three Southern provinces, where, largely as a result of the execution of the leaders of the Easter Rising, public opinion had already moved away from moderate Home Rule to the extreme Nationalism of Sinn Fein.

As early as September 1916, the beaters at a grouse shoot in County Wicklow had all turned up wearing Sinn Fein badges, though they had taken them off without a murmur when the host's wife had told them to do so at once. A more significant straw in the wind was the substantial victory of the Sinn Fein candidate over his Home Rule opponent in the North Roscommon by-election of February 1917. Such was the gloom cast over the local Ascendancy by this result that one gentleman went so far as to say that the Sinn Fein election workers were 'exactly similar in appearance and manner with those who must have carried through the French Revolution'.[30]

After the blow of this election, which was followed a year later by the forcible occupation by Sinn Fein supporters of land belonging to the two spinster sisters Miss Margaret and Miss Maria ffolliott of Hollybrook in County Sligo, it was reassuring for the landowners of this part of Ireland when Field-Marshal Viscount French, as he now was, who succeeded Wimborne as Viceroy in May 1918, began to spend money on improving his house and demesne in County Roscommon. Lord French delighted Miss Margaret ffolliott by paying her a visit; she and others of the Ascendancy felt that they had a real friend in the new Viceroy who was one of themselves. For the Unionist diehards French's belief in the inevitability of Home Rule was outweighed by his military reputation; they saw him as a 'strong man'. The Wimbornes left unlamented; since August 1916 there had not even been the saving presence at Viceregal Lodge of Basil Blackwood, who had gone back to the war and been killed a year later.

The war continued to take its toll. Lord Langford, Herky Langrishe, and Captain Marcus Armstrong of Moyaliffe Castle in County Tipperary were among the tens of thousands who lost a son in 1917; Lord Langford's loss was particularly sad for his other son was of unsound mind. Captain Harry Greer of the National Stud was among those who lost two sons. When the elder of the two, Colonel Eric Greer, was killed, he was commanding a Battalion of the Irish Guards at the age of twenty-five; he was succeeded by another boy-Colonel, Harold Alexander, known to his mother as Tubby and as Alex to his brother officers. Eric Greer was Alex's best friend, the Greers' family home in County Tyrone being close to Caledon.

As Lady Gregory's son, Robert, stood with his wife outside the hall door of

Robert Gregory in flying kit.

Coole in the autumn of 1917, waiting for the carriage that was to take him to the station on his way back to the war, they occupied themselves by seeing who could squeeze the most water out of a wet cloth which the fat housemaid Marian had with her, while their two small daughters watched from an upstairs window. Then the carriage came and he drove off, sitting upright in his Royal Flying Corps uniform, not looking back nor to right nor left. His wife did not wave, but stood looking in the direction of the carriage as it disappeared down the avenue. The fat Marian made the sign of the Cross.[31]

It seems that Robert Gregory knew that he would not see Coole or his wife and children again, as he drove down the avenue and out of the gates and turned right for Gort and the station rather than left for the village of Kiltartan. He died in Italy early in the New Year, when his plane crashed. His mother's friend Yeats makes him foresee his death with the same fatalism that appears in Norman Leslie's last letter, the death-wish of a doomed aristocracy:

> I know that I shall meet my fate
> Somewhere among the clouds above:
> Those that I fight I do not hate,
> Those that I guard I do not love;
> My country is Kiltartan Cross,

My countrymen Kiltartan's poor,
No likely end could bring them loss
Or leave them happier than before.

I balanced all, brought all to mind,
The years to come seemed waste of breath,
A waste of breath the years behind
To balance with this life, this death.

At the beginning of October 1918, when Germany was about to sue for peace, the Dowager Duchess of Abercorn was staying at Shelton Abbey in County Wicklow with her son-in-law, Ralph Wicklow, who had lost his wife in the previous year. Her unmarried daughter, Lady Phyllis Hamilton, was there too, and as well as bringing her maid, the Duchess had brought her cook over from London – a possible reflection on the Shelton cooking.

When it was time for them to return to London, Lady Phyllis decided to stay on another week, in order to see more of her fiancé who lived not far from Shelton and was home on leave from the army. So the Duchess went off on her own, leaving the cook behind to do maid to her daughter. Lady Phyllis and the cook were due back in London on 10 October, and that evening the Duchess sent a brake to meet them at Euston station. The brake returned without them and the driver said: 'The Irish Mail came in empty and there's no news.'[32]

Earlier that day in County Wicklow, word reached Lady Alice Howard and her sister Caroline – Loulie had died a few months before – that the outgoing mail boat, the *Leinster*, had been torpedoed that morning a few miles out of Kingstown. They knew that Phyllis Hamilton was on board, so Lady Alice went into Bray to try and get news. No one could tell her anything there, so she and a friend went on to Kingstown, where there was a great crowd and ambulances and motors taking away the survivors. They met Phyllis's cousin Colonel Douglas Proby, who lived near Shelton at Glenart, which he had inherited from his maternal uncle the last Lord Carysfort; he was looking for his secretary, who had also been aboard the ill-fated *Leinster*. But they heard nothing of Phyllis herself.

Lady Alice ordered the Motor early next morning and went again to Kingstown, but again 'could find no trace of Phyllis'. They gave up hope of her being alive. They heard that between four and five hundred people had been lost, including three of their own contemporaries, the two unmarried sisters of Sir Richard Musgrave of County Waterford, and the widowed Mrs James Jameson of Windfield.[33] Lady Phyllis's family afterwards heard from a survivor, who had seen her as the ship was going down; she had taken off her lifejacket and given it to the cook, saying: 'I'm a strong swimmer.'[34]

9

The last September

— I —

The war was over, but in all too many Irish country houses in 1919 the Young
Master was no more than a memory and a photograph in uniform on a side-table.
The elderly Lord Monck or Lord O'Neill or Lord Langford or Captain
Armstrong now had no heir but a grandson under age or a daughter – in Lord
Langford's case a lunatic son, an ageing and childless brother and a New Zealander
nephew. In some cases the burden of landownership had already fallen on to a
daughter's fair shoulders, as it had onto those of Marguerite Solly-Flood, formerly
Connellan. Or the head of the family was a fatherless child like the eight-year-old
Sir Richard Levinge or the ten-year-old Richard Gregory.

Robert Gregory's widow Margaret and her three children were living at Coole
with her mother-in-law, who was away a great deal in Dublin on Abbey Theatre
business. It was a struggle to keep up the large Georgian house and its romantic
demesne of woods and lake; to raise money they were trying to sell some land, at a
time when prices were very poor. 'The value of an estate in Galway is what you can
get for it,' their agent told them gloomily.[1] Sometimes Lady Gregory wondered
whether they would not be wise to give up Coole altogether, 'with its anxieties and
loneliness, with the burdens of keeping it in order and paying its taxes and rates
and labour'.[2] On the other hand it had been in the family for many generations and
she and her grandchildren loved the place; she wanted Richard to have the chance
of keeping it on if he wished when he grew up.

Coole was lonely because of the departure of several neighbours. By the end of
1919 there was something of an exodus of Ascendancy families from County
Galway, as indeed from the rest of Ireland, but particularly the West. The past
year had been comparatively peaceful, but the signs were ominous.

Coole.

In the general election of December 1918, Sinn Fein won 73 out of the total of 105 Irish Parliamentary seats; the old Nationalist party virtually ceased to exist. Constance Markievicz was among the victorious Sinn Fein candidates, thereby achieving the distinction of being the first woman MP; there was also the County Wicklow landowner Robert Barton, who was related to the Bartons of Straffan as well as to the Brookes. The Sinn Fein members, ignoring Westminster, met in Dublin and declared themselves to be the Dail or Parliament of an independent Irish Republic; a Provisional Government was set up, led by de Valera and with Constance as Minister for Labour. This Government was naturally not recognized by Britain, though it had the legality of being backed by a majority of the elected representatives of the Irish people.

By the end of 1919, a state of guerilla war had developed between the anti-British section of the Volunteers, now called the Irish Republican Army, and the police and military. There were attacks on police barracks and a number of policemen and RMs were shot; the raiding of country houses for arms, which had happened occasionally during the past couple of years, became a frequent occurrence. Coolmore was raided by twelve masked men one night when Marguerite was alone there with her children. One of the intruders held a pistol at the stomach of Patrick Darcy, the old butler, who had appeared on the scene in his pyjamas, and ordered him to hand over Peter Connellan's service revolver. 'I would sooner be shot than let one of ye touch my Captain's things,' Darcy replied indignantly, and after a perfunctory search which did not extend to the nurseries – since Marguerite was anxious that the children should not be frightened – the men departed.[3]

Marguerite Solly-Flood and her children.

The men who raided Carton were polite to the butler and avoided waking the young Duke's uncle Lord Frederick FitzGerald, who was living there at the time,* but they took, among other things, the revolver of Desmond FitzGerald, the fallen hope of the Leinsters, which had been sent back from France. At Paradise Hill in County Clare, where the elderly widow of Francis Henn was living mostly on her own, virtually penniless and keeping going by selling cattle piecemeal and not replacing them, the house was raided repeatedly. The guns had been handed over to the police – except for two which her schoolboy son Tom had secreted among the rafters – but the men took field-glasses, fishing tackle, even an old sword. At Christmas, however, when Tom was home from school, there was a knock on the door and a masked man strode in, flung down a heavy package and went out again. The package was found to contain cartridges, which were then unobtainable; it had a label on it which said: 'Wouldn't it be a pity for Master Tom not to have his bit of shooting, and him home for the holidays?'[4]

As the country became increasingly lawless, so those nocturnal knockings on country-house doors – now bolted, having generally in the past stayed open all night – grew ever more frequent. And other unpleasant things started to happen. When Edward Kennedy, a County Kildare landowner was driving through the streets of Dublin with a friend alongside him and his two schoolboy sons, whom they had met at the boat, in the back, their car was fired upon. As they drove on, unscathed but for a broken windscreen, the friend observed wryly: 'That was worse than a grouse drive.'[5] In December 1919 a genuine shooting party in County Clare was ambushed and the host, Henry Valentine Macnamara of Ennistymon, was shot in the neck and came near to losing his life. Macnamara was a colourful figure who combined the characteristics of an ancient Irish chieftain with those of a Unionist diehard of the old school. His no less flamboyant son Francis was, by contrast, a supporter of Sinn Fein. Francis Macnamara was a natural rebel: a poet, an advocate of free love, a friend of Augustus John whom he introduced to Ireland; he was condemned from the pulpit for encouraging John's children and his to run about naked on the beach near his home at Doolin.

To add to the troubles of the Ascendancy from the end of 1919 onwards, there was a series of strikes. There was even a chauffeurs' strike; when Lady Alice Howard went into Dublin to do her Christmas shopping the Motor was stopped in Fitzwilliam Square by a crowd of striking chauffeurs who tried to prevent Wiggins from driving. Fortunately he proved loyal and drove on.

Despite the raids and the strikes, Ascendancy Ireland was quite gay that Christmas and in the opening months of 1920. Hunting went on the same as ever. The young Lord Waterford and his sisters were among those who danced to

---

* See illustration on page 86.

Lady Alice (right) and Lady Caroline Howard, at about this time.

Percy La Touche out shooting at about the time of his golden wedding celebrations.

Clarke-Barry's music until well into the small hours at a subscription ball held in a country house near Carrick-on-Suir. Lady Annette La Touche gave a dance at Harristown and a month later she and her husband Percy gave a dinner and a ball to celebrate their golden wedding, in honour of which Lord French gave a large luncheon party at Viceregal Lodge. Because of the uncertainties of the Irish situation, Lord French had left his family in England; the Lodge was very much on a wartime footing with the ADCs in khaki and elaborate security measures – which did not prevent the Viceroy from being shot at as his car swung through the gates of Phoenix Park. Lord French's entertaining had little of the old Viceregal splendour about it, yet he gave quite a few dinners and dances and his standards as a host were high. 'Of course one must have good champagne,' he told a Treasury official who was trying to cut down the expenses of the Viceregal establishment.[6]

But although he was performing his social duties very adequately considering the times, he was proving a disappointment in other respects. As so often seems the case with military proconsuls or heads of state, he did not exert sufficient influence over his government, who allowed the situation in Ireland to go from bad to worse. The indiscriminate arrests and reprisals carried out in his name did nothing to restore law and order while antagonizing Irish public opinion still further. Even some of the Loyalists objected; in February Horace Plunkett's supporter Lord Monteagle, a Knight of St Patrick and a moderate Unionist, unlike his Nationalist daughter Mary Spring-Rice, wrote to *The Times* protesting strongly against the wholesale arrests. While Lord French was reigning at Viceregal Lodge, giving his constitutional approval to the policy of repression, his Suffragette sister Mrs Despard was making Sinn Fein speeches in the streets of Dublin. It is a coincidence that Lord Midleton, who nearly became Viceroy instead of Lord French, was the brother of Albinia Brodrick, another daughter of the Ascendancy active in Sinn Fein.

At the beginning of March Ascendancy Ireland was shocked by the murder of Lady Gregory's cousin, Frank Shawe-Taylor, who was shot dead a couple of miles from his home in County Galway while driving in the early morning to a fair. His manservant, who was in the car with him, was critically wounded. Shawe-Taylor's death had nothing to do with the IRA but was an agrarian crime, part of the land agitation now going on all over the West, like that of 1908 only worse. A week before he was shot, he had been visited by a deputation of the locals, who wanted him to sell some of his land to them; but he had said: 'You'll never see a perch of my land!' Shawe-Taylor was the brother of Hugh Lane's champion John Shawe-Taylor, who had died young in 1911. John's widow had recently let Castle Taylor and auctioned the contents of the house; by the time of her brother-in-law's death she was living in England.

The Dublin Spring Show of 1920 was a brilliant success, with a record entry for the jumping. Irish social life was not greatly affected by the curfew from midnight which had been enforced since the beginning of March; parties either ended early, or else people danced through the small hours until it was daylight. Fairyhouse took place as usual, but much to everyone's regret Punchestown had to be cancelled owing to a strike. The strikes continued; there was a strike of farm workers at Lissadell and Sir Josslyn Gore-Booth had to milk his own cows until his hands bled. In the circumstances, it was not very kind of his sister Constance to write to him as she did, reminding him that he came from a family of 'tyrants and usurpers'.[7]

While the strikes went on, so did the raids on country houses, some of which were more in the nature of armed robberies than genuine searches for arms. One night in May, armed men descended on Kilmorna in County Kerry, the family home of Pierce O'Mahony who had lent it to his half-brother Sir Arthur Vicars, the former Ulster King of Arms. Vicars, who was at home at the time, refused to open the door; the raiders broke it down and were confronted by him, alone and resolute, in the hall. Their leader ordered him to hand over the keys of the strong room; when he refused, the men levelled their rifles at him while the leader counted 'one, two, three' slowly and then once again demanded the keys. Once again Vicars refused to hand them over, but showed the men where the strong room was; and after they had tried unsuccessfully to force open the door, they left.

At about the same time as Vicars was raided, there was a robbery at a country house in County Meath. The police failed to trace the thieves, who had stolen some pictures and silver, but the local IRA arrested four of them and returned what they had recovered of the stolen property to its owner. The punishment of malefactors by Sinn Fein, of which this is only one instance, made a considerable impression on loyalists. As Bryan Cooper put it: 'Side by side with the realization that the Government is either unable or unwilling to protect them is coming the yet more startling discovery that on the whole Sinn Fein is trying to prevent anarchy and maintain order.'[8] In some places, Sinn Fein was even controlling the traffic at race meetings.

— *2* —

During the course of that summer, the Government, finding the military and the police inadequate against the guerilla tactics of the IRA, enlarged the Royal Irish Constabulary with recruits of doubtful quality; they also raised a new force, known as the Auxiliaries, largely made up of ex-officers who were misfits and unable to settle down in civilian life. The Auxiliaries and the extra police, who wore an improvised uniform of half police black and half khaki and were consequently nicknamed the Black and Tans after a famous pack of foxhounds, set out to fight the IRA with 'reprisals' of fearful brutality: burning villages, plundering, shooting innocent civilians. It was after the start of these so-called reprisals that the burning of country houses began.

The number of these burnings has been greatly exaggerated by people who, whenever they see the all-too-common sight of a ruined Irish country house, assume that it was 'burnt in the Troubles'. The total number of Irish country houses burnt between 1920 and 1923 was not more than about 200, and when the 'Troubles' started there would have been at least 2000 country houses in Ireland. Most of the burnings took place in Munster and Connaught.

Of the houses destroyed in 1920 and 1921, the majority were burnt in retaliation for reprisals. The military were ambushed, a policeman was shot, a barracks was attacked, and as a reprisal a village was burnt. Then, as a counter-reprisal, the IRA burnt the neighbouring Big House, if its owner was thought to be pro-British. This was hardly fair, in that however pro-British the owner may have been, he or she would almost certainly have deplored the atrocities of the 'Tans' no less than the most ardent supporter of Sinn Fein would have done. Moreover, the British Government was unlikely to be much influenced by the burning of the houses of a handful of politically-unimportant Irish loyalists.

There is one case where a threat to burn a Unionist's country house may have influenced the Government. The local IRA commander in County Longford, Seán MacEoin, was the blacksmith in a village close to Currygrane, the family home of the prominent Unionist James Mackay Wilson. MacEoin had orders from his superiors to burn Currygrane in retaliation for various reprisals in the district, including the burning of his own house and forge, but having always been on the best of terms with Wilson, despite their political differences, he was reluctant to do so. Instead, he promised that Currygrane would not be burnt if Wilson could influence his brother, Field-Marshal Sir Henry Wilson, now Chief of the Imperial General Staff, to have all reprisals in the district stopped. Wilson told MacEoin that he doubted whether his brother the Field-Marshal would listen to him, but in the event the reprisals did stop and Currygrane was saved, at any rate for the present.[9]

Another reason why country houses were burnt by the IRA was to prevent the military or the police from occupying them, or re-occupying them having once been in them. When the military requisitioned Timoleague House in West Cork, its owner, Robert Travers, who was on friendly terms with the officers of the local regiment, protested that the house would be burnt the moment the soldiers left it. The officers assured him that such an outrage would be impossible, since the army would continue to protect his house after the soldiers had moved out. It was burnt none the less, and the officers, who were genuinely distressed, came to see Travers and tried to comfort him. 'It's all right, old boy,' one of them said cheerfully, 'we've avenged you, we've burnt down some of *their* bloody houses.'[10]

Travers pointed out that the cottages in question also belonged to him.

Consorting with the military could in itself put one's house at risk, particularly if one was suspected of passing on information about IRA activities. It became a source of bewilderment and indeed of resentment to simple English officers that people who called themselves loyalists gave the army so little help, but as the army was unable to protect them, the Irish loyalists had no safe alternative but to stay strictly neutral in the conflict. It was also wise to appear to be politically neutral, though a prominent Unionist like Wilson did not necessarily have his house burnt down so long as there were no reprisals in his neighbourhood.

The burning of country houses sometimes had nothing to do with the IRA. Doolin in County Clare, the home of the Sinn Fein supporter Francis Macnamara, was burnt by the Black and Tans as a reprisal. Other burnings were to do with the land agitation; people believed that if they burnt the Big House the family would leave and they would be able to buy the demesne land very cheaply. This is thought to have been the reason for the burning of Tyrone, the great empty house of the St Georges on the shores of Galway Bay, though there was also a rumour that the Black and Tans were going to use it as a hospital. Before setting fire to the straw which they had brought into the house, the incendiaries smashed the statue of Lord St George in the hall. Agrarian burnings differed from those carried out by the IRA in that whereas the former were naturally the work of locals, the latter were almost always done by men from away, the locals being unwilling to help burn the house of someone with whom they were probably on perfectly good terms.

The chances of a house being burnt on the whole bore little relation to the owner's popularity, still less to that of his or her forebears. Robert Travers, for instance, was very popular in his neighbourhood; whereas Lord Ashtown, who was so disliked that even before the Troubles started he had been obliged to go about with a police escort, and who believed that it was thanks to the 'Tans' that people like himself were able to 'stick it' in Connaught,[11] managed to keep the torch away from his principal house, which was in County Galway. However, his shooting-lodge in County Waterford was burnt in May 1920. It had already been damaged by a bomb some years before.

There may, however, be some significance in the fact that the first batch of houses to suffer in June, the month in which the burnings really started, included Oakgrove in County Cork, one of the two family homes of Captain John Bowen-Colthurst, whose rampagings in Dublin during Easter Week 1916 had brought him a spell in Broadmoor, since when he had emigrated to Canada. After Oakgrove was burnt, Bowen-Colthurst's unmarried sister, who had been living there at the time with her mother, received a message telling her to go to a mysterious address in Cork city. There, in an upper room, she found an Aladdin's cave of jewellery from various country houses; she was told to take away whatever was hers and her mother's.

— *3* —

While Lord Ashtown was suffering from the Troubles in Ireland, his kinsman Lord Clancarty was having troubles of a different sort in London. He was on trial for obtaining money and goods under false pretences. He had used cheques which, as a bankrupt, he knew would be dishonoured, to pay for a diamond ring to give to a lady-friend and for meals at various restaurants including the Ritz, the Berkeley and Oddenino's where, as one of the waiters said when giving evidence, they trusted him 'on account of his being a noble earl'. His defence was that his allowance had been stopped altogether for some months by his trustees and that during those months he could hardly have been expected to starve, which drew the unkind observation from the Bench that if Lord Clancarty was starving he need not have gone to the Ritz or the Berkeley.

On 23 July 1920 at the Central Criminal Court, Clancarty was sentenced to three months' imprisonment in the second division. The judge said to him:

> You are one of those unfortunate men who have not been brought up to do anything for a living. You might have been in happier circumstances if you had been called upon to discharge the sufficiently onerous and responsible duties of a landlord. But owing to the state of the country in which you live you were deprived even of that occupation.[12]

— *4* —

On 21 August, after a Dublin Horse Show which had been reasonably successful despite what *The Times* referred to as 'a sensibility of the prevailing political turbulence', Lord Bandon called a meeting of the DLs of the County and City of

Cork. The meeting unanimously resolved that as in recent years the British Government had 'failed to secure the observance of law' and had 'lost the confidence of all classes . . . an immediate effort should be made to settle the question by provisions which, while preserving Ireland within the Empire and safeguarding the security of Great Britain' would 'give effect to the desire of the Irish people for self-government'.[13] This was what was known as 'Dominion Home Rule', a far greater measure of self-government than the scheme put before the Convention. It had been proposed by Lord Monteagle in the House of Lords at the beginning of July and was being widely canvassed by Midletonites like Andrew Jameson, who had come a long way since April 1914 when he had driven north to help with the Larne gun-running; the photograph of Carson, which used to grace the grand piano at his home near Dublin, had by now been banished. Dominion Home Rule was even finding favour among the Unionist diehards, a sign of how greatly the loyalists distrusted Lloyd George's Government and were disgusted by the policy of reprisals – Sir Algernon Coote went so far as to resign his Lieutenancy in protest against the activities of the Black and Tans. It also seemed a way of preventing Ireland from being partitioned; and what was most important to the vast majority of its supporters, a means of restoring law and order.

Less than a week after the meeting of the Cork DLs Barnie Castletown, who was one of their number, was provided with further evidence of the Government's failure to 'secure the observance of law' when a party of armed and masked men held up his car as he was driving back to Doneraile from a grouse shoot in the Ballyhoura Mountains. He jumped out and 'began to abuse them freely',[14] but the men made no reply and merely pointed rifles and revolvers at his head. Meanwhile their leader helped himself to Barnie's gun.

In the car with Barnie on that occasion was Clare Castletown's cousin, Mary Gaussen, who was a niece of Lord Bandon. Although she lived in England, she came often to stay with her relations in County Cork, and being an intrepid young woman she feared neither the Tans nor the IRA. She used to say that she was much more frightened of being hit by a billiard ball while she sat in the hall at Castle Bernard watching her uncle and the other men of the party playing billiard fives, which was their Sunday occupation, it being not done to play cards for money on the Sabbath.

One DL who could not attend Lord Bandon's meeting was Joseph Pike of the celebrated card case: he and his wife were away in Harrogate. But he read of the meeting in *The Times* and immediately wrote to the staunchly Unionist *Cork Constitution* saying that if he had known that the resolution calling for Dominion Home Rule was going to be put forward, he would have returned home especially to vote against it. His letter was published on 26 August.

In the small hours of 29 August, the housekeeper and maids of Dunsland, the

Pikes' country house near Cork, were awakened by loud knockings. On opening the hall door, they were confronted by a crowd of about fifty men, disguised and armed to the teeth. The leader told the housekeeper that he was afraid he would have to ask them to leave, as they were going to burn the house, but that he would give them time to remove their belongings and have a cup of tea. He added that they were doing it because of Pike's letter to the newspaper.

After the raiders had helped the staff to carry out their belongings on to the lawn, the housekeeper told them that there was a pony in the stable adjoining the house. The men set it free and asked if there were any other animals to be rescued. The housekeeper remembered the canary; one of the men went and fetched it and carried it in its cage with great care to a safe place. Then a barrel of petrol from the garage was emptied into the hall and the torch applied. Ten minutes later the front of the house overlooking the Lee estuary was 'like a mammoth furnace',[15] flames a hundred feet high lit up the whole countryside.

− 5 −

September 1920 was the month Elizabeth Bowen had in mind when she wrote her novel *The Last September*, which describes with almost terrifying accuracy what life was like in an Irish country house at this time and how the people living in the house felt. Sir Richard and Lady Naylor of Danielstown – a house modelled exactly on Bowen's Court – were loyalists. The officers from the local garrison came to their tennis parties; that this might have had unpleasant consequences did not worry Sir Richard overmuch.

> 'Listen, Richard,' said Francie; 'are you sure we will not be shot
> at if we sit out late on the steps?'
> Sir Richard laughed and they all shared his amusement. 'We never
> have yet, not even with soldiers here and Lois dancing with officers
> up and down the avenue. You're getting very English, Francie!'

Nevertheless, he was none too happy when Lois showed signs of becoming more than friendly with one of the subalterns, and when she suggested that they should dig up some arms which, it was rumoured, were buried in one of the plantations, he became quite angry. 'You'll have the place full of soldiers, trampling the young trees . . . this country is altogether too full of soldiers, with nothing to do but dance and poke old women out of their beds to look for guns.'

Sir Richard and the other inhabitants of Danielstown were by no means insensitive to all that the soldiers and police were going through. At a tennis party five days after the RIC barracks at Ballydrum had been attacked and burnt out and two of the policemen burnt inside it, Lois remarked to her subaltern friend that one of his brother-officers was looking 'rather sick'.

'Well, we all feel a little rotten about that barrack.'

'*Don't*! Do you know that while that was going on, eight miles off, I was cutting a dress out, a voile that I didn't even need, and playing the gramophone? ... How is it that in this country that ought to be full of such violent realness, there seems nothing for me but clothes and what people say?'

But when the officer, after luncheon one day at Danielstown, announced the capture of a local IRA man, who was wanted over an ambush in County Clare, the reaction was not such as he might have expected.

'I'm sorry to hear that,' said Sir Richard, flushing severely. 'His mother is dying. However, I suppose you must do your duty.'

The Naylors and the other gentry around had been friendly with the garrison at Clonmore – a town recognizable as Fermoy – since Napoleonic times or earlier, when the great barracks on the hill was built. And they were not just friends with the army; they were of the army and it of them. But now their relationship with the officers was full of such frissons.

If their attitude towards the army was ambivalent, they knew exactly how they felt about the Black and Tans. One day when Lois and another girl were driving in a pony-trap, 'they heard a lorry coming. Black and Tans, fortified inwardly against the weather, were shouting and singing and now and then firing shots. The voices, kept low by the rain, the grind of wheels on the rocky road, tunnelled through the close air with a particular horror.'

And all the time a threat hung over Danielstown – though the tall, square house seemed peaceful enough, protected from the outside world by the woods of its demesne – a threat to which only the highbrow undergraduate nephew from England was tactless enough to allude.

'I should like to be here when this house burns.'

'Quite impossible; quite unthinkable,' said the Naylors' friend Mr Montmorency. 'Why don't you fish or something?'

– 6 –

It was bad enough for the fictional Sir Richard Naylor to know that the son of old Mrs Connor up the mountain had been caught by the military and would almost certainly be shot, though there seemed little doubt that the young man had taken part in an ambush. But Reginald Bence-Jones was convinced that a youth from near Lisselane who was going to be executed in connection with an ambush was innocent. So strongly did he feel about it that he went to London to see the Chief Secretary, Sir Hamar Greenwood, who at the time was not on one of his periodic visits to Dublin.

Greenwood received him in his room at the Irish Office, which was heavily sandbagged on account of the situation in Ireland. He was polite, if a trifle unctuous, but totally unhelpful. 'I am afraid the law must take its course,' he kept on saying.

Bence-Jones was the kindest of men, but when riled he would come out with remarks of uncharacteristic ferocity. 'Sir Hamar,' he said, in a voice deceptively mild. 'It would be a very good thing if you could come over to Ireland at once.'

'D'you think that would help?'

'Yes! Because we wouldn't let you live till morning.'

And he stalked out. Whether as a result of this interview, or through the influence of Bence-Jones's old schoolfellow Austen Chamberlain, or for some other reason, the youth was reprieved.

From a purely selfish point of view, it paid an Ascendancy landowner to be seen as the friend of the country people around him, particularly of those who were fighting for Sinn Fein, and indeed, to have friends in Sinn Fein could be very useful. After the death of Sir Algernon in October 1920, the Cootes decided to give up Ballyfin. The new baronet and his family continued to live in a smaller house nearby which had been built just before the war; the great classical mansion, after its contents had been sold, was left empty until a purchaser could be found. It came to no harm, because the family were sensible enough to put in a caretaker who was an ardent Sinn Fein supporter and had been imprisoned by the British at the Curragh Camp.

— 7 —

Irish country-house life in the early months of 1921 was bleak indeed, particularly in remoter districts of the West. Almost as bad as the nightly fear of the knocking on the door by armed men with petrol cans was the boredom. Martial law had now been introduced, the curfew started at eight and people were not allowed to drive more than twenty miles from their homes, if indeed they were able to use their cars at all, for it now required a permit to do so, and these were not readily granted. 'We had a great blow, as we have been refused a permit for the Motor,' Lady Alice Howard lamented on 13 February.[16] The carburettor and the magneto had to be taken out and handed over to the police, and when, a few days later, she made one of her customary forays into Dublin in search of domestics – this time a housemaid – she had to go by train.

Even for those with permits, getting about by car could be difficult if not hazardous on account of such obstacles as felled trees and trenches dug across the road; an axe to deal with the former and a couple of planks to bridge the latter had become an essential part of the Irish motorist's equipment. One wonders if anybody isolated in a lonely Big House in Connaught during the long winter evenings of February 1921 was consoled by the thought that Josslyn Gore-Booth's rebel sister Constance was also isolated – in her case in prison, where she had been since the previous September. Also in prison was Robert Barton, that other Sinn Fein MP from the Ascendancy.

In many parts of the country, there was still hunting to cheer those winter days, though it was stopped from the beginning of February in various parts of Munster by order of the military governor of Cork, on the grounds that it was 'likely to cause disorder'.[17] Shooting was virtually impossible since all guns and cartridges had to be surrendered to the military, who were no respectors of persons in their search for illicit arms. In January Lord Dunsany was arrested for keeping a pair of shotguns, two rook rifles and four Vérey pistols – the latter being useful for giving the alarm in case of a raid – at Dunsany. 'I have fought against Sinn Fein, the Boers and the Germans,' he declared with some spirit when being tried by a court martial in Dublin;[18] nevertheless, he was fined £25. He afterwards heard from an important General that he had always been deeply suspect because of his plays. His fellow-peer Barnie Castletown managed to keep his shotguns until the end of the shooting season, though he never recovered the one taken from him in August. After that episode, he and Clare migrated from Doneraile to Granston, his own family home in the much more peaceful Queen's

County, where he was able to go on shooting right through the season without any trouble.

February was the month chosen by Elizabeth Bowen for the burning of Danielstown. While she was away from Ireland, on the shores of Lake Como, during the worst of the Troubles, she had taught herself to imagine Bowen's Court in flames; what she imagined eventually went down on the final page of *The Last September*.

> Half-way up the avenue under the beeches, the thin iron gate twanged (missed its latch, remained swinging aghast) as the last unlit car slid out with the executioners bland from accomplished duty . . . the first wave of silence that was to be ultimate flowed back, confident, to the steps. Above the steps, the door stood open hospitably upon a furnace.

Of the real-life burnings that February, the most tragic was that of Summerhill, the splendidly dramatic hilltop Palladian house in County Meath where the Empress Elizabeth had found happiness; it was now the home of Colonel William Rowley, uncle of the young mentally-deranged Lord Langford. On the night of 4 February, when Colonel and Mrs Rowley were away, the five servants who lived in the house were sitting together in the kitchen and heard a knock on the back door. The English butler, without opening the door, asked who it was; a voice answered: 'a friend.' The butler was taking no chances and left the door shut, hoping the intruder would go away, but a whistle blew and a few minutes later he and the other servants heard the back door being battered in. They escaped through a door in the basement and went out into the darkness; they could hear windows being smashed and they saw two men heading in the direction of the garage, where the petrol was stored. As the servants walked down the avenue on their way to the farm they came in sight of the house and saw the kitchen wing ablaze and flames coming also from the drawing room. Later, from further away, they could see that the house was on fire in several different places.[19]

As soon as the shooting season was over, Barnie Castletown put his guns into safe keeping. This was just as well, for one evening early that spring, when he and Clare and another lady were at Granston, enjoying a game of bridge after dinner, there was a knock on the hall door and it turned out to be a solitary young raider looking for arms. He asked Barnie in Irish if he was MacGillapatrick, the name of the ancient chieftains from whom he was descended, and Barnie, putting his knowledge of the language to good effect, answered in the affirmative and told him that his guns were no longer in the house. The young man, who was very polite, wished to look over the house all the same, and so Barnie took him round, ending by taking him into the drawing room to see the ladies. They asked the raider if he would like to take a hand at bridge, but he said that he did not know how to play. After the raider had been offered a drink, which he refused, they parted friends.[20]

Not long after this amicable raid on Granston, there was a second raid, even less amicable than the first, on Kilmorna, the Kerry home of Sir Arthur Vicars, whose carelessness with his keys had deprived Barnie of the honour of being invested as a Knight of St Patrick by King Edward. One morning in April when Vicars, who had not been well, was in bed talking business with the manager of the estate, his wife came in to say that there were armed men prowling around the house. The manager told Vicars to get dressed at once and hurried downstairs to secure the doors. But two of the raiders had already come in through the back door, saying to the valet and cook: 'It is all right, we have come only to burn the house.' They gave them two minutes to remove their possessions.

The manager rushed upstairs again to tell Vicars and his wife and then began collecting valuables and putting them outside the hall door until stopped by one of the raiders who placed him under guard. The house was already burning, but although everybody else, including Lady Vicars, was outside, Vicars himself was still in his room. The valet went into the blazing house to fetch him and found him in his dressing gown, having only just got up; he told the valet to go to the dining room and save some of the family portraits. The valet did as he was told and managed to get the pictures out through the window; he then went back to Vicars and at last persuaded him to come down.

The manager, who was standing outside the house being guarded by one of the raiders, saw Vicars emerge onto the terrace and go down the steps. The raiders went after him. The manager heard Vicars say something to them, and then shots rang out. After the raiders had gone, Vicars's body was found at the foot of the steps with a label round the neck which said: 'Spy. Informers beware.' But the IRA disclaimed responsibility for the murder, giving rise to the belief that, like the death of Pierce Mahony, it was somehow connected with the theft of the Crown Jewels.[21]

$- 8 -$

As though to make up for the winter, the spring and summer of 1921 were 'wonderful and unforgettable'. There was day after day of brilliant sun and from seven in the evening onwards, when motor cars were not allowed on the roads, 'the country seemed to belong to the sheep and lambs and birds'.[22] The Spring Show had to be abandoned owing to a coal strike, but Punchestown was particularly

Lord French inspecting a guard of honour of RIC on his departure from Ireland.

successful; there was racing also at Leopardstown and at the Curragh, where Daisy Fingall was to be seen with the veil that had become indispensible to her now that she was approaching sixty. And as though to indicate a change of heart on the part of the Government, Lord French, who had come to be associated in the Irish mind with reprisals and Black and Tan outrages, was replaced as Viceroy by the Catholic Viscount FitzAlan of Derwent, the Duke of Norfolk's uncle. For the first time since the reign of James II, the Sovereign's representative attended Mass in Dublin; but what was more important to the Irish – who set less store by the new Viceroy's religion than the British did – was that FitzAlan seemed to have come as an emissary of peace. After he had been in Ireland a month he publicly admitted that the Black and Tans had committed 'crimes, horrible crimes'.[23] Unlike French, FitzAlan brought his wife with him; he also brought his son and daughter, both of them fortyish and unmarried.

The burnings and shootings continued, all the more frightful in the glorious weather. During the night following French's departure, three country houses in north County Cork were burnt in retaliation for a reprisal, one being Convamore. The Listowels were away at the time, but Lord Listowel's niece, Miss Wrixon-Becher, was living in the house; neighbours found her next morning without her false teeth, which she had lost in the fire. A fortnight later the Ascendancy world, growing accustomed to the burning of country houses, was shocked by the shooting of a young girl. She was Winifred Barrington, only daughter of the Bandons' friends Sir Charles and Lady Barrington of Glenstal Castle in County

Lord and Lady FitzAlan at the time of his appointment to Ireland.

Limerick. She had been driving near her home with two other women, a District Inspector of the RIC and an army officer when a party of armed men opened fire on the car, killing her as well as the police inspector. The IRA maintained that they only intended to shoot the latter, and that Winifred Barrington's death was accidental, which was probably true; it was rash to go driving with a police inspector, who was such an obvious target.

On the day after Winifred Barrington's death another woman was killed, the wife of Captain Blake, also a District Inspector of the RIC, who came from one of the ancient Galway families known as the Tribes. Captain and Mrs Blake, together with Robert Gregory's widow Margaret and two young army officers were driving down the avenue of a country house not far from Coole after a tennis party when they saw that the lodge gates were closed. One of the officers got out to open them and was promptly shot down. The car was then surrounded by armed and masked men, who ordered Mrs Blake and Margaret Gregory to leave. Mrs Blake called out that she would not leave her husband but would die by his side; he and she and the other officer were mown down by volleys fired in quick succession. Meanwhile, hearing the shots, the owner of the house and his two daughters came running down the avenue, only to be held up by three of the armed men while the rest got away. As

The shooting of Captain and Mrs Blake and two young army officers at the lodge gates of a country house in County Galway. Margaret Gregory is on the right, behind the car.

Margaret Gregory's two daughters Anne and Catherine and her son Richard.

soon as it appeared that they had all gone, one of the daughters fetched a horse and galloped over to Gort to give the alarm.

Margaret Gregory, the sole survivor of the ambush, was unhurt; she had been kept standing with her hands up for some time, then allowed to go. She was very shaken and for a week made her two small daughters sleep with her in her four-poster bed. '*How* we hated it,' they afterwards recalled. 'It was all so embarrassing – the nearness of this astral being – clad in a nightdress, and – oh horrors – snoring.'

Not long after the ambush the two girls were stalking a rabbit in the Coole woods when they came upon two young men in hiding, who pointed rifles at them. Then, recognizing them, the men walked back with them to the garden gate. They seemed nice enough and told the girls to stay away from the woods for at least three days, because a lot of men on the run were hiding there. One of them said: 'Tell Her Ladyship that we wouldn't hurt a hair of anyone in Her Ladyship's family.' When the girls told this to their grandmother they were 'rather horrified' because they thought she was crying, but she said that she had a cold coming on.

As a result of the ambush and the encounter in the woods the two girls were taken to London for six months by their mother; it was the first time they had ever been out of Ireland. On the boat, the girls were in the 'open cabin' with a number of other people who were being sick; they themselves were about to be sick when their mother came in and said sternly: 'You are not to be sick. No Gregory was ever sick.' And they were not sick after all.[24]

$$-\;9\;-$$

In the midst of the violence and ill-feeling of that long hot summer, there was an occasion of goodwill on 15 June when the new Arklow lifeboat was launched. Lady Alice Howard christened the boat with a bottle of champagne; it was blessed by the Catholic priest and dedicated by the Church of Ireland minister. The Protestants sang 'For those in peril on the sea'; the Catholics, 'Hail Queen of Heaven the Ocean Star'.

A week later, Lady Alice was horrified to hear that Castle Bernard had been burnt and Lord Bandon kidnapped.

The men arrived at Castle Bernard an hour or so after dawn on yet another glorious summer's morning. The seventy-year-old Bandon and Doty, who was only slightly younger, were awakened and ordered outside, together with their servants. Then the raiders quickly set the castle on fire with petrol which they had brought with them. They appear to have lacked the courtesy so often shown by the burners of country houses. 'The way they treated us was like the French Revolution,' Doty Bandon afterwards recounted. 'The head man was so insulting to me, saying there is no Lord Bandon and that the likes of us had ruined the country. Thank God I kept my head and prevented them being rough to B. when he tried to struggle with them.'[25] Doty saw her husband taken away by the men and then heard shots fired.

Although there was a military garrison in the town of Bandon only just over a mile away, it was not until eight that an armoured car arrived on the scene,

Castle Bernard burning, with such things as were saved out on the lawn in front.

followed by lorries full of troops and police and a fire engine. By then the castle was blazing fiercely and nothing could be done except to try and save some of the contents. The troops rounded up about sixty men in the streets of the town and brought them out to help with the salvage, but even so, only a few things were saved, mostly from the wing where the Bandons had their private rooms: one or two good pieces of furniture, a portrait of Doty as a young girl, some books that were already charred by the time they were rescued.

On the day after Castle Bernard was burnt and Lord Bandon kidnapped, King George V and Queen Mary arrived in Belfast in the royal yacht for the opening of the new Northern Ireland Parliament. The Government, ignoring the call for Dominion Home Rule, had passed the Government of Ireland Act which set up two separate Irish Parliaments: one for the six north-eastern counties of Ulster and another for the rest of Ireland. The latter, apart from the four Unionists elected for Trinity College, was entirely Sinn Fein and continued to regard itself as the Dail of an independent Irish Republic, but the Northern Ireland Parliament met as planned and was opened by the King.

The visit of the King and Queen to Belfast, though they came for less than a day, was a brilliant success. There were flags and bunting everywhere, the pavements and the lamp posts were painted red, white and blue. Cheering crowds lined the route from the docks to the City Hall, so that people were not much aware of the stringent security measures. At the luncheon, the King and Queen sat on either side of Sir James Craig, who was now Prime Minister of Northern Ireland with Lord Londonderry – son of the forceful Theresa and her husband, neither of whom lived to see this day – as Minister of Education. Lady Craig and the Duchess of Abercorn presented the Queen with an address from the loyalist women of Ulster; the Craigs' thirteen-year-old daughter Aileen presented her with a bouquet. In his speech to the new Parliament, the King appealed 'to all Irishmen to pause, to stretch out the hand of forbearance and conciliation, to forgive and forget'.

As soon as Lord Bandon's niece Mary Gaussen read of his kidnapping and the burning of Castle Bernard, she crossed over on the night mail to be with her Aunt Doty, though she still had no idea of her aunt's whereabouts or condition: one paper said that Lady Bandon was in a 'state of collapse'. On her arrival in Ireland, Mary met with kindness on every hand. When, having learnt at the Cork County Club that Doty was still at Castle Bernard, she went to catch the evening train to Bandon, she found a man with whom she had made friends on the train from Dublin waiting to tell her he had reserved a compartment for her.

Mary was met at Bandon station and driven to Castle Bernard. 'I saw the ruins of that best beloved house, no one knows how greatly loved it was,' she wrote in her diary. 'The ruin is absolute and all one can do is to wander across the masses of debris in those precious rooms.'

She found Doty living in the gardener's cottage, guarded by an officer and a platoon from the garrison. Contrary to what newspapers had said, she was 'perfectly splendid'. Her maid, however, was in a state of shock and kept telling Mary horror stories as she tried to undress that night. Mary had a mattress on the floor alongside Doty's bed; being unable to sleep she sat up chatting with the officer of the guard 'in spite of very scanty clothing'.

On the Sunday following, Doty and Mary 'got quite reckless' and drove to church in the brougham without a military escort. That afternoon, they had an unexpected visitor. It was Lord Bandon's cousin Albinia Brodrick, dressed as a nurse for she was looking after IRA wounded and giving shelter to men on the run in her cottage hospital in Kerry. At first Doty would not receive her, but such was Albinia's insistence that, in Mary's words, 'D. finally consented and that terrible woman came in.' She said that she had no news of Bandon, having not seen 'our leaders', but that she had come to advise Doty to put pressure on the British Government to release the prisoners against whose lives he was being held as a hostage.

Mary wrote in her diary:

Doty behaved with extraordinary dignity, but when Alba made this statement I

Mary Gaussen picks her way through the debris in the burnt-out ruin of Castle Bernard.

remarked (with temper) that she ought to withdraw her connection from Sinn Fein, her reply being that she knew more about Sinn Fein than I did (a remark which went no way towards condoning murder). She laid stress upon 'our leaders' and I talked of blackmail; but even the worst interview in one's life comes to an end and my parting shot was, had she seen the house. She had, and she disappeared as mysteriously as she came. We had no officer up here at the moment and I'm afraid that it wouldn't have done if I had asked the Corporal to arrest her.

They were also visited on the Sunday by a woman whose house had been burnt three days earlier, one of fifteen country houses around Bandon to go up in flames that week, another being the home of the widow and children of Captain Jack Longfield who was killed in the motor accident. 'The whole neighbourhood has fled with the crash here,' Mary wrote. '*All* has ended.' To soothe their feelings, she and Doty walked round the rockery after dinner.

On their last night in the cottage, before she and Doty left for Cork where they were to stay in the house of General Strickland, the military governor, Mary wrote: 'I am now sitting in this little room and talking, talking. I feel that we are winding up the whole family; can it be that she and I are spending our last night at our beloved place? One thinks of all who have gone before and yet I am proud to end it all ever as I have loved it, with all my heart and soul.' They went late to bed that night; no sooner had they settled down when firing began. Doty rolled out of bed on to the floor and eventually came and shared Mary's mattress. 'If you wish to enjoy a fight with Sinn Fein,' Mary remarked, 'choose something more substantial than a cottage with a window each end of your room.'[26]

The King's speech in Belfast, in which he expressed his own heartfelt wish for peace in Ireland, was followed two days later by a letter from Lloyd George to de Valera inviting him to discuss peace terms in London. Before accepting, de Valera conferred with his own colleagues and also with Lord Midleton, Andrew Jameson and two other leaders of the Southern loyalists. At the meetings, which took place in the Mansion House in Dublin, Midleton and his colleagues found de Valera and the other Sinn Fein leader Arthur Griffith helpful; they agreed to various safeguards for the Protestant and loyalist minority. They also agreed to release Lord Bandon as an earnest of their good faith for the truce which was to precede a peace conference in London. Midleton then acted as an intermediary between Sinn Fein and the Government and it was through his good offices that a truce was arranged, which came into force on 11 July.

Next day Lord Bandon was brought back to Castle Bernard by his captors. It was a melancholy homecoming, though he did not have to stay long by the ruins, for he was driven immediately into Cork to be reunited with Doty at General

Lord Midleton arriving at the Mansion House in Dublin to meet the Sinn Fein leaders.

Strickland's house. He was said to be looking well, and indeed his captors had been ordered to treat him with consideration and to give him everything he wanted; he had asked for some good brandy and they had scoured the countryside of south-west Cork in search of a bottle. But in fact he never recovered from what he had been through, unlike the indomitable Doty. When she and Bandon left for England a couple of days later, he was a broken man.

The truce brought a general sense of relief; Dublin Horse Show, which opened on 9 August, had something of its pre-war 'charm and vivacity'.[27] But when the Anglo-Irish Treaty was signed on 6 December, with Robert Barton as one of the signatories, setting up an Irish Free State as independent of Britain as Canada or Australia, most of the loyalists felt misgivings. The Treaty contained few of the safeguards for the loyalist minority which de Valera and Griffith had agreed with Midleton and his colleagues before the truce.

Apart from the question of safeguards, there were many who, like Lady Alice Howard, regarded the Treaty as a betrayal. 'The Government have given over everything to the rebels and they are to govern Ireland entirely,' she wrote in her diary on 10 December. 'Too dreadful – with only a nominal oath of allegiance to the King.' And on the last day of 1921, she wrote: 'England has cast us off and given us to the murderers.'[28]

Both sides admired the antirrhinums

— *I* —

Whatever the misgivings of diehards like Lady Alice, the moderates felt hopeful when, in January 1922, the British army left and Dublin Castle was formally handed over to the Provisional Government of the Free State under Arthur Griffith and Michael Collins, the glamorous young generalissimo of the IRA which was now the Free State Army. The constitution still had to be drawn up, and Griffith promised the former Unionists that their position would be adequately safeguarded. Lord Mayo and other leaders of the former Unionists met on 19 January and passed a resolution in support of the Provisional Government.

Meanwhile the Ascendancy was enjoying a Christmas season the likes of which had not been seen since before the war. The Meath and Kildare Hunt Balls were both held for the first time since 1914; Lord Mayo, though over seventy, danced vigorously at the latter. At Leopardstown on St Stephen's Day Lord and Lady FitzAlan and their son and daughter were present in the Viceregal stand which was decorated with 'a bronze plush drapery gorgeously embroidered in gold'.[1] Although the old regime at Dublin Castle ended with a children's fancy dress ball given there in January just before the transfer of power, the Lodge remained Viceregal with Lord FitzAlan continuing to reign over the infant Free State as well as over Northern Ireland. In January the FitzAlans gave a house party which included Lord Midleton and the new Lord Ormonde, who had succeeded his brother in 1919, together with Lady Ormonde and their son and daughter-in-law Lord and Lady Ossory. The Ossorys now lived at Kilkenny Castle since the Ormondes, who were no longer young when they succeeded, preferred to remain at their house in England.

While most of the entertaining that Christmas took place in and around Dublin,

The last social function at Dublin Castle under the old regime: a children's fancy dress ball held in January 1922, just before the transfer of power.

Family group at Curraghmore on the occasion of Lord Waterford's coming-of-age at the beginning of 1922. The young Marquess stands with his mother, his two brothers, Lord William and Lord Hugh Beresford (right), his three sisters, Lady Blanche, Lady Katharine and Lady Patricia Beresford, and his stepfather Lord Osborne de Vere Beauclerk (afterwards Duke of St Albans), who is on the extreme right.

the chief social event was in the South. This was the coming-of-age of Lord Waterford, which was celebrated with a week of festivities at Curraghmore, including a dance and a luncheon for no fewer than 154 employees of the estate who presented the young Marquess with a massive ormolu clock. In his reply to the speeches of congratulations, Lord Waterford thanked everybody who had helped the estate to keep going through difficult times. While regretting that abnormal taxation and the rise in wages forced them to do things on a greatly reduced scale, he nevertheless hoped and trusted that the old place would long survive. They had, he said, been through troublesome times, but he thanked God that the outlook was now brighter and he hoped that a new Ireland would arise in which, forgetting all differences of politics and religion, men would have one ideal to work for, namely the good of their country.

There was tumultous applause and the young Marquess's health was drunk 'with an enthusiasm that is somewhat rare in these days'.[2]

While Lord Waterford faced the future with confidence, his kinsman Major John de la Poer, who lived at Gurteen le Poer, a nineteenth-century Tudor-baronial mansion in the Suir valley some twelve miles to the north-west of Curraghmore, felt less optimistic. At forty, de la Poer belonged to the generation of Irish landowners whose lives stood to be most affected by the change of regime. Whereas men of the generation of Mayo and Barnie Castletown had lived out their lives under the Union and those of Waterford's age were entering manhood under the Free State, de la Poer was old enough to have become a person of consequence under the old dispensation and young enough not to wish to be relegated to the sidelines under the new. He was the Lieutenant for County Waterford, but the public duties attendant on that office had mostly ceased, though in February his wife Patricia was deputed by Lady FitzAlan to collect in the county in order that Princess Mary might receive a wedding present from the 'Women of Ireland'. She managed to raise £22: 'considering the present state of the country, this is not bad,' her husband observed in his diary.[3]

But while Major de la Poer did not miss the duties of his Lieutenancy all that much, being happy enough living quietly with his wife and children at Gurteen, farming and making a water garden, the peace of his existence was being disturbed by men calling themselves the IRA who demanded a levy of £100 from him, and who, when he told them that he did not have it to give them, drove away fourteen of his cattle. They came again and threatened to sell the cattle if he did not pay, and when he told them that he had written to the Provisional Government asking if the levy was authorized, they said they did not recognize the Provisional Government. 'It is very hard to know where one stands with several bodies of men who claim to be the proper government of the country,' he wrote in February. He heard that cattle had also been taken from his two neighbours on the other side of Clonmel,

Major John de la Poer.

Gurteen le Poer, County Waterford.

Lord Donoughmore and John Bagwell of Marlfield, and that motor cars were being purloined. 'If this sort of work is allowed to go on, this country will be no place to live in,' he lamented.[4]

De la Poer's troubles were symptomatic of those afflicting the Free State as a whole during the early months of 1922. On the one hand, the Provisional Government was as yet unable to enforce its writ all over the country; thus de la Poer mentions how a detachment of Free State troops in smart uniforms appeared in Clonmel, but returned to Cahir without having done anything to combat the prevailing lawlessness. And what was more serious, a part of the Irish nation, led by de Valera, was opposing the Treaty settlement on the grounds that it had not produced the all-Ireland Republic for which people had fought. De Valera had the support of a section of the army, troops who continued to call themselves the IRA but were generally known as Republicans or Irregulars.

In March de la Poer left for London, where he attended the Committee of Privileges of the House of Lords which was considering his claim to the sixteenth-century Barony of Le Power and Coroghmore. This peerage had been dormant ever since the senior branch of the family, from which Lord Waterford was descended in the female line, became extinct in the male line at the beginning of the eighteenth century; de la Poer now claimed it as the senior heir-male. The committee decided that he had proved his claim but for the outlawry of a Jacobite ancestor, which would need to be reversed by Act of Parliament. It was in anticipation of becoming an Irish peer that de la Poer did not use the Papal title of Count which he had inherited from his father.

After this lordly interlude, de la Poer returned home to the grim realities of the Irish situation. On 22 April a party of men came to Gurteen in search of arms; a week later the railway beyond Carrick-on-Suir was maliciously torn up. With Irregulars occupying the Four Courts in Dublin in defiance of the Government, the country was in a state of civil war, though the Government was still reluctant to start full-scale military operations against former comrades.

— *2* —

'Excuse me disturbing your Lordship, but the Republicans have taken the Castle.'

George Ossory's first impulse was to tell his butler that that was no excuse for calling him at the unreasonable hour of 5.30 on this May morning. Instead, he dressed quickly and went downstairs to investigate. He remembered that he had heard the sound of rifle-fire coming from the opposite side of Kilkenny during the

Lord and Lady Ossory in the courtyard of Kilkenny Castle.

night; over the past two years he had grown accustomed to such noises.

In the courtyard, he found 'a heterogeneous body of men, about twenty-two in number, dressed in plain clothes, standing by a pile of machine guns, Lewis-guns, rifles, boxes of ammunition and a couple of bombs.' One of the men, having ascertained that George was the 'Boss', informed him that he was the 'Commandant' and had orders from his superior officer to 'defend' the Castle.

George asked whether he and his wife and the servants were to consider themselves prisoners.

'We would not like to be disturbing Herself or your Lordship at all.'

Having gone back upstairs, George talked things over with his wife Sybil. He felt that if they and the servants were to leave the Castle, it would, in all probability be looted and burnt. If they stayed, their lives would be in danger, but they would have 'a slight chance' of saving the Castle from 'fire and robbery'. Sybil suddenly made up both their minds.

'Let's stay and see it through.'

George collected the three menservants and the seven women and informed them of Sybil's and his decision, telling them that if they wished to leave they should go at once, before the siege began. They all wished to stay. Then, having crossed the street to the estate office to put the family jewels in the safe-keeping of his agent, he chose two rooms facing into the courtyard near the gateway as a refuge for Sybil and himself and her Pekinese. The servants established themselves in the coal cellar on the other side of the courtyard.

By now, the rifle fire which George had heard in the night and which came from the attacking Free State troops, had started up again much closer. The Republicans had mounted a machine-gun in each of the towers and another in the passage immediately outside the Ossorys' quarters. The firing grew more intense and the Castle returned fire; for the rest of the morning a battle raged. Every now and then 'a tinkle of glass and a loud smack' told the Ossorys that 'another window had been smashed and that the bullet had lodged in something, whether pictures, furniture, china or merely ceiling or wall'.

At lunch time there was a lull in the firing and one of the menservants appeared with a tray of bread and cold meat. After they had eaten, the Ossorys took the air in the courtyard, and he went to see how the servants were getting on in their coal cellar. They returned to their quarters just before several Free State machine guns opened fire at the nearby tower; there were now two Republican guns firing back from the passage outside their door and for twenty minutes they were deafened and nearly choked by cordite fumes. When, by teatime, the firing had died down, a Republican poked his head through their door. 'I hope Herself is not frightened?'

They assured him that they were quite used to wars.

The firing started up again and George and Sybil passed the rest of the evening playing bezique on the floor and trying to calm the terrified Peke. By edging his way round the courtyard, George was able to reach the larder from which he returned with half a chicken; he and Sybil then made their way along the passage, jumping kangaroo-fashion past each window, and reached their bedrooms in the tower which were undamaged since they faced into the courtyard. Sybil's sitting room, which faced the other way, was in a sorry state, the floor thick with broken glass and fallen plaster and fragments of valuable Royal Worcester china. Before they went to bed the Commandant came to see them; 'two large and wicked-looking revolvers' hung from his belt. He told them that he had put a sentry over them outside their door and that on no account were they to turn on the electric light.

At about six next morning, after not much sleep, they were aroused by 'the now familiar sound of firing'. Before they could get dressed a messenger from the Commandant told them to go immediately to their refuge of the previous day as their bedroom was needed for a machine-gun position. So they went back along the passage, carrying their remaining garments as well as soap, sponges and towels and the Pekinese. After a morning of continuous firing, during which Sybil had a narrow escape when a bullet passed through the bathroom near their quarters where she was washing, they decided to migrate to the opposite corner of the Castle, which was nearer the kitchen. This entailed crawling along a stone passage carrying various necessaries and accompanied by the Peke, but they managed to reach their goal, which was the anteroom to the drawing room. From here George was able to go down to the kitchen and bring back bread and Stilton as well as two syphons and a bottle of port. He also inspected the damage in the drawing room and the picture gallery, both of which had suffered badly. In the picture gallery, many of the paintings were riddled by bullets and the parquet floor was covered with broken glass from the windows and skylight.

While they were settling into their new quarters, the Ossorys were visited by a now somewhat subdued Commandant, who told them with 'too frequent a repetition of a certain adjective' that the Castle was surrounded and would soon be taken by storm. George advised him to surrender at once in order to save his men, but he said that it would be as much as their lives were worth if they surrendered before every round was fired. So George 'urged him to tell his men to loose off the rest of their ammunition as quickly as possible'.

At about seven that evening the firing livened up again and the Ossorys heard a deafening crash, followed by the noise of splintering wood and wild cheering. They rushed to a window in time to see the gate being charged by a Free State armoured car, which drove triumphantly into the courtyard followed by a party of yelling and cheering Free State soldiers. The Republicans surrendered and the Free State General, a returned Irish-American, came upstairs and shook hands warmly with George and Sybil, telling them how pleased he was to meet them and how proud he was to have 'rescued' them. Later that evening, when the Ossorys tried to cross the street to the estate office to send telegrams to their relations, they were almost overwhelmed by a crowd of cheering townspeople who seized them by the hand and showered prayers and blessings on them. The defeated Republicans, before they were marched off to the County Gaol, also insisted on shaking hands with the 'Boss and his Lady'.[5]

— *3* —

The state of civil war extended to Northern Ireland, where ever since the beginning of 1922 a campaign of violence had been waged by Republican irregulars both from within the six counties and from across the Border; Sir James Craig and his Government were finding it hard to combat, even with the help of British troops. In February, Irregulars from Monaghan had invaded Tyrone and Fermanagh, carrying off a number of well-to-do Unionists as hostages for the release of Republican prisoners. One of those taken was the seventy-seven-year-old Anketell Moutray of Favour Royal, a DL for County Tyrone, who got his own back on his captors by singing 'God Save the King' and some of the Penitential Psalms in their ears until it seemed that their ear drums would split; neither appeals, nor commands nor even threats of death could make him desist.

In May there was a campaign of arson in which several country houses perished, including Shane's Castle, Lord O'Neill's family home on the shores of Lough Neagh in County Antrim. The raiders, who are believed to have crossed the Lough in boats, surrounded the castle in the early morning, and while some of them got to work with the burning, others held up the estate employees with revolvers; the carpenter was shot in the hip. The pantry-boy was ordered to bring large quantities of petrol to the castle from the petrol store. Lord O'Neill, who was eighty-two and unable to move without assistance, had to be carried out; he was seen to be deeply affected as he and Lady O'Neill sat watching their home go up in flames.

Lord and Lady O'Neill took refuge with the agent of the Shane's estate, George Young, and his wife at their house near Randalstown. Young was a landowner himself and a DL; he commuted between Randalstown and Culdaff, his family home near Malin Head in County Donegal, now on the Free State side of the Border. A few days after Shane's was burnt, a party of Irregulars broke into the hall of Culdaff at 1.30 in the morning, awakening the cook and the housemaid and Mrs Young's elderly lady companion Miss Clarke, who were the only people living in the house at the time. The leader of the party, who was in uniform, told Miss Clarke that she could take out her belongings, and asked her if there was anything else she specially valued. She asked if they would remove the pictures which, having been warned in advance of the raid, she had already had taken down from the walls. The men helped her to carry them out; she was also able to rescue the silver and Young's private papers, which she had packed up the day before.

The raiders then ordered the yard man to get Young's two motor cars ready, and they loaded them with all the blankets and linen from the house, together with any clothes and boots which they could find. They also took away a pair of guns and a gramophone and records, and they brought out the contents of the wine cellar, most of which they drank on the spot. They then set fire to the house. When the villagers, seeing the blaze, came up to try and help put it out, they drove them away at pistol-point.

Two days later the raiders returned and took away a horse and several chickens, as well as doing some damage to the garden. To make matters worse, the place was overrun with sightseers who came in charabancs and carried off anything they could remove. The Free State police at Carndonagh, a village five miles away, could do nothing; they did not even interfere when they saw Young's two motors, full of loot, standing outside the local Republican headquarters. The pictures and silver rescued through Miss Clarke's foresight were, however, safe, having been stored in the dining room of the parish priest.

During the days following the burning of Culdaff, the man at the gate lodge kept sending telegrams to comfort Young, who was still at Randalstown. 'Don't be worried . . . Things in garden not so bad as at first thought . . . Things looking brighter . . . Servants here all well . . . Bobby working in garden giving out milk as usual.' It was also of some comfort to Young and his wife to hear that the raiders were not local men but had come from another part of Ireland. In fact the local Republicans came to Culdaff a few days after the burning to protect the place, albeit somewhat belatedly. Their leader told Young's manager that the looting was contrary to orders and had been done without his knowledge; he said that the horse and probably also the motors and the blankets would be returned. 'I gather that there was no animus towards yourself,' the manager told Young in a letter. 'While not believing all he says, I feel sure that the fellow means to do his best.'[6]

– *4* –

Fortified by the results of the recent general election, which showed a decisive majority in favour of the Treaty, the Provisional Government of the Free State began waging full-scale war on the Republicans on 28 June. Dublin was cleared of them after a week of heavy fighting in which the Four Courts and the Public Record Office were blown up and much of what the 1916 Rising had spared of Sackville Street – now called O'Connell Street – was destroyed. Lady Alice Howard mentioned the destruction in her diary on 7 July, adding: 'Valera has escaped.'[7] Like many of the Ascendancy in those days, she refused to give the Republican leader the aristocratic 'de'.

During July and August, the Free State forces gradually cleared the Republicans out of Waterford, Limerick, Cork, Clonmel and other places which they had occupied. At the time of the fighting round Waterford, there was an engagement between Free State troops and Republicans in the demesne of Whitfield Court, the home of Lord Waterford's aunt Lady Susan Dawnay, who was away at the time.* 'There was a battle on the lawn this morning,' the gardener reported in a letter to lady Susan. 'There were no casualties and both sides greatly admired your Ladyship's antirrhinums.'[8]

During those two months, people who happened to be behind the Republican lines were completely cut off from the outside world, with no telephones, telegrams or posts, and no road or railway communications owing to the blowing up of bridges. The Castletowns were cut off at Doneraile for a fortnight, living on rabbits and duck. Viscountess Gormanston found herself cut off by Republican troops on 29 June, while she and her four children were staying near Bansha in County Tipperary with her mother Lady Butler, the famous painter of military subjects. 'The boredom of the days that followed is past the telling,' she says in her memoirs. 'No one dared use cars, our nearest neighbours were the mountains, the weather was disgracing the name of summer. One had literally nothing to do but go for very circumscribed walks under an umbrella and read, read, read.'[9] It did not help matters when her eldest small boy came out with measles; a doctor was able to come and see him, but had his car commandeered at pistol-point on his way home. Needless to say, the rest of the children then caught the measles one after the other.

It was nearly six weeks before the noise of battle heralded the approach of the Free State troops, during which time the only bright moments were when the butcher turned up with some fresh meat and when an enterprising newsagent brought them papers which he had obtained by bicycling to a railway station twenty miles away. After the Free State troops had cleared the village, three Republican stragglers came to Lady Butler's house and demanded food, which they were given in the servants' hall. Lady Gormanston went to talk to them; they were polite enough, but it worried her when one of them took a bomb from his pocket and began rolling it about the table among the plates. '*Please* put that back into your pocket,' she urged.

''Tis all right, miss. Yer could play ball wid it yerself and no harm so long as yer didn't pull this pin out.'[10]

The town of Birr was cut off for some weeks in July when it was held by Republican forces. At that time, the fifteen-year-old Lord Rosse – whose father had died of his wounds in 1918 – and the rest of the family were away. The agent, Toler Garvey – one of those agents like Penrose-FitzGerald who were important county figures in their own right – organized a Citizens' Committee to regulate food supplies and generally safeguard the interests of the townspeople. When the Free State troops were approaching, Garvey heard to his dismay that the Republicans intended to burn the Castle before they evacuated the town, but while the military barracks went up in flames, the Castle was spared. 'The place is

* As Lady Susan Beresford, she appears in the illustration on page 88.

now occupied by Government troops and I can feel easy once again as to its safety,' Garvey wrote on 22 July. For the time being, Lord Rosse and his family were particularly fortunate in that the Free State troops were in the stable yard and not in the Castle itself.[11]

The Republicans were inclined to burn country houses after they had occupied them, to prevent them from being subsequently occupied by Free Staters. At the beginning of June they seized Mitchelstown Castle; poor Willie Webber, now nearly ninety, had to take refuge in a house in the square outside the Castle gates. They stayed there until the middle of August; then as the Free State forces were approaching, they evacuated the Castle, burning it as they moved out. They then retreated westwards and seventy of them, mostly very young men, occupied Bowen's Court. Henry Bowen and his second wife were away, so was Elizabeth, but the staff had heard that the Republicans were coming and had removed the family portraits and other valuables to a cottage at the end of the woods.

Having made preparations to blow the house up in case of surprise attack, the Republicans went to sleep, for they were very tired. The leaders lay on the springs of the beds, from which the bedding had gone; the rest lay on the floor. When they woke up, they read; their favourite literature being the works of Kipling, of which they found a complete set in the house, bound in flexible scarlet leather. Mrs Conroy, the caretaker, found them very quiet.

On the third or fourth day after the Republicans arrived, when they were out on their daily reconnaissance, Henry Bowen's sister Sarah descended on the house. As a young girl in the 1870s, she had braved her father's wrath rather than collect the rents of tenants who had difficulty in paying; now, as a formidable elderly spinster, she was fully prepared to brave the Republicans. She was on her way from Cork to Mitchelstown, where she lived; her train had gone no further than Mallow, owing to the destruction of a bridge, and she had been obliged to take an outside car. Rather than have to pay the car-man to drive her all the way to Mitchelstown, she had decided to stop at Bowen's Court, stay the night there and borrow the pony trap to take her on to Mitchelstown next day. When she arrived to find the house shuttered and the hall door barred, she was, in her own words, put out.

After Sarah Bowen had knocked and tugged at the bell for some time, Mrs Conroy peered through a crack in the door and told her that the Republicans were in the house and that she had better fly. She 'replied that that was nonsense: this was her brother's house'. She demanded that the Republican leaders should come and see her at once; when Mrs Conroy told her that the Republicans were all out she entered the house and said she would wait. Having ordered her room to be got ready for her, she went round picking up the volumes of Kipling.

The Republicans never came back.[12]

Sarah Bowen was convinced that the men got wind of her presence and did not return either through timidity or 'nice feeling'. Certainly the IRA in the earlier Troubles and both sides in the Civil War showed a respect for the womenfolk of the Ascendancy; apart from Winifred Barrington and Mrs Blake, whose deaths were unintentional, the only one to lose her life at the hands of the IRA was Mrs John Lindsay, who was kidnapped and shot in County Cork in 1921 for having passed information to the military. Raiders were often subjected to plain speaking by 'Herself', and they put up with it. A Republican, standing guard over a peer's daughter while her house in County Louth was burning, asked her if she was afraid of his gun, to which she retorted: 'No, I'm much more afraid of your fleas!' And when Republicans came to Killadoon in County Kildare and asked Henry Clements and his wife for accommodation, Mrs Clements moved the servants into the guest rooms, and put the Republicans into the servants' rooms.

Unexpected guests of this sort turned up at many country houses during the Civil War. Seventeen Republicans came to Gurteen one night at eleven; they slept in the servants' hall and had breakfast, tea and dinner the next day. 'It is anything but a pleasant experience to have one's house invaded like this, and to see armed men all about the place,' Major de la Poer wrote in his diary. 'However, I must say they have behaved very well and not tried to enter any other part.'[13] Another lot came three weeks later: 'My life here is one of continual anxiety,' de la Poer lamented.[14] The anticipation of these nocturnal visitors – the worry as to what each night would bring – was often worse than the visitors themselves. Not everyone had such strong nerves as Tom Ponsonby who, when Republicans broke into Kilcooley one night, pulled out the main fuse so as to plunge the house into darkness, put on rubber-soled shoes and played hide-and-seek with the raiders. After an hour they could stand it no longer and left.

During the course of that summer, Lord Massy's son and heir Hamon was raided two or three times at Killakee in the Dublin Mountains, where his grandfather used to entertain large shooting parties before 1914. Towards midnight on 19 July, a day after the telephone wires had been cut and their car taken, Hamon Massy and his wife were getting undressed in their bedroom when they heard footsteps on the gravel outside. Massy opened the window and shouted: 'Hello, who is there?'

A man answered, saying that he wished to see him.

Massy went downstairs, carrying a small hand lamp, for there was no electricity in the house. The man, whom he did not know, demanded money, so he opened the safe in the study and gave him £5. This did not satisfy the intruder who would not go; Massy tried to get him out of the house and his wife, hearing shouting, came downstairs and asked the man not to frighten the baby.

The man answered her abusively and then went for Massy, who had taken a

Killakee, the seat of the Massy family in the Dublin Mountains.

revolver out of a drawer. Massy fired a shot over his head, but the man caught hold of Massy's legs. There was a struggle; another shot rang out and the intruder fell mortally wounded.

Massy, who had not intended to shoot to kill or even to wound, was deeply distressed. He sent for the doctor and the priest. In the study, lit only by the small hand lamp, his wife prayed over the dying man.[15]

The 1922 Horse Show took place in beautiful weather and the entries were up on the previous year, but the horses entered from the North were unable to get any nearer to Ballsbridge than Dundalk, which was in Republican hands. Around Horse Show Week there were the usual race meetings as well as Sir Stanley Cochrane's polo tournament, but there had to be some changes in the programme owing to the death of Arthur Griffith on 12 August.

Griffith's death, and that of Michael Collins, which occurred ten days later in an ambush in his native county of Cork, caused dismay in the Ascendancy world where sympathies were overwhelmingly with the Free State against the Republicans. But if the Ascendancy as a whole supported the Free State, there were a few notable Ascendancy figures on the Republican side. Erskine Childers was out with Republican forces in Munster; Constance Markievicz, having toured the United States earlier in the year in an effort to obtain American recognition of an Irish Republic, was now also with Irregulars in the South. Albinia Brodrick was

Mrs Hamon
Massy at the races.

taken prisoner by Free State troops at Kenmare, but escaped down knotted sheets from a third-storey window. Later, in order to warn a South Kerry Republican column of an impending attack, she deliberately drew the Free State fire, receiving a wound in the hip that was to keep her in hospital for six months.

Lord Killanin's brother-in-law Captain Gray Wynne, of a prominent County Sligo family, was unusual in preferring the Republicans to the Free Staters while being himself a Unionist. The Republicans, his wife afterwards maintained, 'had the courage of their convictions' and 'appeared better disciplined than the Free State Army'.[16] It seems that the Wynnes were unfortunate, having been raided for arms at eight in the morning by Free State troops the worse for drink.

The County Sligo Republicans also made a good impression on the Ascendancy when they took over the stewarding of a point-to-point, in which Lord Caledon's brother, Herbrand Alexander, and Captain Delmege's son, Hugh, were among the riders; with strict impartiality the Republicans disqualified two competitors for cheating. On the other hand, when Free State troops occupied Markree Castle, Bryan Cooper's family home in the same county, they did more than £10,000 worth of damage. Furniture disappeared to nearby military camps, books from the magnificent library were thrown in heaps on the floor, their covers wrenched off, their priceless coloured plates torn and scribbled upon.

By the end of August 1922 the Republicans had been more or less beaten in the field, but they were able to carry on a guerilla campaign for some months to come and country houses continued to be burnt. A casualty of about this time was Currygrane, the home of James Mackay Wilson, whose brother the Field-Marshal had been assassinated by Irish Republicans in London towards the end of June.

MacEoin, now a Free State General and a Member of the Dail, was unable to protect the house against the Irregulars.

At Gurteen, the nocturnal visits by Republicans wanting to be put up continued all through the autumn, while the wood on the Tipperary side of the river was being 'slowly but surely cut down' without Major de la Poer being in any way able to prevent this. 'I see no end to it and the country is every day going from bad to worse,' he wrote on 4 November. 'The end of it will be that as far as I am concerned, I shall leave the country, much as it would go to my heart to do so.'[17]

On 24 November the Provisional Government showed its teeth by executing Erskine Childers on a charge of illegally bearing arms. He had been captured by Free State troops at Glendalough House in County Wicklow, the home of his cousin Robert Barton, who had never been happy about signing the Treaty.

While Glendalough was mourning for Childers, other Wicklow country houses mourned for Lady Alice Howard, whose death, the result of a chill, took place within a few days of his. Arriving for the funeral, her nephew saw her sister Caroline standing on the hall door steps, the last survivor of the three, alone in the world at the age of eighty-five. But it was with triumph, rather than with sorrow, that she greeted him.

'It's *my* Motor now.'[18]

− 5 −

At the beginning of December the new Constitution came into force; the Provisional Government, now led by the courageous and statesmanlike William T. Cosgrave, who had succeeded Griffith, became the first Government of the Free State. FitzAlan left and the place of the Viceroy was taken in the Free State by a Governor-General and in Northern Ireland by a Governor. The first Governor-General of the Free State was the veteran Nationalist politician and lawyer Tim Healy. The first Governor of Northern Ireland was the Duke of Abercorn; as Northern Ireland's resident Duke, who had done much for the cause of Ulster Unionism and was the grandson of a Viceroy of Ireland, he was the obvious choice.*

The constitutional safeguards for the former Unionists fell far short of what Griffith had promised at the beginning of the year, in spite of discussions held in London in May and June between him and Midleton, Jameson and others. In fairness to Griffith it must be said that with Ireland in a state of civil war and many

---

* See illustration on page 140.

of his own followers having second thoughts about the Treaty, for him to have given the former Unionists all he had promised them six months earlier would have put the Treaty settlement into jeopardy. And by the end of 1922 some of the loyalist leaders, notably Jameson and Ralph Wicklow, had come to the conclusion that the goodwill of their fellow countrymen was a more valuable safeguard than anything written into the constitution.

Midleton and his colleagues had obtained some concessions with regard to the composition and powers of the Free State Senate, which was not, however, the strong Second Chamber they had hoped for. The Ascendancy was very well represented in the original Senate, which met on 11 December. For while out of the thirty elected Senators only four or five were of Ascendancy background – notably George Moore's brother Colonel Maurice Moore – out of the thirty nominated by Cosgrave, no fewer than twenty came from, or were closely associated with, the Ascendancy. They included Lords Headfort, Granard, Mayo, Wicklow and Dunraven; Lord Desart's philanthropic Jewish sister-in-law Ellen Lady Desart; Horace Plunkett, Andrew Jameson, Yeats, Captain Greer of the

Lord Headfort and General Sir Bryan Mahon arriving at the Senate.

Yeats arriving at the Senate.

National Stud, John Bagwell of Marlfield and the former Nationalist MP Sir Thomas Grattan Esmonde. Cosgrave's nominations also included General Sir Bryan Mahon, who having been General Commanding the Forces in Ireland for two years after the 1916 Rising – during which period he had handled many difficult situations with tact – settled in 1921 at Mullaboden, a country house in County Kildare belonging to his wife. Since then he had been prominent among the stalwarts who helped to keep Irish racing alive during the troubled years.

Joining the Senate required some courage; on 30 November Liam Lynch, Chief of Staff of the Republican forces, had ordered that the houses of all Senators should be burnt. The houses of 'Imperialists (ex-DL type)' were also to be included in the holocaust,[19] but Senators were singled out for attack. The guerilla war between the forces of the Free State and the Republicans went on all through that winter and the following spring.

By 23 December Major de la Poer reckoned that he and his wife had put up a total of 103 Republicans for the night, not counting those who just came for food. More came on the night of Christmas Eve. 'I wonder how much longer I shall be able to stand it,' he wrote on Christmas Day, when he and his wife and children were not even able to go to Mass, the bridge being broken and the river too swollen to be safely crossed in a boat. However, they managed to make the day 'as cheery as possible for the children and they enjoyed themselves'.[20]

As the guerilla warfare continued, so did the lawlessness. On the first Sunday of 1923, Walter Joyce of Corgary in County Galway, who had been boycotted in 1908, was shot and mortally wounded as he was bicycling down his avenue on his way to Mass. Another country house under the shadow of violent death in January 1923 was Birr Castle; there, however, it was no agrarian murder but the execution in the Castle grounds of three Republican prisoners by the Free State troops who now occupied part of the Castle itself as well as the stable yard. The bodies of the three men executed were buried in 'the old laundry drying ground close to the gravel tennis court'; Toler Garvey 'wrote at once on behalf of the Trustees protesting against this having been done in private grounds and requesting that the bodies be re-interred elsewhere'.[21]

January also saw the start of the campaign of burning Senators' houses, in accordance with Liam Lynch's threat, one of the first to suffer being Marlfield. As though this were not enough, the unfortunate John Bagwell was kidnapped three weeks later, though he managed to escape from his captors after a couple of days. Other houses where Lynch's threat was carried out included Palmerstown, Kilteragh, Moore Hall, Mullaboden and Ballynastragh, the ancestral seat of the Esmondes in County Wexford. There was also an attempt to blow up Castle Forbes, Lord Granard's family home in County Longford, with a land-mine, but although very extensive damage was caused, it was not irreparable.

A land-mine was also used in the first place at Kilteragh, and while the house was badly damaged it was not destroyed. Horace Plunkett was away at the time in the United States; when he received the cable telling him what had happened, he said: 'It is not so sad as if it had been a poor man's one-roomed house.'[22] After the explosion, Free State troops were sent to guard the house against further attack; unfortunately they did not stay long enough and the moment they had gone the raiders, who had been watching their chance, moved in again with petrol cans to complete the work of destruction.

When Palmerstown was burnt, Lord Mayo was asked if he would now go and live in England or elsewhere. 'No,' he replied firmly. 'I will not be driven from my own country.' He added that he would not even leave his ruined home, but that he and Lady Mayo would live in the servants' wing, which had survived the fire.[23] As might be expected, George Moore took the burning of Moore Hall less philosophically. When he heard about it, he said: 'Ireland is not a gentleman's country.'[24]

Towards the end of February, raiders from County Tipperary set fire to Desart Court. The seventy-four-year-old Lord Desart, who was in London at the time, hurried over on the night boat to find that the beautiful house he loved was now a burnt-out shell. There was some furniture heaped on the lawn, saved by a courageous housemaid, but everything else of value was lost, including the family portraits and papers. A month later, the van and lorry taking the things rescued from Desart to Kilkenny railway station were stopped on the road by armed men and set on fire, so that even the little that was saved out of Lord Desart's family home was reduced to ashes.

Poor Lord Desart was only the brother-in-law of a Senator; however, the burnings during those early months of 1923 were not confined to Senators' houses. Bessborough was burnt on the same night as Desart, but Lord Bessborough's splendid collection of family portraits had been safely removed to England beforehand. As the glow from Bessborough lit up the sky, Lord Mayo's two nephews, Captain Richard Wyndham-Quin and his brother Valentine, stood on the steps of the neighbouring great house, which was then their parents' home, and said to one another: 'They'll be coming here next.'[25] But they did not come, even though the Wyndham-Quins, as well as being related to Mayo, were cousins of Lord Dunraven who was also a Senator; Lord Dunraven's own house, Adare Manor in County Limerick, likewise escaped. There was, however, an attempt to burn Glin Castle, the home of Dunraven's son-in-law the Knight of Glin, though the raiders were three local men and may have had nothing to do with the campaign against Senators. When the men arrived, the Knight, who was paralysed as a result of a stroke which he had suffered in 1914, refused to move. He remained in his wheelchair in the study, successfully resisting all attempts to put him out,

Punchestown, April 1923. Edward Kennedy escorting Tim Healy, the recently-appointed Governor General of the Irish Free State.

until the incendiaries, not wanting him to be burnt to death in his own castle, called off the burning and left.

On 17 April, soon after midnight, there was a fearful hammering on the hall door of Gurteen. 'This is the end,' Major de la Poer thought to himself. 'The IRA have come to burn the house.' But this time the nocturnal visitors were Free State soldiers, forty-eight of them; they spent the night, as the Republicans had done, in the servants' hall and next day moved into the stables, where they were to remain for some months.[26] By now, the Republicans were at the end of their tether, having lost several of their leaders, and on 27 April de Valera ordered a cease-fire

The ending of the Civil War was anticipated earlier in April by a Punchestown that was particularly successful, though there had been threats of violence and armed guards were much in evidence. Tim Healy, smiling genially through his beard, was welcomed on his arrival at the course by Edward Kennedy, who had taken over the management of Punchestown after Percy La Touche's death in 1921. The new Ireland was represented by Cosgrave; the honour of the old Ireland was upheld by the gentleman rider Harry Beasley who rode in a race and won it though he was more than seventy years of age. Northern Ireland were represented

Punchestown, April 1923. Lord Mayo
with his nephew, Captain Richard
Wyndham-Quin, whose father was
Lord Dunraven's cousin and heir.

by another septuagenarian sportsman, the Earl of Enniskillen. Lord and Lady
Powerscourt, Lord Kenmare and Sir Timothy O'Brien were among the large
crowd, as well as Lord Mayo and Sir Bryan and Lady Mahon. The Mahons, like
the Mayos, had not allowed the burning of their house to drive them out of their
country, but the burnings had driven out many, including Lord Desart, and the
exodus was by no means confined to those whose houses had been burnt. 'Most of
the people one knew have left already or will go,' Major de la Poer had observed
gloomily in March;[27] though the neighbourhood of Gurteen was not nearly as bad
in this respect as other parts of Ireland.

'No petty people'

— I —

The exodus which had begun in 1919 showed little or no sign of abating after the Civil War ended. There were those who, like Bandon and Desart, left heartbroken, their houses burnt; there were those who escaped the burnings but for whom the disturbances had been more than they could stand; there were the loyalist diehards who did not wish to live in an Ireland no longer part of the United Kingdom. There were those who left because their friends had left and those who left simply because the money had run out. This was the most usual reason for going, the real reason in the case of many who left ostensibly because of the unrest or the loneliness or their dislike of the new Ireland.

Many of those who left were glad to go, like Christopher Lynch-Robinson, last of the RMs and grandson of old Sir Robert Lynch-Blosse of Athavallie. 'I was sick to death of the country and of everything in it, of clever talk, of intellectual posturings and of philosophic radicalism,' he afterwards wrote.[1] The Catholic Mrs Gray Wynne, whose father, old Lord Killanin, had spoken with a brogue, felt even more bitter. 'Where could one live in Ireland now, but in the tragic past of horrors, for the present is also one of gloom?' she wrote, after she and her husband had left Ireland for good. 'All the fun and laughter of olden days is gone, it is unpatriotic to be cheerful, and disloyal to "Ireland as a nation" to be witty.'[2]

Another Catholic, Sir Timothy O'Brien, predicted that the policy of Ireland's new rulers towards the Ascendancy would be to 'squeeze you dry and throw away the empty skin' – the same treatment which, in 1887, Tim Healy had hoped would be accorded to the then Lord Granard by his mortgagee. Sir Timothy eventually moved to London, but there were many loyalists who remained in the Free State while being as pessimistic as he. They continued their dire prophesies even after

1925, by which time Ireland had become one of the most peaceful countries in Europe and the Free State Government had reduced income tax by a shilling in the pound.

Those landowners who had not sold their tenanted land under the Wyndham Act felt badly treated by the new legislation for land purchase, which now became compulsory in the Free State as well as in Northern Ireland. Not only was the purchase price for the tenanted land based on the current rents, which in most cases were about 20 per cent lower than they had been in 1919, but it was paid in low-yielding bonds which could not be sold except below par. Major de la Poer, who regarded the Free State Land Act as 'disastrous to the landlord', mentions an estate which had brought in £7806 a year in 1919, but for which its owner was subsequently compelled to accept only £52,500 in bonds producing a mere £2362 a year.[3]

The Free State authorities also caused ill-feeling over the question of compensation for houses burnt during the recent disturbances. According to the law, people who suffered malicious damage to their property could apply to the courts for compensation which in normal times was charged against the ratepayers but now, owing to the number and extent of the claims, had to be met by the State. The Provisional Government promised that all claims would be paid promptly and in full; moreover the Irish authorities were obliged to follow the recommendations of a Committee set up by the British Government in London to which appeals could be made. But as the total amount claimed greatly exceeded the sum allocated for paying the compensation, claims were scaled down so that they eventually bore little or no relation to the damage suffered. The compensation money was slow in coming and awards were generally conditional on all but a small amount being used for rebuilding. For those who did not wish to rebuild, this condition could be interpreted as spending the money on building anywhere within the Free State, so that it was possible to build urban or suburban houses and then sell them.

After Summerhill was burnt, Colonel William Rowley obtained an estimate for rebuilding from the architect Richard Orpen, brother of the portrait painter. Orpen's figure was £72,540, which did not include any elaborate interior plasterwork or fine chimneypieces such as there had formerly been. Colonel Rowley accordingly put in a claim for £100,000 for the house and £30,000 for the contents, which had been valued for probate in 1919 at £19,297; in September 1921 the Court awarded £65,000 for the house and £11,000 for the contents. This award had to be agreed by the Government Inspectors, who appear to have done nothing about it all through the following year.

Colonel Rowley, who succeeded his nephew as Lord Langford in September 1922, now lived in Middlesex and was personally not in favour of rebuilding

Summerhill. Before deciding finally, he wrote asking the opinion of several cousins who were in remainder to the property after his New Zealander nephew. They all agreed with him. 'Much as I should like to see the old house rebuilt, one must remember that even if this was done you could not put back the old things that formed part of it,' Douglas Rowley wrote from the Riviera, adding that it would be pointless to rebuild for the benefit of the New Zealander and his wife who had never seen the place.

'Living in Ireland would be, for all loyal subjects, quite impossible for many years to come,' Douglas Rowley's brother Arthur wrote from Barcelona, where he

The ruin of Summerhill. Approaching up the avenue, one first became aware that it was a ruin by noticing the daylight showing through the hall door.

was British Consul-General. 'I, personally, have no wish to reside in that unfortunate country.'

Their sister, Mrs Edward Milner, who lived in Nottinghamshire, expressed herself even more forcibly. 'Nothing would induce me to live in Ireland if I was paid to do so, a country of murderers.'[4]

When at last the Inspectors came to a decision in April 1923, they cut the award for the house from £65,000 to £16,775 of which at least £12,000 had to be spent on building a new house in the demesne, or else used towards the rebuilding of the original house. If no building were done, the award would be a derisory £2000. The Inspectors blithely suggested that for £15,250 Lord Langford could build himself a house with drawing room, dining room, library, hall, billiard room and ten bedrooms.

Lord Langford's counsel told the Inspectors that a house such as this could not be built for the sum mentioned and that even if it could it would be 'totally inadequate for the requirements of a person in Lord Langford's position'. Mr Barker of the Irish Compensation Associates in London suggested having a question asked in Parliament. Eventually, after an appeal had been lodged in August 1923, the award for the house was raised to £27,500 with no obligation to build. The award for the contents had already been raised to £14,000 and there was an extra £2000 for 'consequential loss', making a total of £43,500 which was paid early in 1924 and invested in gilt-edged stocks.[5] The ruin of the great Palladian house was left uncared for on its hill.

For the burning of Mitchelstown Castle, a claim in the neighbourhood of £150,000 was put in by Willie Webber and after his death in 1924 by Colonel Alec King-Harman who succeeded to the property. Nearly two years of delays and negotiations brought an award of no more than £27,500, of which £25,000 had to be spent on building, and it was another year again before the money was actually paid. 'The methods of the Government are not much better than those of card-sharpers,' King-Harman remarked bitterly.[6] He tried appealing to the Committee in London, but with no success.

King-Harman, who was a cousin of the Stafford-King-Harmans of Rocking-ham, lived in County Longford at Newcastle, another of the great houses of his family. He did not, therefore, wish to build at Mitchelstown, so was allowed to spend the stipulated sum on building seventeen houses in the suburbs of Dublin. He was no businessman and worried himself sick over such details as the type of basins to be put in, and when he came to sell the houses they each fetched about £300 or £400 less than it had cost him to build them, though subsequent legislation brought a 10 per cent addition to the award which enabled him to recoup his losses.

Most of what remained of the Mitchelstown estate was sold. The ruin of the castle was demolished, the ashlar having been bought by the monks of Mount Melleray for their new church. That garden party of August 1914, after a little more than ten years, seemed to Elizabeth Bowen 'like a dream'; and the castle itself was 'a few bleached stumps on the plateau'.[7]

Some ten miles south of Mitchelstown, the ruin of Convamore continued to stand, the stucco flaking off its façades, the bushes growing up to hide the views of the Blackwater from its sightless windows. Whereas the Convamore demesne had been sold and the Listowels had passed for good from the Irish scene, the young cousin who succeeded Bandon in 1924 kept the lands of Castle Bernard though he did not rebuild the Castle which stood as a ruin. When the new Lord Bandon came here on leave from the Royal Air Force, in which he was making his career, he occupied the cottage where Doty had taken refuge after the burning of the Castle.

While the new Lord Bandon made do with a cottage, others, like Robert Travers's cousin and successor, built new houses to take the place of houses that had been burnt. Others again, like Lord O'Neill, made houses for themselves out of their former stables. Those who actually rebuilt their original houses generally

The ruin of Convamore.

Elizabeth Bowen, with another Irish writer, Sean O'Faolain (left), visiting the ruin of Convamore.

Miss Pamela Pilkington, Lord Desart's great-niece, at Desart in 1926 after the house had been rebuilt by her mother.

did so on a smaller scale. At Glenart, which had been partially burnt in 1921, the surviving part was made into an occasional residence for Colonel Proby and his family when they came here on visits from their English seat. Houses rebuilt more or less as they were included Palmerstown, Marlfield, Mullaboden, Culdaff and Gardenmorris, the home of the Poer O'Shee family in County Waterford which was burnt in 1923. The bathroom fittings for the rebuilt Gardenmorris were obtained in France; as the house was in the style of a French château, it made guests wonder if they had not been magically wafted from County Waterford to Normandy when they found taps labelled chaud and froid.

Another house completely rebuilt was Desart, which Lord Desart, who had no male heir, had handed over to his niece, for whom the work was done. It was finished in 1926, when a tea party was given as a house-warming; soon afterwards a hunt ball was held in the house. While Desart thus came back to life, Bessborough, which had been burnt on the same night, was rebuilt by Lord Bessborough – the former Vere Duncannon – but left unfurnished and never again occupied by the family.*

*His architect for the rebuilding was his friend Harry Goodhart-Rendel, who appears in the photograph of a pre-war house party at Bessborough on page 147.

The Bessboroughs had migrated to Sussex, where they had acquired a fine country seat and were more grandly housed than other expatriates such as the Desarts who had bought a much smaller property in the same county. Lord Desart tried to take an interest in this 'little country place', but when his daughter saw him here one summer evening, discussing the planting of a rock-garden, she 'suddenly noticed the look of great weariness and deep indifference that came over his face. I knew he was thinking of Desart, of the long borders in the kitchen-garden and the great flowery terrace in the sunset. He could not easily become attached to a garden-plot in Sussex.'[8]

If Lord Desart, who was prominent in English public life, and Horace Plunkett, who in Surrey was, if anything, better placed for carrying on his worldwide activities than he had been at Kilteragh, both felt the bitterness of exile, the Ascendancy émigrés of lesser degree who settled in England felt it all the more. Few of them could afford to buy country seats such as they had possessed in Ireland; their names carried little weight in an English county. Those who settled in the country mostly found themselves relegated to that village world of which Lady Naylor in *The Last September* speaks with some distaste, as though subconsciously aware that it was to be her own fate.

> I remember a year ago when I was staying with Anna Partridge in Bedfordshire – she is always so full of doing things in the village, little meetings and so on. Well, I went to one of her meetings and really – those village women sitting round in hats and so obviously despising her!

Many of the expatriates preferred a villa in a south coast resort such as Bournemouth or Eastbourne. Some were happier abroad; Christopher Lynch-Robinson felt more at home in France than he did in England. Among those who went further afield was Lord Carbery, who having sold Castle Freke settled in Kenya. He was now divorced from the beautiful José; there were rumours that when they were in Kenya together, he had whipped her. People on his side maintained that he had been using the whip on some wild beast which had invaded their bedroom and that she had got in the way.

Even further from Ireland was the eccentric Miss Kathleen ffrench of Monivea Castle in County Galway, who lived among the Russian émigrés at Harbin in Manchuria. She felt reasonably at home here being half Russian herself; from her mother she had inherited estates and palaces in Russia where she had lived in preference to Monivea, which was also hers. Having lost all her Russian property in the Revolution and been imprisoned by the Bolsheviks, she had returned to Monivea where her cousin Miss Rozzie ffrench was living; Rozzie gave her a cold reception, feeling that it was thanks to her own popularity in the neighbourhood that the house had escaped being burnt and that the presence of the returned absentee owner would not help matters. So Kathleen said goodbye to her ancestral home and retreated to Harbin.

Hardly any of the loyalists who did not wish to remain in the Free State seem to have thought of moving across the Border into Northern Ireland, where they would have known people and where the old life still went on, a sign, perhaps, of their bitterness over what they regarded as Ulster's betrayal of them. Such migration of Ascendancy as took place within Ireland at this time was mostly from the remoter parts of the country to somewhere nearer Dublin, particularly to the villa belt along the South County Dublin coast. In 1923 Sir Ralph Coote gave up the house which he had built in the Ballyfin deer park only ten years before and moved with his family to a villa at Killiney named Palermo. Most of the Ballyfin estate, which was still more or less intact, was sold to the Land Commission in 1925.

— 2 —

Those of the Ascendancy who continued to live in the Free State gradually accustomed themselves to the changes. Friends and neighbours had gone and so had the British army with its unfailing supply of young officers for hunts, shoots, tennis parties and dances. Lady Gregory tells of how Lady Ardilaun, now 'a lonely figure in her wealth, childless and feeling the old life shattered around her' lamented for 'those nice young officers who used to write their names in our book'.[9] As a sad reminder of the departed garrison, there was the charred skeleton of the military barracks, burnt during the Civil War, which brooded over many a country town such as Fermoy – the original of the barracks where Lois in *The Last September* went dancing. Gone, too, was cricket, except in the Dublin area and in one or two other places, notably Cork, where the Mardyke ground still flourished under the patronage of Sir George Colthurst and, after his death in 1925, of his son and namesake. Na Shuler did not survive the Great War, though it was to have a brief revival in the 1930s.

Though life in the country was now much quieter than it had been, there was plenty of entertaining in some of the surviving great houses. The youthful Lord Rosse, whose interests were artistic rather than scientific, together with his sister and his younger brother, had many of their fellow 'Bright Young Things' to stay with them at Birr. At Headfort, Lord Headfort and the still-beautiful Rosie had a succession of house parties. On the other side of Ireland at Westport, Lord and

The revived Na Shuler, a match at Castlemore, County Carlow, against Mr Hardy Eustace-Duckett's XI. Sitting third from the left is the younger Sir George Colthurst.

Lady Sligo were in residence for only part of the year, coming over from their London house with a dozen English servants, but while they were here they entertained constantly. As most of the county neighbours had gone, they relied for society on house parties of friends from Britain, who came by the mail boat and made the long train journey across Ireland, ending with the Mayo branch line on which all and sundry would invade the first class. If Lord Sligo himself was travelling, the guard would get rid of the intruders with cries of 'Howt with ye, now! Howt ye all get. Shligy's on the train.'[10].

When Tom Ponsonby was expecting guests from England, he would arrange for them to be given a hamper by the station master in Dublin to sustain them on their journey south to Kilcooley. The station master would insist on the Kilcooley guests going first class, even if they had only bought third-class tickets, and he would select a compartment for them with care. 'No, not that one, Ma'am, poor Lord Ashtown, too much of the drink, you know.'[11]

Life at Kilcooley in the 1920s was centred on farming and sport. When the two Ponsonby boys were home from school they would spend their days hunting, walking the bogs after snipe or performing various feats of horsemanship. They

Bright Young Things at Birr in the late 1920s. Lord Rosse with his sister and friends on the roof of the castle.

Yeats at Coole in
the 1920s.

would tether their horses to the ranch fence outside the front of the house – a reminder of their great-uncle Horace Plunkett's days in Wyoming – rush indoors for a quick luncheon and then rush out again and back into the saddle.

One day when the local doctor was expected to luncheon, the boys persuaded the cook to do an oxtail stew, and into the doctor's helping they slipped a small human vertebra which had come from the ruined abbey in the demesne. The doctor must have been exceptionally good at anatomy, for while eating his stew he suddenly went green in the face. Other exploits of the Ponsonby boys included nearly drowning an objectionable tutor in a bog and making General Sir Hubert Gough, of Curragh Mutiny fame, ride a pony which they knew would buck him off.

Certain Irish country houses in the 1920s had the distinction of being visited by Yeats. When he arrived to stay with the Leslies at Glaslough the local 'Fiddler of Dooney' started to play in the hall. 'It was a weekend wreathed in Celtic mist,' Shane Leslie recorded in his diary. 'With sad solemnity Yeats told us that Cuchulain died having in his eyes the secrets of many women.' Shane Leslie also describes how he and his American wife Marjorie encountered Yeats at Muckruss near Killarney which now belonged to a wealthy compatriot of hers. 'Marjorie and I, strolling in the woods, heard what we mistook for a swarm of humming bees. We lay low and the great poet passed us, head in the air mouthing melodious poetry about Byzantium.'[12] The country house where Yeats was most frequently to be found was Coole. Lady Gregory's daughter-in-law Margaret used to say that he came when the sedum was out, the sedum being in flower for most of the year.[13]

— 3 —

Yeats and Lady Gregory were among those who, in the social life of Dublin, served as links between the old Ireland and the new. Such links were far from numerous; Shane Leslie would have been another, only he lived mostly in London. There were the Senators of Ascendancy background; there was Bryan Cooper, who since 1923 had represented his old constituency of South County Dublin in the Dail. There were the young Lord and Lady Longford, who like Lady Gregory were deeply involved in the theatre; thanks to Lord Longford's financial backing, Dublin would soon have a second theatre company.

Most of the Ascendancy, when in Dublin, had no social contacts with the new Irish ruling class, but kept within the pale of the Kildare Street Club, more than ever so now that the Viceregal Court, which had formerly brought them in touch with some of the other Dublin worlds, was a thing of the past. On the face of it, the Club had been remarkably little affected by the upheavals; what it had lost in membership through the exodus and the departure of the military, it had gained through the demise, soon after the Treaty, of the Sackville Street Club. There had, however, been two significant changes in the Kildare Street Club's rules. Since 1922, people living in and around Dublin had been allowed into the Club as guests. Since 1923, new members had been elected by a committee rather than by the Club as a whole, so that candidates were much less likely to be blackballed for political or sectarian reasons. Nevertheless, there was still no question of any of the leaders of the new Ireland becoming members. Perhaps the only two people elected in the 1920s who might not have managed to get in before 1914 were Yeats and the former Nationalist MP Sir Walter Nugent, who, incidentally, joined in 1922, before the system of election was changed. Yeats's politics had modified considerably since his pro-Boer days; Nugent's impeccable family background and his position in the racing world made up for his early defection from the Unionist fold.

Apart from going to the Club, the Ascendancy now tended to think of Dublin purely in terms of the Horse Show and the Spring Show, of Punchestown and other race meetings outside the city but within easy reach of it. During the 1920s, the Horse Show superseded Punchestown as the chief event of the Irish social calendar, particularly after the Aga Khan had presented his trophy for the international jumping competition. At the first of these competitions, the British team – which included two Irishmen, one of them being Sir Timothy O'Brien's son-in-law Captain Edward Boylan – was greeted with tremendous cheers. And when the band struck up 'God Save the King' in the team's honour, the entire Members' Stand rose to its feet and sang the words in chorus – except Lord Longford, who remained seated and kept his hat on until somebody knocked it off. This spontaneous demonstration showed that, in the case of most of the Ascendancy, 'support for the new regime came from the head, not the heart'.[14] The wheel had come full circle since the days when the Ascendancy was Unionist from the dictates of the head but gave its heart to Erin.

The Royal Dublin Society, which ran the Horse Show, provided its members with a club house in its premises adjoining the Showground at Ballsbridge. For many of the widows and unmarried daughters of the Ascendancy who lived in and around Dublin, life was centred on the afternoon pilgrimage to the RDS to read the English newspapers and magazines while sipping tea and nibbling currant cake. The Misses Mary and Theresa Netterville, granddaughters of the penultimate Viscount Netterville, would come here from their 'big damp house' in Killiney. In 1925 their undergraduate nephew Pierce Synnott brought his Oxford friend John Betjeman to tea with them here and the result was a verse:

> 'Netterville! Netterville! Where have you been?'
> 'I've been to Dublin to read *The Queen*.'
> 'Netterville! Netterville! What did you do there?'
> 'I drank some weak tea and sat on a chair.'[15]

While people like the Misses Netterville had no contact at all with the new Ireland, the grandees at any rate met the Free State leaders at the Horse Show, on the racecourse and elsewhere. In particular they met the Governor-General, Tim Healy, who ran Viceregal Lodge with simple dignity. Healy's attitude towards the Ascendancy had greatly mellowed since the days of the Plan of Campaign, when he had spoken so unkindly about the father of Senator the Earl of Granard. When he took Lady Gormanston into supper at a charity ball in Horse Show Week of which she was a patroness, he got on so well with her that towards the end of the meal he was calling her 'Mee dear gurl'.[16] Major de la Poer went to see him about getting the outlawry of his Jacobite ancestor reversed so that he could become Lord Le Power and Coroghmore, the British Government being reluctant to bring in the necessary Bill for fear of constitutional difficulties with the Free State. Healy was 'very nice' and made helpful suggestions;[17] though in the event de la Poer got no further in obtaining his peerage.

In 1928 Healy was succeeded by James McNeill, an Ulster Catholic who cut short a distinguished career in the Indian Civil Service in order to take part in the movement for Irish independence. McNeill and his young and elegant wife did much to bring together the old Ireland and the new during their reign. In the autumn of 1928, when Lady Gregory was staying with them at the Lodge, there was a royal visit, albeit a brief one: Princess Mary and her husband Viscount Lascelles came to breakfast on their way to Portumna, which Lord Lascelles had inherited from the notorious Lord Clanricarde who was his great-uncle.

$$- 4 -$$

In Northern Ireland royal visits were a frequent occurrence and the Duke and Duchess of Abercorn kept up Viceregal state at Government House, Hillsborough, the former seat of the Marquesses of Downshire south of Belfast, a rambling late-Georgian mansion of which one side bore a striking resemblence to Viceregal Lodge. On becoming Governor, Abercorn was made a Knight of St Patrick. Since then no other non-royal Knights had been made, though the British Government had plans to revive the Order and in 1928 approached the Government of the Free State through Lord Granard to find out their reaction, which was unfavourable.

Government House, Hillsborough.

Government House is only one example of how the old Ascendancy world survived north of the Border. County society had not been depleted here as in the Free State – though families left from time to time for financial and other reasons – and there was still a garrison. The Ascendancy kept an official position, continuing to serve as Lieutenants of counties, DLs and JPs, as well as having a certain political influence. The Northern Ireland Government included Edward Archdale of the Castle Archdale family and – until 1926 – Lord Londonderry. Lord O'Neill's surviving son was one of the Northern Ireland MPs at Westminster as well as being Speaker of the Northern Ireland House of Commons, other members of which included the widow of the Marquess of Donegall's cousin Colonel Robert Chichester of Moyola. Lord Dufferin was Speaker of the Northern Ireland Senate.

The Northern Ireland Ascendancy also moved in the Ascendancy world of the Free State; people went south across the Border to race meetings and the Dublin Horse Show; they belonged to the Kildare Street Club as well as to the Ulster Club in Belfast. In the counties along the Border, there were constant comings and goings between Northern Ireland and the Free State to visit neighbours who were now in a different country – the Border separated the Leslies of Glaslough from their neighbours the Caledons and the Stronges of Tynan, though their demesnes actually marched.

While most of the Northerners, secure in their enclave of Unionism, took little or no interest in the new Ireland of the Free State, there were some who strove for better understanding between North and South, among them General Hugh Montgomery of Blessingbourne in County Tyrone, who founded the Irish Association. General Montgomery's father, Hugh de Fellenberg Montgomery, who was a member of the Northern Ireland Senate until his death in 1924 and also a Privy Councillor, had been a staunch opponent of sectarianism, though this had not prevented him from disinheriting his eldest grandson when he became a Catholic. As in the case of Shane Leslie, it was done in an amicable way.

$$- 5 -$$

Although some of the Ascendancy nominated to the original Free State Senate gave scandal by their poor attendance, those of them who took their duties seriously, such as Lord Mayo, Sir Bryan Mahon and Andrew Jameson, made a valuable contribution to the proceedings of the Second Chamber, showing that former Unionists and Nationalists 'could work harmoniously together in

Parliament for the good of their common country'.[18] Donal O'Sullivan, the Clerk of the Senate, himself a Nationalist and a Catholic, pays tribute to them in his book:

> I never knew one who was not, in the most genuine sense, a lover of Ireland, or who regarded Ireland as other than his own country. I never knew one who, at any time, put the interests of England before those of Ireland. And, except for one solitary incident . . . I never knew one who showed a trace of bigotry in the religious sense.[19]

The 'solitary incident' occurred in 1925, when Yeats made what O'Sullivan, rather unfairly, regarded as an attack on the Irish Catholic Church in his speech on the question as to whether or not divorce was to be allowed in the Free State. The speech ended with what O'Sullivan calls 'bombastic references to the superiority of the Ascendancy class', but while Yeats's words are certainly arrogant, and made a bad impression at the time, they are the best panegyric that has ever been spoken on the Ascendancy:

> We are no petty people. We are one of the great stocks of Europe. We are the people of Grattan; we are the people of Swift, the people of Emmet, the people of Parnell. We have created the most of the modern literature of this country. We have created the best of its political intelligence.

In the Dail, where the power lay, the Ascendancy was naturally not so well represented as in the Senate. During the period from 1923 until the end of the decade, there were only about half-a-dozen Deputies from the Ascendancy class. In addition to Bryan Cooper, they consisted of Osmond Esmonde, son of Sir Thomas; Dermot O'Mahony, brother of the ill-fated Pierce Mahony; John Hewson of Castle Hewson in County Limerick; and Richard Wolfe of Forenaghts in County Kildare, a descendant of Theobald Wolfe after whom Wolfe Tone was named. Of this small company, the one who made the greatest impact was undoubtedly Bryan Cooper. He got on well with everybody and enjoyed the political life of the new Ireland, happier in his villa on the Dublin coast, which had the romantic name of Khyber Pass, than at Markree, where he did not begin to make good the damage caused by the Free State troops until 1927, when he restored and modernized part of the castle.

Cooper entered the Dail as an Independent, but supported Cosgrave's Government in any measure which he considered to be for the good of the country. He did a great deal of useful but unobtrusive work in legislation, acting, in the words of his biographer, as 'an invisible mender'.[20] In 1927, after de Valera and his

Bryan Cooper.

followers entered the Dail – having hitherto stayed out owing to their refusal to take the Oath of Allegiance to the King – Cooper saved Cosgrave's Government from being defeated by one vote. He called at the hotel of a Deputy known to be against the Government, a Sligo man like himself, and offered him a drink. In the words of Lord Dunsany, who chronicled the episode, 'The other man did not shirk. Drink for drink they had, with absolute fairness, until Bryan Cooper strode out over his opponent's recumbent body.'[21] Cooper was back in the Dail in time to vote for the Government in the crucial division. Alas, his prowess as a drinker was born of over-indulgence which ruined his health, so that he died at the early age of forty-six in 1930.

The Ascendancy has frequently been criticized for playing so little part in the politics of the new Ireland, but this was not really the Ascendancy's fault. Someone of Ascendancy background wishing to enter the Dail suffered from the same disability as that which prevented a cousin of Lady Ardilaun's from obtaining a diplomatic appointment under the Free State Government. When he applied for one, he was asked: 'What did you do in the war – the war against England?'[22] In fairness to those Irish who asked this question – whether openly or in their minds – it must be said that there were a great many candidates for government posts and Parliamentary seats who had taken part in the 'war against England' who might well have been considered more deserving than former Unionists whose support for the new regime all too obviously came from the head rather than from the heart.

Those of the Ascendancy who were most active in the 'war against England' had virtually no political careers after the end of the Civil War. Robert Barton, who was never really happy in the pro-Treaty camp, retired altogether from politics in 1923. Albinia Brodrick busied herself with local affairs in Kerry. Constance Markievicz was a Dail Deputy, but died in 1927 a month before her leader, de Valera, decided to subscribe to the Oath of Allegiance and take his seat; had she lived, she would certainly not have followed his example. After Constance's death, Yeats wrote his celebrated lament for her and for her sister Eva Gore-Booth, the poet, who had died a year earlier, remembering them as girls at Lissadell:

> The light of evening, Lissadell,
> Great windows open to the south,
> Two girls in silk kimonos, both
> Beautiful, one a gazelle.
> But a raving autumn shears
> Blossom from the summer's wreath;
> The older is condemned to death,
> Pardoned, drags out lonely years . . .

'No bells ring here'

— I —

The general election of 1932 brought de Valera and his Fianna Fail party into power – something which the Ascendany had dreaded. Colonel Proby's son Granville, a scholarly bachelor who was a Clerk in the House of Lords, felt so strongly about it that he came over from England to Glenart specially in order to vote, but not understanding the complexities of the Irish system of proportional representation, he voted for de Valera's man by mistake. Having managed to come to terms with the Free State, the former loyalists now faced the prospect of being governed by those who had fought on the Republican side in the Civil War.

Their fears seemed confirmed when de Valera proceeded to dismantle the Free State constitution, abolishing the Oath and, as a preliminary to abolishing the office of Governor-General, replacing McNeill with a minor politician who did not even take up residence at the Lodge. Then, in 1934, he introduced a bill to abolish the Senate. 'The Granards and the Jamesons and the like are no longer to be in a position to block the progress of the Irish Nation,' one of de Valera's principal lieutenants proclaimed in the Dail when the bill was being debated.[1] By now, through death, resignation and electoral defeat, the number of Ascendancy Senators had dwindled to a mere six, three veterans of the original Senate – Bagwell, Jameson and Colonel Moore – and three newcomers, but the abolition of the Senate meant that the Ascendancy was almost completely excluded from Irish political life. In the Dail, there were three Deputies of Ascendancy background: Esmonde, O'Mahony and a solitary newcomer, Frank MacDermot, half-brother of The MacDermot Prince of Coolavin. When somebody once complained in the Dail about Frank MacDermot's English accent, he replied proudly: 'I am the only person in this House who can trace back twenty-three generations that have been nothing but Irish and Catholic.'

By the middle of the 1930s, the Ascendancy was even more turned in on itself and 'West British' than it had been ten years earlier. There was a general feeling of disenchantment with the new Ireland in Ascendancy circles. 'Now one rarely talks of Ireland at all,' Daisy Fingall remarked sadly, remembering how she and Horace Plunkett and their friends used to talk of nothing else.[2] Since Fingall's death in 1929, the ageing Daisy had lived in Dublin, where she kept a small weekly salon. She occasionally found herself next to de Valera's Cabinet colleagues at dinner, and complained that their sole topic of conversation was their prison experiences.

Since Irish had become the official language of the new State, appearing on road signs and income tax demands, the Ascendancy had grown bored with the Gaelic revival. A few old stalwarts kept their enthusiasm for the language, notably Douglas Hyde, though he had resigned from the Gaelic League twenty years earlier when it had become political. Almost the only new recruit to the movement from the Ascendancy world after 1920 was the former Lord Chancellor's son Lord Ashbourne, who like Shane Leslie wore a saffron kilt. He refused to speak English, so that those who knew no Irish had to speak to him in French.

Lord Ashbourne wearing his plaid.

It was unusual even to find an enthusiasm for Irish folk culture among the Ascendancy of this period – particularly among the younger generation – such as was shown by Anthony Vere Foster and his two sisters, who in 1931 revived the annual midsummer festival known as the 'Patrun' or 'Pattern' which had been held in former times in the village of Tallanstown near Glyde Court, their home in County Louth. Anthony, who was born soon after his parents and sisters were painted by Orpen, was now a handsome and charming if slightly eccentric subaltern in the British army. His parents were still living at Glyde; Lady Foster's eccentricity now took the form of hibernation – she went to bed for the winter. Her elder daughter kept up the fantasy that she was a boy, of which Orpen had remarked; she was known as John, she wore a tweed jacket, breeches and gaiters, a tie and a man's hat, and she had her hair cropped by a men's hairdresser.

At the opening of the first Tallanstown Patrun, the local band marched through the village, a symbolic bough was ceremonially set up, and Anthony Vere Foster blew a trumpet. Afterwards there were songs and old Irish dances, 'humorous items' and recitations; in the evening there was a play, and the proceedings ended with another fanfare from Anthony's trumpet. When the revived Patrun had been going a number of years, Anthony's sister John wrote of it in a local paper: 'The Patrun is a festival by the people for the people . . . the war pipes of Old Ireland reverberated through the hills and echoed down the river to tell that Tallanstown was en fête.'[3]

Writing from India to Dorothy, the younger of his two sisters, in the autumn of 1933, Anthony told her what he would like his parents to give him for Christmas. 'Let them put thirty shillings aside for my return, when we can have a dance to which the band, the Patrun Committee and all my friends are invited and that will pay for their refreshments. *That's what I'd love most in all the world.*' He wrote another letter to Dorothy, to whom he was devoted, at the beginning of 1934. 'I've ridden ponies in the best game in the world and been mistaken by Indians for an Indian, and with my nightingales and men I've laughed, lived and sung uproariously and felt beyond all words outrageously happy.'[4]

Later that year, his regiment moved from India to Khartoum, where, in September, he was found dead in tragic and mysterious circumstances.

— *2* —

Soon after coming into power, de Valera withheld the Land Annuities, the payments due to Britain in respect of land purchase, which had been largely financed by the British Exchequer. The British Government retaliated by levying customs duties on imports from the Free State. There ensued the so-called Economic War, which ruined Irish farming, yet another blow to the finances of the landowning Ascendancy. Many of the more impoverished landowners were forced to sell up altogether. Tom Ponsonby was one of those rich enough to survive, but having hitherto farmed extensively and with notable success at Kilcooley, he was now obliged to lease most of his land to the Forestry Department.

In the middle of the Economic War, the Ascendancy was shocked by two crimes which appeared to be ushering in a new era of violence. Early in 1935, when Gerald More O'Ferrall and his wife were at dinner at Lisard in County Longford, together with a grown-up son and daughter and two guests, a band of armed men

Lisard, County Longford.

forced their way into the house. They had come for More O'Ferrall, probably on account of a dispute over the rents of some houses in the neighbourhood, and tried to drag him from the room. His wife, his son and daughter and another girl came to his assistance; in the ensuing struggle his son was felled by the butt of a revolver and shot through the back as he lay stunned on the floor. The raiders made off; the unfortunate young More O'Ferrall, paralysed from the waist down, was taken by car to a Dublin nursing home where he died after eleven days of suffering.

A year later, Admiral Boyle Somerville, brother of Edith, was shot dead on his own doorstep at Castletownshend in the presence of his wife. His murderers left a card accusing him of being a British recruiting agent; in fact all he had done was to give advice and references to young men of the neighbourhood wishing to join the Royal Navy. The crime was attributed to the extremist organization calling itself the IRA which Cosgrave had declared illegal in 1931. De Valera had lifted this ban in 1932, but he imposed it again three months after Admiral Somerville's murder, which in the event was followed by no further outrages against the Ascendancy.

During the lean years of the Economic War, Ascendancy life became simpler. Even before the collapse of farming, there had been retrenchment in many country houses, particularly when an extravagant older generation was succeeded by an impecunious younger one. Right up to his death, through a hunting accident, in 1927, Bertram Barton had sixteen servants at Straffan, including three footmen; there were orchids on the dinner table at Christmas. Had he lived another two months, the bank would have foreclosed. His son and daughter-in-law managed to carry on, but had to make drastic economies. They lived very quietly; Mrs Barton, who had trained as a VAD in the Great War, devoted much of her time to acting as an unpaid district nurse, for the medical services in rural Ireland were then rudimentary. By the middle of the 1930s, the Bartons had decided that the great Italianate mansion at Straffan was too big for them, so they pulled down two-thirds of the main block, making what was left into a house designed to be run by only four servants.

Straffan House, before it was reduced in size.

Stradbally Hall.

Most of the larger Irish country houses still had more servants than four, even where there had been retrenchment. Many people still had butlers, though they tended to be old or eccentric or addicted to the bottle, and frequently all of these things. There was an occasion when the butler at Caledon, fortified by his diligence as a wine-taster, leant over Lady Caledon's shoulder during a dinner party and proposed marriage. She afterwards told a friend: 'Of course I accepted him and told him to continue serving. Next day it was all forgotten.'[5] During the tea party at Blarney Castle following the funeral of Sir George Colthurst's widow the butler entered the drawing room carrying the large silver tea tray, stark naked. The lady who had been companion to Lady Colthurst went up to him. 'I think we need a little more sugar.' And he immediately left the room.

At Stradbally Hall, the Cosbys had a butler and footman right through the 1930s as at Carton, where the aunts of the profligate Duke of Leinster lived until about 1937, when the house was closed up. Carton was one of the many grander Irish country houses which did not possess electricity, another was Middleton Park in County Westmeath, a house in other respects luxurious, with excellent food and plenty of bathrooms and hot water. Here lived Captain and Mrs Arthur Boyd-Rochfort and a gentleman who, soon after the Great War, had come to stay a night before going off on a camping holiday. The weather had been bad so he had stayed on; he was still there more than ten years later.

Bowen's Court was one of the houses where, in the 1930s, people still had to

A hip-bath in one of the bedrooms of Bowen's Court in the 1930s.

Group on the steps of Bowen's Court in the 1930s. Elizabeth Bowen second from the left; Evelyn Waugh on the right.

make do with hip-baths. A son of Elizabeth Bowen's neighbours the Annesleys of Annes Grove, staying here for a hunt ball, had the misfortune to upset a hip-bath full of water. During the 1930s, Elizabeth Bowen, whose husband, Alan Cameron, worked in England, only came to Bowen's Court for holidays; but while she was here she had many friends to stay, including fellow-writers such as Evelyn Waugh.

Even in straitened circumstances, the Ascendancy's traditions of hospitality were maintained. There were few Irish country houses where people could not turn up unannounced for a meal, or even to stay; they would simply push open the hall door and call out: 'Is anyone at home?' Hall doors were seldom locked, even at night; it had been necessary to do so when there was the danger of raids, but with the return of peace the old easy-going ways had also returned. Those who attempted to ring the bell usually found themselves pulling the yard-and-a-half of rusty wire out of its hole in the masonry many times over before anything happened. A nephew from England, arriving at the home of Lord Ashtown's younger brother in County Limerick – a vast nineteenth-century baronial castle from which most of the pictures and furniture had been sold in the previous decade – told the woman who opened the door to him that he had been ringing for some time. 'No bells ring here,' she replied laconically.

At some of the more run-down houses, the hospitality, though readily offered, was a little rough. Guests at Kilcoleman Abbey in County Kerry, where the

Tervoe, County Limerick, home of Lord Emly, who in his old age would move from room to room as the rain came in.

widowed Lady Godfrey and her middle-aged step-daughter Miss Phyllis Godfrey were looked after by one woman, had to put up with crusts of bread in the bread sauce and cream that was always sour through being left too long in the bowl. To make matters worse, Phyllis Godfrey, who acted as her own motor mechanic, was always covered in oil. When she was staying with her uncle and aunt in County Waterford, the maid said to another guest: 'Have ye seen the bath after Miss Phyllis has been in it? It's all grace and scoom.'

There were all too many dilapidated country houses in Ireland at this time, but Kilcoleman stood high in the league; it actually smelt of dry rot. Others ran it close; at Tervoe in County Limerick the portly widower Lord Emly, smoking innumerable cigars, moved from room to room as the rain came in. The rain came no less abundantly through the leaky roof of Lismehane in County Clare, clattering into enamel jugs and basins put out to catch the drips. The fine furniture was warped, the carpets were threadbare, the wallpaper was peeling off the walls. As though in concert with the drips, the shaky old Colonel George O'Callaghan-Westropp slobbered his food, as he sat at breakfast, bull-necked and bearded, 'surrounded by a pack of mangy terriers clothed in old vests to stop them scratching'. In addition to his grown-up children, his household included an elderly female relation who always wore a hat, decorating it sometimes with 'a home-made brooch made out of the small bones of a rabbit'[6] and sometimes with the skull of a snipe.

Though a loyalist and a Protestant and an ADC to the King, Colonel O'Callaghan-Westropp admired de Valera, seeing in him 'the purest nationalism, unsullied by class hatred'.[7] The Colonel's love of Ireland was intensified by his pride in what he believed to be his ancestry. He convinced himself that he was The O'Callaghan, Chief of the Name, and having heard that in ancient times the Chief was elected from among the members of his family by the whole Sept, decided to clinch matters by holding a formal election. So he put an advertisement in the paper stating that he would be at an hotel in Mallow, which was in the old O'Callaghan territory, on a certain day in 1937, and called upon all the O'Callaghans of that region to gather there for the purpose of electing him Chief if they saw fit. A large crowd assembled, and having been regaled by the Colonel with whiskey and porter elected him with acclamation. The Colonel was happily unaware that there were less than a dozen O'Callaghans in the crowd.

A few years later, he managed to persuade the Chief Herald of Ireland to recognize him as The O'Callaghan. On further investigation it was found that his pedigree could not be authenticated. But out of consideration for the old Colonel, who by then was nearly eighty, the Chief Herald allowed him to keep the title for the rest of his life.

— *3* —

According to a list drawn up by Colonel O'Callaghan-Westropp, the number of Ascendancy families in County Clare went down from about eighty in 1919 to a mere ten in the early 1930s. The exodus was worse in Clare than in most parts of Ireland; nevertheless, it went on all over the country during the years following the ending of the Civil War. As well as those who went away altogether, there were those who did not actually leave but had to give up their family seats. Of the latter, perhaps the most unfortunate was Hamon Massy, now Lord Massy. He had inherited very little money with Killakee, he was no good at managing his affairs, and he had a drink problem, the result being that, in 1924, Killakee had been taken over by the bank. He and his wife were now living in poverty in a single-storey gate-lodge at one of the entrances to his former demesne; his old home stood empty, the once-famous formal gardens a wilderness, trees growing out through the roof of the great conservatory.

By 1927, Lady Gregory had realized that there was no hope of Coole remaining in her family. She had therefore sold it to the Forestry Department, continuing to live in the house as a tenant until her death in 1932. Since then, like Killakee, it had stood empty.

In 1935, the Ossorys found that they could no longer afford to live at Kilkenny Castle and also keep their house in London. They decided to keep the London house and abandon the Castle, which since 1922 they had lovingly restored, redecorated and modernized – though it still had no more than four bathrooms. So they sold all the contents apart from the portraits and other heirlooms; the sale, in the autumn of 1935, lasted a full ten days.

Though the Castle, after 1935, stood 'grim and deserted',[8] empty but for the portraits in the picture gallery, it still belonged to the Ormonde family, which kept up its links with Kilkenny. The Ossorys came on visits, staying in a flat which they had made for themselves in the castle stables. In 1937 Lady Beatrice Pole-Carew and Lady Constance Butler, daughters of the previous Lord Ormonde, came to Kilkenny and gave a tea-party at the Imperial Hotel for people who had worked at the Castle in their parents' time. There were only six of them left, but they also invited the son of another old retainer who had died recently.

The closing of Kilkenny Castle was followed a couple of years later by the sale of Desart; the house, so recently rebuilt, was dismantled and after standing for some

Desart Court in its final state of ruin after the recently-rebuilt house had been dismantled. It was subsequently razed to the ground.

years as a ruin was razed to the ground. Among the many other houses that were eventually demolished was Monivea, which became very run down during the years when Kathleen ffrench was away in Harbin. By 1935 her cousin Rozzie was existing with no servants at all, being too poor to pay the wages which they now expected; there was nobody even to bring in the turf for the fires. And no amount of turf could have rekindled the fire which formerly welcomed the arriving guest in the big hall, for a piece of masonry had fallen and blocked the hall chimney. When the male cousin who acted as agent for the property proposed selling some timber to raise money for essential repairs, Kathleen cabled him from her Manchurian retreat: 'Not a stick or stone of my dear old home must be removed.'[9]

Kathleen died in 1938, bequeathing Monivea to the Irish Nation as a 'Home for Indigent Artists'. The bequest was refused and, after Rozzie's death in 1939, Monivea passed to another spinster cousin living in England, who sold it to the Land Commission.

$$-4-$$

While other great Irish houses were being closed up, the former Viceregal Lodge, now called Áras an Uachtaráin, was re-opened in 1938 to receive Douglas Hyde, the first President of Eire, as the Free State was now called. The office of President, which under de Valera's new constitution of 1937 replaced that of Governor-General, gave the impression that Ireland was now a Republic, whereas the actual Head of State was still the King. As President, Hyde was an inspired choice, appealing to the new Ireland as a Gael and to the old Ireland as an Ascendancy Protestant; he was to perform his social duties remarkably well considering he was nearly eighty.

Hyde's appointment was one of several moves by de Valera to conciliate the Protestants, who were beginning to wonder if they did not prefer him to Cosgrave, whose strict adherence to the Catholic line had provoked Yeats's outburst. Another of de Valera's conciliatory moves was to revive the Senate, though the electoral system of the new Second Chamber made it almost entirely political. In 1938 the number of Senators who came from the Ascendancy was down to three. They consisted of the County Waterford baronet Sir John Keane and The McGillycuddy of the Reeks, both veterans of the old Senate – Keane had first become a Senator in 1922 – and Frank MacDermot, who was no longer in the Dail, where, after the 1938 general election, there were only two Deputies of Ascendancy background. One was the young Erskine Childers, whose father's support of the Republican cause in the Civil War had cost him his life; the other was Captain John Esmonde who sat for his late cousin's constituency of Wexford.

The year 1938 saw the ending of the Economic War, de Valera having come to an agreement with the British Government over the Land Annuities. The negotiations also brought to an end the agreement that had existed since the Treaty whereby Britain retained the use of the Irish naval bases. This made it possible for Eire to be neutral in the European war which was now imminent.

'Tubby will be there'

— I —

Whereas 1914 was as fateful a year for the Ascendancy as 1789 was for the old nobility of France, the same cannot be said of 1939. Unlike the earlier conflict, the Second World War was followed by no upheavals in Ireland. And while the Ascendancy was never quite the same after Mons, Gallipoli and Passchendaele had taken their toll, the casualties of the Second World War were not only fewer than those of the First, but their collective impact was less severe. Individual families suffered. Sir Basil and Lady Brooke – he became Prime Minister of Northern Ireland in 1943 – lost two sons; so did Sir Josslyn and Lady Gore-Booth. The Stafford-King-Harmans lost their only son and heir; Lord Hugh Beresford* went down in HMS *Hood*; George Ponsonby of Kilcooley was severely wounded. The young Lord Dufferin, one of whose uncles, Lord Ava, had died in the Boer War and another, Basil Blackwood, in the Great War, was killed near the Burmese city of Ava, from which the Viceroy took his second title. But the Ascendancy as a whole had become inured to the horrors of war.

The fact that so many more of them survived does not mean that the sons of the Ascendancy who were young in 1939 were not just as ready to fight and if necessary die as the First War generation had been, though it is doubtful if they went into battle with the stoic fatalism of a Norman Leslie. And it was not only the sons who went off to the war; the fathers went also, though they generally failed to get any nearer to the front line than some depot in Britain. Having heard Chamberlain's declaration of war on the wireless at Coolmore, Dick Solly-Flood, now a retired Brigadier-General aged sixty-two, 'spent the rest of that day sorting out his

---

* See illustration on page 216.

uniforms'.[1] He left for London as soon as he could, only to be told by the War Office that there was little hope of his being able to re-join the army; eventually, with Lord Donoughmore's help, he became second-in-command of a battalion of Home Guard in Sussex. His wife Marguerite was as anxious to help in the war effort as he was: she gave a ball at Coolmore in aid of the Red Cross within a few weeks of the outbreak of hostilities; later she followed her husband to England and became Secretary of the Essex Women's Land Army.

Those who through age or for some other reason were obliged to stay in Eire for the duration managed to do their bit in various ways. Two old Generals who lived near each other in County Cork – one was married to a Godfrey of the Kilcoleman family – helped recruiting by boycotting their local church because the parson's son did not go to the war. It meant going to another church several miles away; the two old couples had to drive there and back every Sunday in a trap, for there was no petrol. But they cheerfully endured this hardship as their part in the war effort.

Over the question of Eire's neutrality, Ascendancy opinion was divided. There were those who regarded it as the latest in the catalogue of de Valera's misdeeds; people with naval connections tended to be of this mind, indignant that the Royal Navy could not use the Irish harbours. There were also those who felt that, by remaining neutral, Eire was more likely to be invaded by the Germans. Granville Proby, believing a German invasion of Ireland to be imminent, sold Glenart for a knock-down price, much to his family's sorrow.

On the other hand, many believed, as de Valera himself did, that by remaining neutral Eire stood a better chance of not being invaded than by entering the war, certain that Britian did not have the resources to be able to defend Eire against a German attack. They saw the neutrality as an act of statemanship on de Valera's part; he went up in their estimation. Those who supported Eire's neutrality fought in the war just as much as those who opposed it. Fighting alongside the British, paradoxically, gave them a greater bond with de Valera's Ireland: the more their British comrades abused de Valera in their presence, the more they rallied to his defence. This, of course, has aways been the way of people from the Ascendancy ever since Ireland became independent; they may speak of the new Ireland in the most outrageous terms among themselves, but woe betide any Englishman who dares say a word against it. Philip Bence-Jones, serving as a colonel in India, would forestall any remarks about Eire's neutrality from his young officers by saying to each new batch, when they arrived: 'And remember, gentlemen, your Colonel is a neutral volunteer.' Bertram Barton's daughter managed to get the Germans out of the family wine château near Bordeaux by arriving on the scene brandishing her neutral Irish passport.

Since Northern Ireland was in the war, many of the Ascendancy from north of the Border, particularly the older generation, did not soldier in Britain or overseas

General Sir Alan Brooke, afterwards
Field-Marshal Viscount Alanbrooke.

General Sir Harold Alexander,
afterwards Field-Marshal Earl Alexander
of Tunis.

but served in the defence of their homeland. So heavily was Northern Ireland
garrisoned that some of the Ascendancy from Eire found military employment by
going north for the duration.

The Ulster Ascendancy had the distinction of producing the four greatest
British military commanders of the war: Field-Marshals Dill, Alanbrooke,
Montgomery and, of course, Alexander. Lady Caledon showed no anxiety when
she heard that war had been declared, but just said: 'Tubby will be there.'[2]
Unfortunately she died in October 1939 so did not live to see her favourite son
leading the Allied armies to victory. Lady Leslie, the neighbouring grande dame,
felt no less confident of the outcome, being Winston Churchill's aunt. She wrote
frequent letters to her nephew after he became Prime Minister, sending them off
from a post office on the northern side of the Border to which she drove in a horse-
drawn brougham brought back into commission when petrol became short. Being,
like her daughter-in-law, an American, Leonie Leslie took a special interest in the
GIs who, after America came into the war, did sentry duty along the Border
between the demesne walls of Glaslough and Caledon; she would greet them as she
passed them in her carriage by putting out an elegant hand and making a 'V sign'.[3]

Caledon.

Glaslough.

Leonie and her husband, both over eighty, had an English butler and numerous other servants to look after them at Glaslough, but owing to the shortage of coal the great Victorian house was so cold that they had to wear wraps indoors. Candles were the only form of lighting, for there was no electricity and paraffin was unobtainable. At the end of a passage on the top floor, Norman Leslie's bedroom was kept exactly as it was when he left it for the last time in 1914. As his niece recalls, 'a curious sad atmosphere lingered in this room . . . on the walls there still hung trophies of his army days in India – the hooves and antlers of animals he had shot – and on tables stood those yellowing photographs of his sweethearts and his polo ponies.'⁴ On the pillow lay a bunch of wilted flowers, with rosemary for remembrance. Every year on Norman's birthday his mother would spend long hours in solitary vigil here.

− 2 −

The fuel shortage caused most of the hardships of Irish country-house life during the Second World War. There were many families like the Toler-Aylwards of Shankill Castle in County Kilkenny who for most of the duration never went outside an eight-mile radius of their home, which was as far as they could go on bicycles or in a trap. The elder of the two Vere Foster sisters, who dressed like a man and was known as John, could not afford to keep a trap at the glebe house in County Louth where she was now living, neither did she possess a bicycle, so that she could not go anywhere at all beyond walking distance. She also could not afford a wireless, so would walk down to the nearest cottage which had one to listen to the news.

A limited amount of petrol was available for taxis and for agricultural purposes. A County Louth lady and her daughter, both of whom dressed rather more elegantly than John Vere Foster, had the idea of going to a summer tea party reclining on rugs and cushions in their farm trailer, pulled by the tractor, but no sooner had they turned out of their lodge gates than the tractor wheels began to spatter them with dung.

Those within reach of a railway station could visit friends similarly situated in other parts of the country; the journey there and back was very slow, but as food and servants were plentiful, nobody minded how long their guests stayed. People also tended to forgather in Dublin or some other town easily reached by rail. Major and Mrs Bertram Bell, the son-in-law and daughter of Lord Barrymore, whose title had died with him, had no difficulty in getting to Cork from Fota, where they had their own railway station on the island; they were able to meet friends such as the younger Sir George Colthurst at the County Club. Young officers serving in Northern Ireland would come south to Dublin to eat steaks; they would organize dinner parties at Jammet's restaurant with girls who were able to come into the city from the neighbouring counties. Officers with longer leave came south to stay in country houses and hunt – at times it almost seemed as though the old days of the garrison had returned.

People gave hospitality to officers from the Dominions on leave. When a number of Australian officers came to stay in a house in County Westmeath, a young stoker off an Australian ship was somehow included in the party. The hostess saw that the officers were being rather unkind to this young man, so she arranged for him to go and stay on his own in a neighbouring country house with an old and very grand dowager. So well did the young Aussie get on with the dowager that he married her, much to the horror of the County.

As in the First War, a number of country houses were closed for the duration while their owners were away. The Irish army, which was increased in strength on account of the emergency, occupied some of these houses. An infantry battalion established itself at Coolmore, the officers in the house, the men under canvas in the demesne. The officers promised Dick Solly-Flood that there would be no damage done and they were as good as their word. Other houses, including the empty Kilkenny Castle, were treated less kindly.

The number of houses taken over by the military in Northern Ireland was naturally greater than in Eire; they included Caledon, which was occupied by American officers – Leonie Leslie would drive over the Border in her brougham to visit them. In County Fermanagh all country house demesnes were requisitioned

Castlecoole.

because of the flying boat base on Lough Erne. Lord Belmore, an elderly and autocratic bachelor of elephantine build, tried to keep the military out of his own demesne of Castlecoole, but it was discovered that the place was held originally by a Plantation grant which obliged the grantee to help with the defence of the country. So the authorities declared Castlecoole escheated, giving it back to Lord Belmore when the military left. The military did not, however, go into the house, where Lord Belmore lived on undisturbed.

Living with Lord Belmore in that palatial classical mansion overlooking a lake inhabited by a flock of greylag geese were his rather sad bachelor brother and his four unmarried sisters, the Ladies Lowry-Corry, with whom he was not on speaking terms. When Lord Belmore first inherited Castlecoole there were eight unmarried sisters living with him there; since then one had married and three had died – one drowned in the lake and, according to the legend, turned into a greylag goose. Lord Belmore and his brother and sisters had always occupied the same places in church, strung out in a line according to age; there were gaps where the deceased Ladies Lowry-Corry had been, for when they died the survivors had not closed ranks.

〔14〕

The heart is still sound

— I —

By the end of the Second World War the exodus had virtually ceased. Then the tide turned and the younger generation of families that had left in the 1920s and 1930s started to come back. Country houses which had been empty or inhabited by farmers were once again lived in by the Ascendancy, in some cases by people with roots in the neighbourhood. Many of those who returned had never really had a proper home except in Ireland, having soldiered or followed some other peripatetic career since their parents went into exile. Others had established themselves in England, only to find life under the postwar Labour Government not to their liking.

'The Flight from Moscow', as this influx of refugees from socialism and shortages has been called, also brought many English settlers with no Irish roots. On the whole, they were welcomed by the Ascendancy, particularly if they hunted, but some of the more formidable old ladies had doubts regarding these 'new squatters'. The octogenarian Mrs Richard Grove Annesley, whose husband was still adding to his wonderful gardens at Annes Grove in County Cork, was certain that all the settlers were in trade, for which she had the proverbial contempt. 'Her father was nothing much – he made corsets in Australia,' she would say of a connection of hers. She had a habit of assuming that anybody whose name reminded her of some well-known product must be 'in' that product, often a product with a name different from that of its manufacturer. 'I hear Killowen has been bought by people called Worcester. Worcester Sauce, I suppose.'

One of the two Generals' wives of the wartime church boycott was even more concerned about the newcomers' origins, for she set great store by ancestry; she even despised perfectly good Ascendancy families if they were Cromwellian, getting round the fact that, as a Godfrey, she was a Cromwellian herself by saying: '*We*, of course, came over with Charles II.' If she thought that any of the newcomers smelt of the counting-house, she would tell her friends: 'Have nothing to do with them. Have *nothing* to do with them.' She imposed her veto for other reasons as well. Of an elderly Old Etonian widower whose uncle was a lord, she said: 'Have nothing to do with him. He has *three* dreadful women living with him who call themselves Belgians, but they look much more like *Bulgarians*.'

Of the expatriates who came back to Ireland immediately after the war, some came only on visits, generally on a pilgrimage to their old family home. The now Sir Christopher Lynch-Robinson, who had so gladly shaken the mud of Ireland off his feet in 1922, returned for a visit in the summer of 1946 and was struck by how kind and helpful everybody was, though it saddened him to find that the nuns who now owned Athavallie had removed all the creepers from the house and painted it yellow. Tom Henn, who came over in 1948, found Paradise Hill, his old home in County Clare, empty and desolate, 'with that peculiarly "blind" look of a house where the windows have long been shuttered and the frames decayed.' He felt that it would really have been better if the house had been burnt rather than 'left to linger on like a dying animal'.[1] One of Lady Gregory's granddaughters went back on a visit to Coole with her husband just after the end of the war. She had heard that the roof had been taken off the house and expected to find only a ruin, but when they rounded the last bend of the avenue she found that the house had disappeared altogether. There was literally nothing there. The shock was terrible,[2] yet she might have expected that Yeats's prophecy, when he sang of Coole in 1929, would come true.

> Here, traveller, scholar, poet, take your stand
> When all those rooms and passages are gone,
> When nettles wave upon a shapeless mound
> And saplings root among the broken stone . . .

While the influx of returned exiles and new settlers saved many country houses from the fate suffered by Coole, there were some houses past saving. In 1946 Lord Rossmore and his family abandoned Rossmore Castle, which was badly infested with dry rot; the fructifications in the great drawing room were of monstrous proportions and the bottles of wine from the cellar carried spores to the dower house to which the family moved, causing a fresh outbreak there. Other houses were too big for even the richest settlers, like Kilkenny Castle, which continued to stand empty and forlorn, none the better for its wartime military occupation. The rain came through the skylight of the picture gallery, the portraits were stacked against the walls from which the crimson wallpaper hung down in swathes.

The picture gallery at
Kilkenny Castle in 1951.

Even as remodelled by Bryan Cooper, Markree was too big for his son and
daughter-in-law, who having lived there for a few years after the war with a staff of
eight including a butler, decided to close the greater part of the castle, moving into
a wing where they could manage with only two servants. Rosie Headfort's son and
daughter-in-law also moved into a wing at Headfort, turning most of the house
into a boys' school. When the new Lord Wicklow inherited Shelton and an indoor
staff of twenty-one from his father in 1946, he came to the conclusion that his only
hope of carrying on was to run the house as an hotel. The venture was not a
financial success and in 1950 he decided to sell up and to live the whole time in his
Dublin flat.

The Solly-Floods moved into a smaller house, having decided after the end of
the war that Coolmore was too big and would cost too much to modernize. It still
had no electricity, which continued to be the state of affairs at a number of other
Irish country houses. Some houses still did not have telephones; the elderly
Captain Charles Barton of Grove in County Tipperary acquired one at about this
time. 'You'll be able to ring up your friends,' a neighbouring county lady said to
him brightly, but he replied: 'Oh no, the cook knows how to work that instrument.'

There were still those who could afford to modernize their houses and occupy
them fully, however large they might have been. Some kept up considerable state,
as the Rosses did at Birr. At Powerscourt, after the younger generation succeeded
in 1947, there was a butler and a footman in livery. At Kenure Park, Colonel
Roderick Fenwick-Palmer's Corinthian mansion on the North County Dublin
coast, there was also a butler and footman and the house was full of guests

Fota.

The dining room at Fota. A portrait of Lord Barrymore by William Orpen over the mantelpiece; a portrait of his son-in-law, Major Bertram Bell, to the left.

Major Bertram Bell (centre, with dog) and Mrs Bell (on his right) with the indoor and outdoor staff at Fota in the 1940s. Some of the botanical treasures of the Fota gardens can be seen in the background.

throughout the summer. One day the Colonel's setter grabbed the housekeeper's pet hen, and appeared with it outside the window. The Colonel, who was very kind-hearted, rushed out to the hen's assistance, followed by the butler with a bottle of whiskey on a silver salver with which to revive the unfortunate fowl.[3]

The indoor and outdoor staff at Fota immediately after the war numbered more than fifty, the former headed by the admirable butler Russell. The famous gardens were perfectly maintained with new plantings being carried on all the time, Mrs Bell having inherited her father's great knowledge of plants. The grass in the arboretum was kept tidy by a fleet of horse-drawn mowers, each driven by a pensioner with a straw hat and a drooping moustache.

Major and Mrs Bell continued their weekly visits to Cork, always on a Thursday, to meet Sir George Colthurst and other friends at the County Club. They would all have luncheon together, then, with the exception of Mrs Bell, who usually had things to buy for the garden, they all went to the cinema. They did not go to the same film but dispersed, in pairs or singly, to different picture-houses.

Afterwards they forgathered again at the Club for tea, and compared notes about the films they had seen.

'Hullo Georgie, what was yours like?'

'It was quite good, but I couldn't understand a word. How was yours?'

'Couldn't understand a word.'

'Ah, here's Billy. Did you enjoy your film?'

'Couldn't understand a word. All about babies in cages.'

As a sign of how the old customs lingered on, many Irish country houses still had a clientèle of occasional visitors, like those who had visited Mrs Brooke of Summerton in the 1870s, to be rewarded by her with coppers and cold meat sandwiches. Some of the postwar clientèle of old Lady Dunalley, who lived in the north of County Tipperary, would come all the way from Dublin in a hired motor with a driver in order to receive her bounty.

— 2 —

In 1948 de Valera's long reign came to an end. Having greatly regretted his accession to power sixteen years before, the Ascendancy was now on the whole sorry to see him go, not only on account of the uncertainties of the new regime, but because they had come to admire him for his statesmanship and his stature. The new Interparty Government was a coalition consisting principally of Fine Gael, Cosgrave's party, now led by John A. Costello, Cosgrave himself having retired; it also included Labour and an extreme Republican group led by Sean MacBride, son of Yeats's old flame Maud Gonne. The presence of the two latter elements was enough to make the Ascendancy apprehensive, but when, a few months after coming into power, Costello made Eire into the completely independent Republic of Ireland, breaking the remaining ties with Britain and the Commonwealth, he forfeited much of the support which the Ascendancy had given his party since 1922.

The Ascendancy can be said to have got its own back on Costello, for an episode in which two Ascendancy figures played a leading part helped to bring about his Government's downfall. This was the so-called Battle of Baltinglass, a row over a sub post office in County Wicklow that grew into national proportions. The sub post office in the village of Baltinglass had been run by members of the Cooke family since about 1870; in 1950 it was expected that Miss Helen Cooke would succeed her aunt, who was retiring. Instead, the Minister for Posts and Telegraphs in the Interparty Government appointed someone else. Under the vigorous leadership of the local landowner, General Meade Dennis of Fortgranite, the entire village rallied to Miss Cooke's support. General Dennis, a collateral descendant of Dean Swift, felt a special responsibility towards Miss Cooke, for his grandfather, as a JP, had been instrumental in giving the original postmastership to her grandfather.

Miss Cooke also found a champion in Dermot O'Mahony of Grange Con, the former Dail Deputy, who now styled himself 'The O'Mahony of Kerry'. O'Mahony threw himself into the fray with the same passionate concern for the oppressed that his father had shown towards the Bulgarians and Sir Arthur Vicars; he resigned from Fine Gael, having run the party in West Wicklow. There were deputations to Costello and angry exchanges in the Dail; telegraph poles were cut down and an aeroplane, flying low over Dublin, broadcast an appeal on behalf of Miss Cooke whose sympathisers grew ever more numerous and included even the Pope. Towards the end of December 1950, after the battle had been raging for several weeks, the interloping postmaster resigned. Justice and Miss Cooke triumphed. The minister, one of the Labour members of the coalition, also resigned, so that the Government was weakened and consequently unable to survive a more serious crisis which blew up a few months later.

During the weeks when he led Baltinglass in the fight for Miss Cooke, General Dennis was temporarily restored to that position of local leadership which his forebears had held as a matter of course. Others were able to recover this position to some extent by involving themselves in non-political bodies such as the new National Farmers' Association. By now, the ill-feelings engendered by the agrarian disturbances, the Troubles and the Civil War had mostly died down.

After a generation, the Ascendancy had really come to terms with the new Ireland, while remaining entirely unofficial, as much divorced from the governing class as the old nobility of France under the Third Republic. In the 1950s, the occupants of the Members' Stand at Ballsbridge would not have sung 'God Save the King'; they would also have been most punctilious about standing to attention for the National Anthem of the new Ireland, 'The Soldiers' Song'. Yet the old loyalty to the Crown was as strong as ever – as strong as the monarchical allegiance of French monarchists, to whom the Ascendancy might well be compared. The death of King George VI and the Queen's coronation brought great manifestations of this loyalty on the part of the Ascendancy.

$$- 3 -$$

This dual but by no means conflicting allegiance to the British monarchy and the Irish Republic was particularly noticeable in Elizabeth Bowen, who was now living at Bowen's Court the whole time, apart from an annual winter visit to the United States, having until 1951 been obliged to live mostly in London because her husband Alan Cameron, who died in 1952, worked for the BBC. The tall, square, eighteenth-century house, 'with its rows of dark windows set in the light façade against dark trees'[4] had been used only for holidays and she had sold most of the Victorian furniture with which her grandfather had cluttered it up; since coming back to live here permanently she had refurnished the house with a rather sparse elegance. This sparseness suited the large and lofty rooms, with their big windows which seemed, in her own words, 'to contain the weather itself';[5] but it was dictated by her limited means. She did up the house in excellent taste, but on a

Elizabeth Bowen at Bowen's Court with Eddie Flynn and the cart.

A dinner party at Bowen's Court in the 1950s. From left to right, Lady Ursula Vernon (daughter of 'Bend Or', 2nd Duke of Westminster), Major Jim Egan, Mary, Lady Delamere, Elizabeth Bowen, Major Stephen Vernon, Iris Murdoch.

shoestring; thus the pink curtains which went so well with her grandfather's white Victorian watered silk paper and gilt pelmets and mirrors in the drawing room were made out of corset material, a friend connected with a London department store having let her have some rolls of it on the cheap. The drawing room contained a grand piano seldom played yet kept in tune by an old piano-tuner who used to come from time to time on a bicycle. On one occasion his advent was immediately followed by a heavy fall of snow, so that he and Elizabeth were snowed up together for several days.

Upstairs, each of the bedrooms, with their wonderful views of the mountains, had been given a character of its own by Elizabeth, and they were all in full use, for when she was here the house was always filled with her friends. They came from all walks of life, Irish, English, American, but needless to say, there was a large

Lord and Lady David Cecil at Bowen's Court.

proportion of writers: Lord and Lady David Cecil, Lady Cynthia Asquith, Edward Sackville-West, Rosamond Lehmann, Iris Murdoch, Antonia White. From nearer at hand there was Molly Keane.

Life followed a pattern. Unless there were people coming to luncheon, Elizabeth would work for most of the day in her upstairs study. At five she would come down and join her guests for tea in the library, which was always full of new books sent to her for review. After tea, if it was summer, there might have been an expedition – up the mountain, perhaps, or to the Annes Grove gardens. Later, there would be people in for drinks – not a party, though the drawing room would very quickly be full. After dinner, the talk would go on late into the night until the moment when Elizabeth would rather regretfully ask someone to help her to put the great iron bar in place which kept the hall door shut. She would much rather have left the door open all night, just as it always stood open during the day, but although burglaries in Ireland were still rare, they were no longer unknown.

To keep the house going, there were a few devoted retainers, notably Molly O'Brien the cook who years later remarked: 'We were always laughing at Bowen's Court.'[6] She also remembered how she and her colleagues sometimes found the basement kitchen rather cold; to warm themselves up they would go and play handball in the garage. The coldness of the house was a perpetual source of worry to Elizabeth, who could not afford to instal central heating. For the benefit of guests used to overheated apartments in New York, she would put oil stoves beside every bed, sofa and armchair; so that the rooms were always comfortably warm though there was a serious fire hazard.

Doneraile Court, a few miles to the west of Bowen's Court – which, but for various additions, it would have closely resembled – was now once again the home of a Lord Doneraile, having passed back to Clare Castletown's family after Barnie's death, at the age of nearly ninety in 1937. The present Lord Doneraile had spent most of his life in New Zealand and had been not far off eighty when he and his wife, a New Zealander much younger than himself, came to live here. They found the house very run down, for Barnie had neglected it in his extreme old age, and nothing much had been done to it by Lord Doneraile's elder brother and predecessor. They themselves could do little more, being not particularly well off, but they valiantly kept the house going. They became much-loved figures in the neighbourhood, he spare and bearded, usually wearing an eyeshade of the sort traditionally worn by men in newspaper offices, she austere of countenance but with a kindly and cheerful disposition.

The house was full of beautiful and interesting things, but faded and a little dusty; damp patches on the ceilings and stained wallpaper bore witness to the poor state of the roof. The conservatory, where Harold Nicolson and his parents sat with the Castletowns on that wet August afternoon in 1905, was now derelict; plants ran riot through openings where glass had been. There was, however, another and much smaller conservatory at the opposite corner of the house which was more or less intact and served as a downstairs lavatory; when the intervening doors were open, it terminated the vista from the hall. The doors were open one

Lord and Lady Doneraile.

Doneraile Court in the 1950s. The conservatory, with plants growing out through holes in the glass roof, is on the left.

day when a lady of royal descent called; she looked along the vista and saw, at the far end, Lord Doneraile enthroned playing the violin.

After Lord Doneraile's death at the end of 1956, Lady Doneraile lived on in the house and her sister came from New Zealand to keep her company. A third member of the family was a tame goat named Gigi, who inhabited the slightly-unkempt formal garden over which the principal reception rooms faced. He would come into the Pink Drawing Room through the French window to be fed with cigarettes, a box of the best Benson and Hedges being always kept in readiness for him on the mantlepiece.

$-4-$

At the time when Lord Doneraile died, the Suez Crisis was still the chief topic of conversation at Ascendancy dinner tables. There were just enough dissentients to provoke the occasional heated argument, though the vast majority were in agreement that Eden had been abominably treated. A retired colonel living in a

Dublin suburb felt so strongly about it that he had not allowed a lady who was playing bridge with him at the time to listen to Gaitskell's speech on the wireless. Her son afterwards remarked: 'It appears that the great heart of Protestant Dublin is still sound.'[7]

Second only to Suez as a topic of conversation that autumn and winter was Lissadell. When Sir Josslyn Gore-Booth died in 1944, he was succeeded by an invalid son incapable of managing his affairs who was made a ward of court. The Lissadell estate, which was large by Irish standards – nearly 3000 acres, mostly woodlands planted by Sir Josslyn for the sake of his posterity – passed under the control of a court official, who appointed Miss Gabrielle Gore-Booth, Sir Josslyn's youngest daughter, to manage it. By 1955 the estate was showing a substantial overdraft and Gerald Maguire, who was then the official responsible for it, accused Miss Gabrielle of incompetence; she and her family for their part criticized Maguire's system of accounting and blamed him for not allowing her sufficient money to pay adequate wages. Eventually Maguire appointed a new manager, but when he came to Lissadell to take charge, forty-one out of fifty-three workers on the estate refused to take orders from him. Maguire accordingly dismissed them, whereupon Miss Gabrielle announced that she would pay their wages herself, and began selling crops and timber off the estate to raise the necessary money.

The court put an injunction on the Gore-Booths; and then ordered the entire Lissadell estate to be sold to the Land Commission. The Gore-Booth family managed to stop the sale, but at about the time of Suez Maguire decided to sell some cattle from the estate and sent an auctioneer named McGarry to collect them; anticipating trouble with the locals, who were very much on the family's side, he arranged for McGarry and his drovers to be escorted by twenty Gardai.* McGarry was confronted by Miss Gabrielle in the road bounding the field in which the cattle were grazing. When he announced that he had instructions to seize them, she jumped on to a bank and over a bramble hedge, tearing her nylon stockings to shreds, and then, with blood streaming from the scratches on her legs, she ran towards the cattle and drove them away. She was joined in the chase by her sister Aideen; McGarry and his men followed in hot pursuit. After a few minutes the sisters gave up, and the cattle were with difficulty loaded into McGarry's lorry.

Maguire tried to have Miss Gabrielle and Miss Aideen sent to prison for contempt, but the court dismissed the application; it would certainly have caused an outcry if the nieces of Constance Markievicz had been gaoled by the Republic for the sake of which she had herself endured prison. Instead, an eviction order was made against the Gore-Booths. It was like the Land War in reverse; now it was the landlord's family who were to be evicted. However, the order was only used as a

* Police.

threat to prevent the Gore-Booths from interfering any more in the management of the estate.

Among the many unmarried or widowed ladies of the Ascendancy struggling to keep large country houses and demesnes in the 1950s, the Misses Gore-Booth had the advantage of being still young. Miss May Power of Kilfane in County Kilkenny – which had come to her through the death of her two brothers in the South African War – was about eighty in 1956. She lived alone in the dilapidated Big House, her sister, with whom she was not on good terms, living in a cottage on the place.

Mrs Norton Barry of Castle Cor in North Cork was reputed to be well up in her nineties when she died in 1959, though nobody knew her exact age. By the time she died, her fine Georgian house not only to all intents and purposes lacked a roof, but even the walls were rotten; her kitchen garden had the name for being the best woodcock shoot in the neighbourhood. Inside the house, little or nothing had been done in the way of cleaning or polishing for years. Elizabeth Bowen once spent a night here and was startled to see a strange white glow on the floor of her bedroom, as if the bed were floating in ectoplasm; it was the moon reflecting on the hard shiny layer of the candle-grease of ages that covered the bare boards.

Mrs Barry was looked after by an ancient manservant named Thady, who also acted as her groom and her bone-setter, for she hunted right up to the end, as well as playing a hard game of tennis, wiry and athletic despite her weakness for chocolates and cream cakes – Edward Sackville-West used to say that the only person he had known to rival her consumption of the latter was Queen Mary. As the widow of a former Master of the Duhallow Hunt, descended on her father's side from the Wrixon-Bechers who ran the hunt for more than a century, and on her mother's side from the Listowels, Mrs Barry was a formidable figure in the hunting field, riding as fearlessly as people half her age, a bunch of violets always in her button-hole. Once, towards the end of her life, she rode into somebody's back garden while hunting and was knocked off by the clothes-line. As she lay prostrate on the ground, apparently unconscious, while other Hunt members attempted to revive her, the English lady who was then Master said: 'Be careful of her false teeth.' Whereupon, from the lifeless body, there came a sepulchral voice.

'Leave them. They're my own.'[8]

Elderly ladies of less advanced years living in decrepit country houses at this time included Miss Phyllis Godfrey, soldiering on alone at Kilcoleman after her stepmother's death in 1950, Miss Frances Bagwell of Jamesbrook in County Cork, and Miss Dorothea O'Neill Daunt of Kilcascan Castle in the same county. Miss Bagwell once said to her neighbour Mrs Bell of Fota, who was visiting her at Jamesbrook: 'We will now have luncheon,' and proceeded to cook some potatoes over the drawing room fire. Miss O'Neill Daunt lived by selling things out of her house. 'I've sold out my drawing room,' she announced one day, when there was nothing there left to sell.

There was also a lady in the Wicklow Mountains who hadn't the heart to turn her dog out into the cold night. The dog therefore took to relieving himself against one of the legs of a gilt baroque table in her hall. When, eventually, the leg rotted, she simply sawed pieces off the other three so that they matched.

It is remarkable how long the houses of these ladies lasted with roofs like sieves; the ladies generally avoided the worst of the leaks by moving from room to room, as Lord Emly had done. They learnt to live with dry rot, hoping the fungus would keep to its own quarters, so to speak; they shut the door on it, as on the Monster of Glamis, and with any luck it stayed put. Or else it claimed another room every so often as tribute, leaving the lady enough space until she died. Occasionally people were too slow in dying and the fungus got impatient. By the time Phyllis Godfrey lay on her deathbed at Kilcoleman in 1959, the dry rot had attacked the staircase, with the result that the people looking after her insisted on carrying her out of the house to die in a cottage at the gates, because they feared the stairs would not take the weight of her coffin.

The twice-widowed Mrs de Sales La Terriere, who as Miss Joan Grubb shocked people before 1914 by riding astride, was fortunate in that her castle in County Tipperary was solidly built so that although totally neglected it did not actually fall down. She cooked her dogs' food in the hall and had no vehicle except a horse and trap. She wore a man's cap, jacket and tie, rather in the manner of John Vere Foster, whose avenue, which was exceptionally long for a glebe, was now almost completely choked with brambles.

– 5 –

If John Vere Foster's eccentricities originated in her mother's desire for a son, those of Raymond Lecky-Browne-Lecky of Ecclesville in County Tyrone – known to his friends as Tibby – can be blamed on his mother's longing for a daughter. She continued to dress him as a girl after he had passed the age when this was customary, and while as a male adult he was prohibited by law from indulging in transvestism in real life, he made quite a name for himself as an actor of female parts in amateur theatricals, which were his ruling passion. Irish newspapers and magazines of the early years of this century contain frequent pictures of him as Mrs Tanqueray or Lady Windermere; one of the captions speaks of 'the peculiar proclivity of Mr Lecky-Browne-Lecky', probably in all innocence.

In later years, when he dressed with a faded effeminate elegance, Tibby used to give musical parties at Ecclesville, which was now a little dilapidated and full of old theatrical pictures. A local paper has an account of one which he gave at Christmas time in about 1950.

> From the standpoint of culture this was a most delightful treat, and Mr Lecky-Browne-Lecky entertained upwards of 120 guests. The spacious reception rooms with their beautiful floral decorations were much admired by all. Great interest was aroused by the first appearance in Ireland of the beautiful young professional singer Lydia de Burgh, who sang an Italian Aria and several songs, much to the delight of everyone . . . a feature at the conclusion of the party was the handing round of mince pies.*

The programme also included a pianoforte solo played by Tibby himself, who always liked to be at the centre of the stage.

About 1960, when he was nearly eighty, Tibby gave a tea party at which one of the guests was Miss Helen Bonaparte Wyse, a member of a County Waterford Ascendancy family descended in the female line from Lucien Bonaparte. After tea Miss Bonaparte Wyse, who appeared to be a typical Ascendancy spinster of a certain age in tweeds, went out to her car and returned carrying a suitcase from which she produced some sheaves of manuscript and a Napoleon hat. Donning the latter, she proceeded to give very long and very stirring Napoleonic recitations of her own composition. Tibby, in his mauve velvet jacket, began to shift about uneasily. If anybody was to steal the stage it should be himself. He turned to one of the male guests and in his high-pitched voice said: 'Rather amateurish, don't you think?'

Miss Bonaparte Wyse was impervious to such asides. On she went: Austerlitz, Jena, La Grande Armée, the retreat from Moscow, the Old Guard; no detail was missed. 'Rather amateurish, don't you think?' repeated her host, in an even more penetrating voice. But Miss Bonaparte Wyse went on. When at last her recitations were over, they turned out to have been only the first part of the performance, for she sat down at the piano and crashed into Rachmaninoff. Her chords were not enough to drown the voice of Tibby as he turned yet again to his neighbour.

'Rather amateurish, don't you think?'[9]

Tibby's cousin Mervyn Knox-Browne, who died in 1954, also fancied himself as an actor. At Aughentaine Castle, a few miles south of Ecclesville, he had a private theatre, where he always played lead parts such as Romeo. Aughentaine

---

* Miss de Burgh, who comes of the County Kildare branch of the Clanricarde family, later became a well-known portrait painter, achieving the distinction of being the only portrait painter resident in Ireland to whom the Queen and other members of the British royal family have sat.

was close to Blessingbourne, the home of a more serious devotee of the arts, Captain Peter Montgomery, a keen and knowledgable musician who became President of the Northern Ireland Arts Council. As well as being prominent in the musical and artistic world, Captain Montgomery was an honorary ADC to Lord Wakehurst, the then Governor of Northern Ireland, and he followed the example of his father in maintaining as many contacts as he could south of the Border. He was a friend of Erskine Childers who was a Minister in Fianna Fail Governments from 1951 onwards. At the same time he was on very friendly terms with his neighbours Viscount and Viscountess Brookeborough. When his disinherited elder brother, now a Monsignor in England, came to stay, he would take him over to dinner with them. Whatever might be said about Lord Brookeborough's politics, he did not allow religious differences to affect personal relationships.

Lord Brookeborough, who as Sir Basil Brooke became Prime Minister of Northern Ireland in 1943, was very much of the Ascendancy, unlike the two previous Prime Ministers who came from the Northern Ireland business community. He was head of the great Brooke clan which had many ramifications south of the Border, notably the branch formerly at Summerton near Dublin. The Brookes were typical of the Ascendancy in their strong military tradition; Field-Marshal Lord Alanbrooke was Lord Brookeborough's uncle.

The only outward sign of Lord Brookeborough's importance at Colebrooke, his family home in County Fermanagh, was a constable patrolling the sweep. While the policeman walked up and down, Lord and Lady Brookeborough were often hard at work in the sunken garden which they had made at one end of the rather austere classical house. They lived mostly in the small rooms at this end, the larger rooms, including the dining room which Lord Craigavon, the former Sir James Craig, christened 'Golgotha' on account of the numerous deer skulls covering the walls, being used only on special occasions, such as when the Queen Mother came to stay in 1962.

Although Lord Brookeborough himself, for reasons of policy, did not venture south of the Border, Lady Brookeborough and also their son and daughter-in-law, Captain and Mrs John Brooke, frequently visited friends in the Republic. Captain Brooke and his wife Rosemary – a cousin of Lord O'Neill and of Captain Terence O'Neill who was to succeed Lord Brookeborough as Prime Minister in 1963 – sometimes took part in equestrian events at Ballsbridge. The Ascendancy from north and south of the Border continued to mix freely; if there was the occasional clash of opinions, this did not make relations any less cordial. Amongst themselves, those who lived south of the Border sometimes told satirical anecdotes of how their friends and relations in Northern Ireland took Ulster Unionism a little too seriously. Perhaps the best story of this kind is that told – and very likely invented – by a member of a County Kildare family about his own mother, who came from County Derry. One day, mother and son were expecting Dr Maurice Craig, the architectural historian, and another gentleman whose name happened to be Carson to luncheon. 'We mustn't forget that Craig and Carson are coming today,' the son told his mother that morning, whereupon she corrected him, saying reverently, 'Carson and Craig, dear' – as though he had got two of the Persons of the Blessed Trinity in the wrong order.

15

Dior and dogs' dinners

— *I* —

Fashionable Ascendancy life, by the beginning of the 1960s, was becoming less exclusively sporting. Racing still flourished, but fewer people hunted owing to the ever-increasing cost and difficulty of keeping hunters. And since the break-up of the big estates, there were only a very few first-class shoots left in Ireland; most Irish shooting was now rough by British standards. Now, alongside the traditional sporting world, an artistic world was growing up within the Ascendancy, in which those associated with the new Irish Georgian Society – founded in 1958 by Mr and Mrs Desmond Guinness to take the place of one founded early in the century and since defunct – were very much to the fore.

The Ascendancy world, particularly in and around Dublin, was also becoming more cosmopolitan. The foreign embassies were filling the gap left in the Irish social scene by the passing of the Viceregal Court and there was now an increasing number of continentals and Americans among the new settlers. There were also people of different nationalities who had married into the Ascendancy; there was the Russian Mrs Prescott, there was Prince Ferdinando d'Ardia Caracciolo, whose wife was a Purcell-FitzGerald from County Waterford. There was Lady Cochrane, half Lebanese and half Neapolitan, married to Sir Desmond Cochrane of Woodbrook, the nephew of the singer and patron of cricket and polo Sir Stanley. There was Mrs Desmond Guinness, of a German princely family and a great-grandniece of the Empress Elizabeth.

Having been rather English-orientated between the wars, the Guinnesses were now very much back on the Irish social scene. In 1958 Mr Desmond Guinness, a great-grandson of the first Lord Iveagh, had bought Leixlip Castle in County Kildare; he and his wife had worked hard to restore and furnish it and it was now

Leixlip Castle

one of the most attractive as well as hospitable country houses in the neighbourhood of Dublin. Mr Guinness's cousin, Mrs Plunket – formerly Miss Aileen Guinness – lived a short distance away at Luttrellstown Castle, where she entertained regally, inviting people from all walks of life in Ireland together with friends from Britain and abroad. Since the war, she had done up the interior of the Castle in a palatial manner; what seemed like an army of footmen, something now very rare in Ireland, adding to the splendour. Mrs Plunket's sister lived at Luggala, a sugary white castellated lodge in the Wicklow Mountains, where she gave parties of a more bohemian nature; Brendan Behan and his wife were among her guests. In Northern Ireland, Mrs Plunket's nephew Lord Dufferin and his artist wife Lindy – herself a Guinness of the banking branch of the family – gave frequent house parties at Clandeboye after their marriage in 1964.

Away from the Guinness connection, the best-run of the greater Irish country houses in the early and middle 1960s included Curraghmore, Birr, Dunsany, Glin, Kildangan and Mount Juliet. At Curraghmore, where Lord Waterford's coming-of-age celebrations in 1954 were reminiscent of his father's, the house and its vast demesne were still kept up very much in the old style; there were plenty of horses in the stables, for Lord and Lady Waterford both hunted and he played polo. The castles at Birr and Dunsany had both been elegantly redecorated by their present owners – in the case of the latter, the son and daughter-in-law of the poet and playwright. At Birr, Lord and Lady Rosse had also greatly added to the gardens. Glin was now more beautiful than at any other time in its history, thanks to the excellent taste of the young Knight of Glin who was already making a name for himself as an authority on architecture and the decorative arts. The Castle had recently benefited from a much-needed restoration carried out by the Knight's wealthy Canadian stepfather.

Mr Roderic More O'Ferrall, a very successful breeder of bloodstock, was making another great Irish garden at Kildangan, as well as having carried out many improvements to the house. Mount Juliet, also closely connected with the Turf, now belonged to General McCalmont's son Dermot, who together with his son Major Victor McCalmont ran the Kilkenny Hunt in a style unknown to most of the hunting world since 1914. To add to the pre-1914 atmosphere of Mount Juliet, it had a cricket ground, and was the only place in Ireland where country-house cricket still went on, the matches being organized by a neighbour, Sir William Blunden of Castle Blunden.

If at country houses such as these it seemed as though the wars and upheavals of the past half century had never taken place, the same was true of the Kildare Street Club, even though in about 1955 it had been obliged to retrench by selling off the part of the club house nearest to Nassau Street, including the original hall and the room in which Lord Fermoy nearly got shot. The good old club servants were far more numerous than in the best London clubs at this time; the table and the cellar were as good and as inexpensive as ever, although oysters now had to be ordered in advance and the muffins from London had long ceased. The membership in 1965 was almost as high as it had been at any time during the past century, and out of the 750 or so members, about half were still of the Ascendancy or closely connected with it, though some of them were expatriates. The other half was largely drawn from the Dublin professional and business worlds and from the new settlers, British, continental, American. Only three members had any sort of footing in the new Irish ruling class. One of these was Sir Anthony Esmonde, now representing Wexford in the Dail; he was elected to the Club in 1960, the first of the family to be a member since Sir Thomas Grattan Esmonde and his brother resigned in the 1880s. The other two were the economist, historian and lawyer Professor George O'Brien, a Senator until 1965, and Dr Frederick Boland, the former Irish Ambassador to the Court of St James's and Irish Representative at the United Nations. While Sir Anthony Esmonde belonged to the Ascendancy by birth, Professor O'Brien and Dr Boland were both, so to speak, honorary members of it through being, or having been, Directors of the Guinness Brewery. The scarcity of Ireland's rulers in the Club was as much due to their reluctance to join as to the Club's unwillingness to have them.

Catholics in the Club, though numerous, were still outnumbered by Protestants; the Club Masonic Lodge flourished. In short, as a bastion of the Ascendancy, the Club appeared, in the middle 1960s, to be going on very well. Few would have believed that within a very few years its finances should have taken such a turn for the worse as to oblige it to leave the old club house in Kildare Street altogether and to amalgamate with the University Club in St Stephen's Green.

Though the Dublin life of the Ascendancy was no longer limited to the Club, the Royal Dublin Society and the race meetings, as it had been between the wars, the Horse Show still had pride of place in the social calendar. Horse Show Week was as crowded with gaieties as ever – private parties and a succession of hunt balls that were always lively and often riotous. Such was the attraction of the parties that some people 'did' Horse Show without going near Ballsbridge, or at any rate not except on the Friday, and then only in the afternoon. Few of the really dedicated party-goers were up early enough to get to the Show in the morning. One afternoon at about five during the 1964 Horse Show, Mrs Desmond Guinness was taking some friends round Leixlip. 'This is King John's Room,' she said, opening a door. In the depths of the great canopied bed, there was a sudden stirring. '*That*,' said Mrs Guinness, ever tactful, 'is King John.'

Because of the smallness of Irish society, foreign visitors staying for Horse Show in the more fashionable country houses around Dublin did not mix exclusively with their 'smart' hosts and their hosts' equally smart friends, as would be the case in England, but would also be taken to see people like the three old Hamilton sisters who lived in a fine but dilapidated house named Woodville on the banks of the Liffey a few miles away from Hamwood, their family home. The 'Hams', who eked out a modest income by taking in paying guests – ranging from Trinity students to a retired Group-Captain – had known many people in their time, including Yeats; the eldest, May, was a painter of distinction. And while the three old ladies were excellent value in themselves, there was always a sense of the unexpected in a visit to Woodville; one never knew who one would meet there. During one Horse Show week, somebody dropped in and found Princess Maria-Pia of Italy standing gracefully among the dogs' plates on the doorstep. This blending of the very smart cosmopolitan world with homely, tweedy, animal-loving county folk was a feature of Ascendancy life during the 1950s and 1960s, not only in and around Dublin but all over the country. Dior and dogs' dinners went hand in hand.

— 2 —

May Hamilton, the eldest of the the Hams, died in 1964. During the 1960s, the grand old ladies of the Ascendancy were dying fast, with nobody to take their place; those growing old now were not the same, having not reached adult life before 1914. One who survived the decade, though she was already eighty in 1960, was Miss Ethel Dillon, sister of the last Lord Clonbrock. She lived alone at Clonbrock, a beautiful Georgian and Victorian house in County Galway which had the rare quality of being faded but not run-down. Though very shaky and walking with two sticks, she still did things well here. No poky sitting room smelling of dog for her; she sat in the long early Victorian drawing room with its walls of silky grey, its crystal chandeliers and its closely-hung paintings in gilt

Miss Ethel Dillon. She appears as a young girl at the turn of the century in the illustration on page 105.

Clonbrock.

frames. Her father, as a young diplomat in Vienna, had written home giving instructions on how the floor of this room was to be laid, so that it might be suitable for dancing the latest waltzes. She had an old butler waiting at table; he would join her for morning prayers in the hall, just the two of them. They sang hymns to the accompaniment of an eighteenth-century chamber organ which they took it in turns to play.

Another house which was faded and old-fashioined but well-kept was the rambling Moyaliffe Castle, seat of the Armstrongs in North Tipperary. After her husband's death in 1965 the childless Mrs William Kemmis, who was an Armstrong, lived here the whole time, having previously migrated between Moyaliffe and Ballinacor, Captain Kemmis's family home in County Wicklow. She was looked after by an old butler and an even older cook, who in the vast antiquated kitchen had a bed on which to take the occasional nap. There was also an elderly uniformed housemaid who would take up early morning tea with very thin slices of bread and butter to anybody who was staying. An old gardener kept the expanse of lawn between the house and the river perfectly mown.

At Moyaliffe, nothing had been touched since about 1914. The family brougham still stood in one of the coach houses. The hall and staircase were a shrine to Mrs Kemmis's brother, who was killed in the First World War; his photograph, showing him looking incredibly handsome, was flanked by the heads of animals he had shot in India, as well as by his full-dress uniform and his ceremonial saddlery. The rather dark sitting rooms were crammed with furniture

The drawing room at Clonbrock in the 1960s.

The hall at Clonbrock. On the left is the organ which
Miss Dillon and her butler used to take it in turns to
play, when the two of them met here for morning
prayers.

and objects, their walls covered with water colours and photographs. Every bedroom had its washstand with jug and basin; and somewhere in the labyrinthine back premises – 'It's such a *convenient* house' Mrs Kemmis used to say – there hung an array of massive china hip-baths, complete with the cans in which the hot water for them was carried. In the match-boarded downstairs lavatory, there were ivory-backed hairbrushes and little hand towels neatly arranged. On a table lay a 'Confession Book', a kind of autograph book in which, as the young Miss Winona Armstrong of First World War days, Mrs Kemmis had got her young men friends, mostly officers from the garrison, to write. The pages were divided into columns, with printed headings, such as 'Your Greatest Ambition', under which most of the men had gallantly written: 'To marry Miss Winona Armstrong'.

– 3 –

'My two loyalties are to Ireland and the Crown,' a certain Irish peer says, even to this day, and there are still plenty of people living south of the Border who feel the same as he does. Nevertheless, even in the 1960s, the attitude of some of the Ascendancy in this respect was changing. 'Head or harp?' the writer and broadcaster Lionel Fleming, a cousin of the Castletownshend cousinhood, asks himself in his autobiography of that name, a name derived from the call, still heard in Ireland, at the spinning of a coin – Irish money having formerly borne the British Sovereign's head on one side and the harp on the other. By 1965, when his book was published, an increasing number of people in the Ascendancy world would have come to the same conclusion as he does when he says, 'Harp it is.'[1]

This, of course, was particularly true of some of the younger generation who had far fewer regrets than their elders had for the broken links with Britain and the Commonwealth. The decline in the Ascendancy's romantic allegiance to the Crown coincided with a decline in the great service tradition, a result, perhaps, of the improvement in the Irish economy. By the 1960s the sons of the Ascendancy were finding it easier to make their careers in Ireland. But such employment as they found was almost invariably in business. However friendly they may have been with individual members of the Irish official world, that world was still largely closed to them. It was the same with the political world. The number of Dail Deputies of Ascendancy background had, for some time now, stood at three: Childers, Esmonde and Gerard Sweetman, head of a family of Catholic gentry in County Kildare who had been a minister in the second of the two Interparty

Governments of the 1950s. And all through the 1960s, the only Senator who came from the Ascendancy was Mr Michael Yeats, son of the poet.

While the leaders of the new Ireland were probably now more friendly towards the Ascendancy than they ever had been – if only because they now saw it as a picturesque survival, unlikely 'to block the progress of the Irish Nation' as Lord Granard and Andrew Jameson and others of their kind had been accused of doing in the 1930s – yet they still did not see fit to make any tax concessions for the upkeep of country houses, let alone give grants for their repair. Yet they appreciated the value as a tourist attraction of Westport, which Lord Altamont, son of the present Lord Sligo, had opened to the public. Without grants or tax concessions, there was very little incentive for opening houses, for the takings alone seldom justified the trouble and expense of opening. Including Westport, there were only about half-a-dozen private houses in the Republic open during the 1960s; one of them was Bantry House, Lady Ardilaun's girlhood home, which had been open for many years. Another was Lissadell.

In the case of the latter, the Gore-Booth sisters and their younger brother were able to take visitors round themselves, which kept expenses to a minimum. And they needed any money they could get, having incurred the heavy costs of an unsuccessful High Court action over the running of the Lissadell estate. Apart from the takings from visitors, they had little income other than what Miss Gabrielle earned working for their neighbour Lord Mountbatten as his manager. In winter, the Gore-Booths now lived mainly in the kitchen, to save coal.

In Northern Ireland, there was a flourishing National Trust, to which several important houses had been made over since the end of the war, including Castlecoole; the families still lived in some of them and the necessary endowments had been provided by the State. But no organization comparable to the National Trust existed in the Republic, where the owners of country houses which they could no longer afford to maintain were faced with the alternative of selling up or allowing the house to become derelict.

Most country house owners in the Republic had to rely on farming as the only way of keeping going. While there were great hopes that things would improve if Ireland joined the Common Market, in all too many cases the land was just not enough to support the house, however efficiently it may have been farmed. Where a large country house was well maintained, there was almost invariably some other source of income – generally from outside Ireland.

Against a background of growing prosperity, the sale of country houses by their families had gone on unabated since the end of the war. Gormanston Castle was sold in 1947, Straffan a couple of years later, being by now too large for the Bartons even in its reduced state. At about the same time as Straffan went, the trustees of the Leinster family sold the unlived-in Carton. In 1953 Lord De Freyne sold

The ruin of Rockingham, County Roscommon, after it had been burnt down in 1957.

French Park and the son of Fingall and Daisy sold Killeen. So the melancholy catalogue goes on. The demesne of Rockingham was sold by the Stafford-King-Harmans after the house had been accidently burnt down in 1957.

In 1959 Elizabeth Bowen decided that she could no longer afford to keep Bowen's Court, and so she sold it to a local man, under the impression that he and his family were going to live in the house and care for it. 'What I dread are not my own feelings but other people's,'[2] she wrote at the beginning of 1960, when she was about to leave the house for the last time. She left before the furniture was sold; Molly O'Brien closed the hall door behind her and 'saw her drive away as if it were just an ordinary day – all emotion withstood, withheld or by now simply over'.[3] Unlike most of those who sold their family homes since the end of the war, she did not stay in Ireland, eventually settling in Hythe, where she had spent some happy years as a child. A few months after Elizabeth left Bowen's Court, a friend in County Cork heard alarming rumours about what was happening to the house and went to investigate. He found only the hall door and a window on either side of it still standing.

The year 1961 saw the sale of Powerscourt, perhaps the most famous of all Irish country houses. There was some consolation in the thought that the splendid baroque house and its formal gardens in the grand manner would be well maintained by the new owner, who also bought most of the contents. In fact the house was destined to survive intact for only another thirteen years before the greater part of it was accidently gutted by fire.

'This is the end,' Major Bell said one day in the 1960s, when he heard that Russell, the butler, had died. Though the octogenerian Major did not live to see it, Fota would indeed be sold within ten years of Russell's death. The servant shortage, having not been much of a problem in the 1950s, grew progressively worse during the 1960s. The change from an adequate staff to hardly any help at all seemed particularly abrupt in Irish country houses for the reason that so many of them had relied on old retainers who died within a short time of each other and could not be replaced. Ballinamona Park in County Waterford, the home of Major Robin Carew – whose third birthday had been celebrated here with 'a feast and sports' at which he had given away the prizes – was a very well run house in the middle 1960s. A few years later Major Carew, now a widower of nearly ninety, had a melancholy tale to tell:

> A couple of years ago the housemaid died suddenly – she had been here 26 years. Last year 3 old retainers died and last April my housekeeper died. She had been here nearly all her life. So now I have no help in the house. It is sad to lose all these old friends.[4]

Sir Terence Langrishe, Herky's son, was more fortunate than Major Carew in that he at any rate had one woman to look after him at Knocktopher in his old age. He still put on a dinner jacket every night, to dine by himself off shepherd's pie.

About 1960, the daughter of another great house had called at Stradbally Hall one sunny afternoon in the middle of harvest and found the Cosby family playing tennis, the men in white flannels, the old butler bringing out a silver tray with glasses and a jug of lemonade. Having been brought up to take farming seriously, she had been scandalized. Ten years later, the butler was no more and Mr Adrian Cosby was leading the life of a working farmer, as well as acting as his own carpenter in the battle to keep the roof of his ancestral mansion in repair. Such are the contrasts of Ireland, that when, at about this time, he brought his bride back to Stradbally, they were pulled in an open carriage by the townspeople, who presented them with an illuminated address.

For families less resilient than the Cosbys, the combination of no servants and a troublesome roof often proved too much. All too many houses which somebody more energetic might have saved belonged to 'a wistful, defeated old couple' as Evelyn Waugh called the owners of a castle in County Waterford which was for sale when he was contemplating settling in Ireland.[5] And it was not only the old who were defeated by Irish country houses. The young cousin, usually from

Mr Adrian Cosby (right) with friends, setting out from Stradbally Hall for the Irish Derby in the 1960s.

England, who inherits a house, comes over and lives in it for a couple of years, then sells it and goes away again, has long been a phenomenon of the Ascendancy world. While it is hard enough for people who are merely ineffective, it can be imagined how much more difficult it was for the spendthrifts, the gamblers and the alcoholics.

The Ascendancy of County Galway is supposed to have had more than its fair share of such people. This is certainly borne out by the decline in the number of Galway county families living in their ancestral homes, though this decline can also be attributed to the fact that Galway was one of the counties worst affected by the Troubles and the Civil War. A Galway lady who died in her ninetieth year in 1959 reckoned that in her time she had stayed in eighty different country houses in the county, and that there were at least another thirty in which she did not stay. By 1959, the number was down to about twelve. Since then, a further eight had gone, including Clonbrock – Miss Dillon ended her days in an old people's home. To drive through County Galway is to follow a succession of crumbling demesne walls, with occasionally a ruined house half buried in ivy, though more often than not the house has, like Coole, been razed to the ground.

– *4* –

When so many Irish country houses were ruins, it was fully expected by about 1960 that Kilkenny Castle would soon be a ruin also. Still empty, it was fast deteriorating; various schemes for its use had come to nothing. Then the State agreed to buy the castle for a nominal sum with a view to restoring it. The Castle's future seemed assured, though it was sad that the Ormondes should now be parting with it, having owned it since 1391. Nearly six hundred years of history were coming to an end.

The formal handing-over of the Castle by Lord Ormonde – who had succeeded his brother, the former George Ossory, in 1949 – took place on 12 August 1967 during the first Rally of the Butler Society, a world-wide association of members of the great House of Butler which had recently been founded. It was hoped that the south tower would eventually become the Society's headquarters, which served to mitigate the sadness of the occasion; for this meant that a small part of the Castle would, so to speak, stay in the family.

It had rained heavily at the Dublin Horse Show on the previous day, but the afternoon of 12 August was fine. The ceremony was held in the Castle courtyard. On three sides were the massive buildings of grey stone, on the fourth side, gently rising parkland, trees heavy with the spinach green of August, a distant blue

Scene in the courtyard of Kilkenny Castle on 12 August 1967 during the formal handing-over of the Castle by Lord Ormonde (right).

mountain. The gathering was large and distinguished. There was the septuagenarian Lord Ormonde himself, a genial cavalryman, with steel-grey hair and moustache. There was Lady Ormonde and Lord Ormonde's cousin and heir from America, Mr Charles Butler, another soldierly figure. There was Lord Carrick, son of the elder of the twins who had been Pages at the Viceregal Court before 1914. There were two other Butler peers and their wives, Lord and Lady Mountgarret and Lord and Lady Dunboyne. There was Miss Marye Pole-Carew and her sister Mrs Du Cane, granddaughters of the Lord and Lady Ormonde of Edwardian days, with whom they had stayed here frequently as children. There was Sir Thomas Butler of Ballin Temple, a former Colonel of the Grenadier Guards, now Governor of the Tower of London. There was Mr Hubert Butler the historian. There were Vicomtes de Butler from France, Barons von Buttlar-Elberberg from Germany and Austria. The new Ireland was represented by the Minister for Finance, Mr Charles Haughey.

It was more like a garden party than a rally. Before the actual ceremony began, people wandered about the courtyard, chatting. The ladies wore their smartest dresses and hats; the gentlemen were not actually in morning coats, but the kind of suits they wore were the next best thing. There was, however, one discordant note, a foursome who stood out strangely in the garden party crowd. They consisted of two young men with hair down to their shoulders, one wearing a grey-green cloak almost to the ground, and two tousled girls in trousers. There was speculation as to who they might be; some thought they were the singers of old Irish songs due to perform next day in a medieval house in the city. Others thought they must have come from the Kilkenny Design Centre, which now occupied the Castle stables.

While Lord Ormonde spoke a few words of welcome, the photographers clicked their shutters in a somewhat desultory way. And then suddenly, like dogs sniffing the scent, they became alert, turned quickly and disappeared with their cameras into the crowd. A moment or two later they could be seen running up the rise, led by the strange foursome.

Gradually the assembled Butlers learnt what was happening. The foursome consisted of one of the Rolling Stones and his friends, who wished to be photographed with the Castle in the background. To the media, they were far more interesting than Lord Ormonde, the 6th Marquess, the 24th Earl, the 30th Hereditary Chief Butler of Ireland, more exciting than six hundred years of history.

Select Bibliography

ANSON, LADY CLODAGH: *Victorian Days*, London 1957.

ANTRIM, ANGELA: *The Antrim McDonnells*, Belfast 1977.

ARNOLD, BRUCE: *Orpen, Mirror to an Age*, London 1981.

BAMFORD, FRANCIS and VIOLA BANKES: *Vicious Circle*, London 1965.

BENCE-JONES, MARK: *Burke's Guide to the Country Houses of Ireland*, London 1978.

—: *The Remarkable Irish*, New York 1966.

BENCE-JONES, MARK and HUGH MONTGOMERY-MASSINGBERD: *The British Aristocracy*, London 1979.

BENNETT, GEOFFREY: *Charlie B*, London 1968.

BERESFORD, ADMIRAL LORD CHARLES: *Memoirs*, 2 vols. London 1914.

BOWEN, ELIZABETH: *Bowen's Court*, London 1942.

BOWEN, MURIEL: *Irish Hunting*, Tralee ND.

BROOKE, RAYMOND F.: *The Brimming River*, Dublin 1961.

BRUCE, H. J.: *Silken Dalliance*, London 1946.

BUCKLAND, PATRICK: *Irish Unionism I*, Dublin and New York 1972.

—: *Ulster Unionism*, Dublin 1973.

CASTLETOWN, LORD: *Ego*, London 1923.

DESART, EARL OF and LADY SYBIL LUBBOCK: *A Page from the Past*, London, 1936.

DE STACPOOLE, DUKE: *Irish and Other Memories*, London 1922.

DEVAS, NICOLETTE: *Two Flamboyant Fathers*, London 1966.

DICKINSON, P.L.: *The Dublin of Yesterday*, London 1929.

DONNELLY, JAMES S. Jr.: *The Land and the People of Nineteenth Century Cork*, London 1975.

DUNRAVEN, EARL OF: *Past Times and Pastimes*, 2 vols, London ND.

DUNSANY, LORD: *Patches of Sunlight*, London 1938.

EVERETT, KATHERINE: *Bricks and Flowers*, London 1950.

FINGALL, ELIZABETH COUNTESS OF: *Seventy Years Young*, London 1937.

FLEMING, LIONEL: *Head or Harp*, London 1965.

GALLOWAY, PETER: *The Most Illustrious Order of St Patrick*, Chichester 1983.

GAUGHAN, J. ANTHONY: *The Knights of Glin*, Dublin 1978.

GLENDINNING, VICTORIA: *Elizabeth Bowen*, London 1977.

GORMANSTON, EILEEN: *A Little Kept*, London 1954.

GREGORY, ANNE: *Me and Nu*, Gerrards Cross 1970.

Lady Gregory's Journals (ed Lennox Robinson), London 1946.

GURNEY, SAMUEL: *Isabel*, Norwich and London 1935.

HEADLAM, MAURICE: *Irish Reminiscences*, London 1947.

HEALY, MAURICE: *The Old Munster Circuit*, London 1939.

HENN, T.R.: *Five Arches*, Gerrards Cross 1980.

HONE, JOSEPH: *The Life of George Moore*, New York 1936.

HONE, PATRICK: *Cricket in Ireland*, Tralee 1955.

Irish Unionism 1885–1923 (Documents ed Patrick Buckland) Belfast 1973.

LESLIE, ANITA: *The Gilt and the Gingerbread*, London 1981.

LESLIE, SEYMOUR: *The Jerome Connexion*, London 1964.

LESLIE, SHANE: *Long Shadows*, London 1966.

Letters of a Noble Woman (Mrs La Touche of Harristown) (ed Margaret Ferrier Young), London 1908.

LYNCH-ROBINSON, SIR CHRISTOPHER: *The Last of the Irish RMs*, London 1951.

MALINS, EDWARD and PATRICK BOWE: *Irish Gardens and Demesnes from 1830*, London 1980.

MARRECO, ANNE: *The Rebel Countess*, London 1967.

MIDLETON, EARL OF: *Records and Reactions 1856–1939*, London 1939.

MORE, JASPER: *A Tale of Two Houses*, Shrewsbury 1978.

NEELY, W.G.: *Kilcooley: Land and People in Tipperary*, Belfast 1983.

O'BRIEN-FFRENCH, CONRAD: *Delicate Mission*, London ND.

ORIGO, IRIS: *Images and Shadows*, London 1970.

O'SULLIVAN, DONAL: *The Irish Free State and its Senate*, London 1940.

ROBINSON, SIR HENRY: *Memories Wise and Otherwise*, London, New York and Melbourne, 1923.

ROBINSON, LENNOX: *Bryan Cooper*, London 1931.

ROBINSON, LENNOX, TOM ROBINSON and NORA DORMAN: *Three Homes*, London 1938.

ROSSMORE, LORD: *Things I Can Tell*, London 1912.

SOMERVILLE, E. OE. and MARTIN ROSS: *Irish Memories*, London 1917.

—: *Some Irish Yesterdays*, London 1906.

TUMIM, STEPHEN: *Great Legal Disasters*, London 1983.

VAUGHAN, W.E.: *Landlords and Tenants in Ireland 1848–1904*, Dublin 1984.

WELCOME, JOHN: *Cheating at Cards*, London 1963.

WYNNE, MAUD: *An Irishman and His Family*, London 1937.

Source references

Chapter I   'The happiest country I ever knew'

1. Brigadier Bryan Fowler, in conversation with the author.
2. Lord Castletown, *Ego*, London 1923.
3. Admiral Lord Charles Beresford, *Memoirs*, 2 vols, London 1914.
4. C.P. Crane, *Memories of a Resident Magistrate*, Edinburgh, privately printed, 1938.
5. Castletown, op cit.
6. Ibid.
7. Bisbrooke papers.
8. Diary of Lady Alice Howard.
9. Lord Rossmore, *Things I Can Tell*, London 1912.
10. Bence-Jones papers.
11. W.G. Neely, Kilcooley: *Land and People in Tipperary*, Belfast 1983.
12. Sir Christopher Lynch-Robinson, *The Last of the Irish RMs*, London 1951.
13. Ibid.
14. Elizabeth, Countess of Fingall, *Seventy Years Young*, London 1937.
15. Sir William Nott-Bower, *Fifty-two Years a Policeman*, London 1926.
16. Maud Wynne, *An Irishman and his Family*, London 1937.
17. Rossmore, op cit.
18. *The Letters of a Noble Woman* (Mrs La Touche of Harristown) (ed Margaret Ferrier Young), London 1908.
19. Beresford, op cit.
20. E. OE. Somerville and Martin Ross, *Irish Memories*, London 1917.
21. Mayo papers.
22. W. Bence-Jones, *The Irish Church from the Point of View of one of its Laymen*, London 1868.
23. Nicolette Devas, *Two Flamboyant Fathers*, London 1966.
24. Katherine Everett, *Bricks and Flowers*, London 1950.
25. Ibid.

Chapter 2   The Land War

1. I am indebted to Dr W.E. Vaughan for this information.
2. *Letters of a Noble Woman.*
3. Hart papers.
4. e.g., James S. Donnelly, Jr., *The Land and the People of Nineteenth Century Cork*, London 1975; W.E. Vaughan, *Landlords and Tenants in Ireland 1848–1904*, Dublin 1984.
5. A.M. Sullivan, *New Ireland*, 2 vols, London 1877.
6. Ibid.
7. W.E. Vaughan, *Landlords and Tenants in Ireland 1848–1904*, Dublin 1984.
8. Lady Clodagh Anson, *Victorian Days*, London 1957.
9. Elizabeth Bowen, *Bowen's Court*, London 1942.
10. *Letters of a Noble Woman.*
11. Ibid.
12. Calendar of the Ashbourne papers, Belfast, HM Stationery Office, 1974.
13. *Letters of a Noble Woman.*
14. Castletown, op cit.
15. Bence-Jones papers.
16. *The Times*, December 25, 1880.
17. Bence-Jones papers.
18. Bowen, op cit.
19. Hart papers.
20. Blackwood papers.
21. Ibid.
22. Lynch-Robinson, op cit.
23. Hart papers.

Chapter 3   Dramas in muslin

1. Diary of Lady Alice Howard.
2. Earl of Dunraven, *Past Times and Pastimes*, 2 vols, London ND.
3. Diary of Lady Alice Howard.
4. Ibid.
5. In *A Drama in Muslin.*
6. Raymond F. Brooke, *The Brimming River*, Dublin 1961.
7. Viceregal Court records.
8. Fingall, op cit.
9. Ibid.
10. Ibid.
11. Joseph Hone, *The Life of George Moore*, New York 1936.
12. Ibid.

13. Ibid.
14. Viceregal Court records.
15. Fingall, op cit.
16. Diary of Lady Alice Howard.
17. Ibid.
18. *Letters of a Noble Woman.*
19. Rossmore, op cit.
20. H.J. Bruce, *Silken Dalliance*, London 1946.
21. Major Hugh Delmege, in conversation with the author.
22. Diary of Lady Alice Howard.
23. *Letters of a Noble Woman.*
24. Ibid.
25. Quoted Neely, op cit.
26. Diary of Lady Alice Howard.
27. Bruce, op cit.
28. Ibid.
29. *Letters of a Noble Woman.*
30. Diary of Lady Alice Howard.
31. Ibid.
32. Quoted in *Journal of the Society of Arts*, November 23, 1888.
33. *Letters of a Noble Woman.*
34. Ibid.
35. Wynne, op cit.
36. Mayo Papers.
37. Diary of Lady Alice Howard.

Chapter 4   Celtic Unionism

1. Duke de Stacpoole, *Irish and Other Memories*, London 1922.
2. Quoted J. Anthony Gaughan, *The Knights of Glin*, Dublin 1978.
3. T.W. Russell, letter to *The Times*, January 20, 1889, in *Irish Unionism 1885–1923* (ed Patrick Buckland), Belfast 1973.
4. Castletown papers.
5. *The Times*, 8 November, 1887.
6. de Stacpoole, op cit.
7. Carew papers.
8. Wynne, op cit.
9. Somerville and Ross, op cit.
10. Report of Proceedings, Unionist Convention, June 1892.
11. Quoted Patrick Buckland, *Ulster Unionism*, Dublin 1973.
12. *Irish Unionism.*
13. Fingall, op cit.

14. Angela Antrim, *The Antrim McDonnells*, Belfast 1977.
15. Fingall, op cit.
16. Ibid.
17. Ibid.
18. *Letters of a Noble Woman.*
19. Diary of Lady Alice Howard.
20. Mr Claud Proby, in conversation with the author.
21. Diary of Hon. Charles Monck.
22. Earl of Desart and Lady Sybil Lubbock, *A Page from the Past*, London 1936.
23. Quoted Hubert Butler, 'Anglo-Irish Twilight. The Last Ormonde War', in *Journal of the Butler Society*, 1978–1979.
24. Marguerite Solly-Flood typescript.
25. Butler, op cit.
26. Anson, op cit.
27. Castletown, op cit.
28. Butler, op cit.
29. Gaughan, op cit.
30. E. OE. Somerville and Martin Ross, *Some Irish Yesterdays*, London 1906.

Chapter 5 'George, George, the Bonus!'

1. Solly-Flood typescript.
2. Told by this lady's grandson to the author.
3. Information given to the author by Lady Anthea Forde.
4. Information given to the author by Major Hugh Delmege.
5. Solly-Flood typescript.
6. Coote papers.
7. *Leinster Express*, 30 December, 1905.
8. Solly-Flood typescript.
9. Told by Major Hugh Delmege to the author.
10. Lennox Robinson, Tom Robinson and Nora Dorman, *Three Homes*, London 1938.
11. Langrishe papers.
12. *Letters of a Noble Woman.*
13. Solly-Flood typescript.
14. Langrishe papers.
15. Hone, op cit.
16. Ibid.
17. Ibid.
18. Quoted Anne Marreco, *The Rebel Countess*, London 1967.
19. Harold Nicolson, *The Desire to Please*, London 1943.
20. Quoted Fingall, op cit.
21. Major Hugh Delmege, in conversation with the author.

22. Diary of Lady Alice Howard.
23. Brooke, op cit.
24. Kildare Street Club records.
25. Quoted Stephen Tumim, *Great Legal Disasters*, London 1983.
26. Fingall, op cit.
27. Kildare Street Club records.
28. Ibid.

Chapter 6   'A doomed aristocracy'

1. James White, in catalogue of Orpen Centenary Exhibition, Dublin 1978.
2. Orpen letters.
3. Ibid.
4. Ibid.
5. Bruce Arnold, *Orpen, Mirror to an Age*, London 1981.
6. Orpen letters.
7. Ibid.
8. Fingall, op cit.
9. In conversation with the author.
10. Harold Nicolson, *Helen's Tower*, London 1937.
11. Coote papers.
12. Mayo papers.
13. Diary of Lady Alice Howard.
14. Lord and Lady Aberdeen, *More Cracks with 'We Twa'*, London 1929.
15. Sir Henry Robinson, *Memories Wise and Otherwise*, London, New York and Melbourne 1923,
16. Francis Bamford and Viola Bankes, *Vicious Circle*, London 1965.
17. Aberdeen, op cit.
18. Vaughan, op cit.
19. Lennox Robinson, *Bryan Cooper*, London 1931.
20. Maurice Headlam, *Irish Reminiscences*, London 1947.
21. Quoted Patrick Buckland, *Irish Unionism I*, Dublin and New York 1972.
22. Coote papers.
23. Quoted Gordon St George Mark, 'Tyrone House', in *Irish Georgian Society Bulletin*, July-December 1976.
24. Ibid.
25. Ibid.
26. Brooke, op cit.
27. Maurice Healy, *The Old Munster Circuit*, London 1939.
28. *The Times.*
29. *Irish Times.*
30. Ibid.

31. Souvenir Album presented to Marquis and Marchioness of Aberdeen and Temair by Members of their Staff and reproduced for publication, Dublin 1915.
32. *Irish Life*, 29 November, 1912.
33. Headlam, op cit.

Chapter 7   The shadow of Home Rule

1. *Irish Unionism*, op cit.
2. Miss Catharine Clements, in conversation with the author.
3. Robinson, *Bryan Cooper*.
4. Marreco, op cit.
5. *Irish Life*.
6. Ibid.
7. Fingall, op cit.
8. Quoted Samuel Gurney, *Isabel*, Norwich and London 1935.
9. Patrick Hone, *Cricket in Ireland*, Tralee 1955.
10. Miss Marye Pole-Carew and Mrs Peter Du Cane, in conversation with the author.
11. Sir Cecil Stafford-King-Harman, in conversation with the author.
12. Mrs Edmund Boyle, in conversation with the author.
13. Colonel Kendal Chavasse, in conversation with the author.
14. Hannay, *Westminster Gazette*, loc cit.
15. Ibid.
16. Lady Betty Clarke, letter to the author.
17. Buckland, *Ulster Unionism*.
18. Solly-Flood typescript.
19. Buckland, *Ulster Unionism*.
20. Earl of Birkenhead, *F.E.*, London 1959.
21. Buckland, *Ulster Unionism*.
22. Sir Cecil Stafford-King-Harman, in conversation with the author.
23. *Irish Times*.
24. Harold Nicolson, *King George the Fifth*, London 1952.
25. Solly-Flood typescript.
26. Bowen, op cit.

Chapter 8   Terrible beauties

1. Diary of Lady Alice Howard.
2. Quoted Brooke, op cit.
3. Vere Foster papers.
4. Countess of Wicklow, in conversation with the author.
5. Bryan Cooper, *The Tenth Irish Division in Gallipoli*, NP 1918.

6. Quoted Shane Leslie, *Long Shadows*, London 1966.
7. Lord Dunsany, *Patches of Sunlight*, London and Toronto 1938.
8. Diary of Sir Shane Leslie.
9. Lady Cynthia Asquith, *Diaries 1915–1918*, London 1968.
10. Quoted Buckland, *Irish Unionism*.
11. Anne Gregory, *Me and Nu*, Gerrards Cross 1970.
12. Headlam, op cit.
13. Fingall, op cit.
14. Headlam, op cit.
15. Dunsany, op cit.
16. Headlam, op cit.
17. Max Caulfield, *The Easter Rebellion*, London 1963.
18. Marreco, op cit.
19. Coote papers.
20. Castletown papers.
21. Ibid.
22. Quoted Buckland, *Irish Unionism*.
23. Diary of Sir Shane Leslie.
24. Blackwood papers.
25. Diary of Lady Alice Howard.
26. Bisbrooke papers.
27. Everett, op cit.
28. Earl of Midleton, quoted Desart and Lubbock, op cit.
29. Earl of Midleton, *Records and Reactions 1856–1939*, London 1939.
30. *Irish Unionism*.
31. Mrs Robert de Winton, in conversation with the author.
32. Countess of Wicklow, in conversation with the author.
33. Diary of Lady Alice Howard.
34. Countess of Wicklow, in conversation with the author.

Chapter 9   The last September

1. *Lady Gregory's Journals* (ed Lennox Robinson), London 1946.
2. Ibid.
3. Solly-Flood typescript.
4. T.R. Henn, *Five Arches*, Gerrards Cross 1980.
5. Mr Robert Kennedy, in conversation with the author.
6. Headlam, op cit.
7. Marreco, op cit.
8. Robinson, *Bryan Cooper*.
9. Letter from General Seán MacEoin in *Irish Times*.
10. Lionel Fleming, *Head or Harp*, London 1965.

11. Quoted Buckland, *Irish Unionism I*.
12. *The Times*.
13. *Cork Constitution*.
14. Castletown, op cit.
15. *Cork Constitution*.
16. Diary of Lady Alice Howard.
17. *The Times*.
18. Quoted Buckland, *Irish Unionism I*.
19. Langford papers.
20. Castletown, op cit.
21. Bamford and Bankes, op cit.
22. Fingall, op cit.
23. Quoted Marreco, op cit.
24. Anne Gregory, op cit.
25. Rosse papers.
26. Bisbrooke papers.
27. *The Times*.
28. Diary of Lady Alice Howard.

Chapter 10   Both sides admired the antirrhinums

1. *Irish Life*.
2. Ibid.
3. Diary of Major John de la Poer.
4. Ibid.
5. Earl of Ossory, 'The Attack on Kilkenny Castle', in *Journal of the Butler Society*, 1972.
6. Young of Culdaff papers.
7. Diary of Lady Alice Howard.
8. Mark Girouard, 'Whitfield Court', in *Country Life*, 7 September, 1967.
9. Eileen Gormanston, *A Little Kept*, London 1954.
10. Ibid.
11. Rosse papers.
12. Bowen, op cit.
13. Diary of Major John de la Poer.
14. Ibid.
15. *Irish Times*.
16. Wynne, op cit.
17. Diary of Major John de la Poer.
18. Countess of Wicklow, in conversation with the author.
19. Quoted Donal O'Sullivan, *The Irish Free State and its Senate*, London 1940.
20. Diary of Major John de la Poer.
21. Rosse papers.

22. Quoted O'Sullivan, op cit.
23. Ibid; *Irish Times.*
24. Quoted Joseph Hone, op cit.
25. Told to the author by the late Captain the Hon. Valentine Wyndham-Quin.
26. Diary of Major John de la Poer.
27. Ibid.

Chapter *11* 'No petty people'

1. Lynch-Robinson, op cit.
2. Wynne, op cit.
3. Diary of Major John de la Poer.
4. Langford papers.
5. Ibid.
6. Robert Douglas King-Harman, *The Kings, Earls of Kingston*, Cambridge, privately printed, 1959.
7. Bowen, op cit.
8. Desart and Lubbock, op cit.
9. *Lady Gregory's Journals.*
10. Jasper More, *A Tale of Two Houses*, Shrewsbury 1978.
11. Neely, op cit.
12. Diary of Sir Shane Leslie.
13. Told by Mrs Robert de Winton to the author.
14. Terence de Vere White, 'Social Life in Ireland 1927–1937', in *Studies*, Spring 1965.
15. Pierce Synnott, *The Netterville Monument and Family*, privately printed.
16. Gormanston, op cit.
17. Diary of Major John de la Poer.
18. O'Sullivan, op cit.
19. Ibid.
20. Robinson, *Bryan Cooper.*
21. Dunsany, op cit.
22. *Lady Gregory's Journals.*

Chapter *12* 'No bells ring here'

1. O'Sullivan, op cit.
2. Fingall, op cit.
3. *Dundalk Democrat.*
4. Vere Foster Papers.
5. Diary of Sir Shane Leslie.
6. Devas, op cit.

7. L.P. Curtis, Jr., 'The Anglo-Irish Predicament', in *Twentieth Century Studies*, November 1970.
8. *The Post*, Kilkenny.
9. Conrad O'Brien-ffrench, *Delicate Mission*, London ND.

Chapter *13* 'Tubby will be there'

1. Solly-Flood typescript.
2. Diary of Sir Shane Leslie.
3. Seymour Leslie, *The Jerome Connexion*, London 1964.
4. Anita Leslie, *The Gilt and the Gingerbread*, London 1981.

Chapter *14* The heart is still sound

1. Henn, op cit.
2. Mrs Robert de Winton, in conversation with the author.
3. Mr Richard Ball, in conversation with the author.
4. Bowen, op cit.
5. Ibid.
6. In conversation with the author.
7. Told by Mr Richard Tottenham to the author.
8. Mr Malcolm Lysaght, in conversation with the author.
9. Told to the author by Captain Peter Montgomery.

Chapter *15* Dior and dogs' dinners

1. Fleming, op cit.
2. Quoted Victoria Glendinning, *Elizabeth Bowen*, London 1977.
3. Ibid.
4. Major Robin Carew to the author.
5. *The Diaries of Evelyn Waugh* (ed Michael Davie), London 1976.

Manuscript and other unpublished sources

Bence-Jones papers, in the possession of the author.
Bisbrooke papers, in the possession of Mr George Boyle.
Blackwood papers, in the Public Record Office of Northern Ireland.

Carew papers, in the possession of Mr Peter Pearson.

Castletown papers, in the possession of Mr George Boyle.

Coote papers, in the possession of Sir Christopher Coote, Bt.

Diary of Major John de la Poer, in the possession of Count de la Poer.

Diary of Lady Alice Howard, in the National Library of Ireland.

Diary of Sir Shane Leslie, in the National Library of Ireland.

Diary of Hon. Charles Monck, in the possession of Mr Daniel Gillman.

Hart papers, in the Public Record Office of Northern Ireland.

Kildare Street Club records.

Langford papers, in the possession of Mr Peter Pearson.

Langrishe papers, in the possession of Sir Hercules Langrishe, Bt.

Mayo papers, in the possession of Mr Peter Pearson.

Orpen letters, in the National Gallery of Ireland.

Rosse papers, in the possession of the Birr Scientific Heritage Foundation.

Solly-Flood, Marguerite, *Memories of Six Reigns*, unpublished typescript in the possession of Mrs David Thomas.

Vere Foster papers, in the Public Record Office of Northern Ireland.

Viceregal Court records.

Young of Culdaff papers, in the Public Record Office of Northern Ireland.

Index